THE REPEALER REPULSED

GW00493908

THE REPEALER
REPULSED

William McComb

edited by
Patrick Maume

UNIVERSITY COLLEGE DUBLIN PRESS
PREAS CHOLÁISTE OLLSCOILE BHAILE ÁTHA CLIATH

First published 1841
This edition first published by
University College Dublin Press, 2003

Introduction and notes © Patrick Maume 2003

ISBN 1 900621 97 5
ISSN 1383–6883

University College Dublin Press
Newman House, 86 St Stephen's Green
Dublin 2, Ireland
www.ucdpress.ie

Cataloguing in Publication data
available from the British Library

Typeset in Ireland in Baskerville by
Elaine Shiels, Bantry, Co. Cork
Printed on acid-free paper in Ireland
by ColourBooks, Dublin

CONTENTS

INTRODUCTION

Patrick Maume

Biographical note

William McComb was born in Coleraine, County Londonderry
on 17 August 1793, son of a draper. While apprenticed to a
Belfast draper, McComb founded a Sunday school to coun-
teract Painite religious and political ideas. He subsequently
trained as a schoolmaster with the Kildare Place Society and
taught and managed the Society's Brown Square school (near
the top of the Shankill) until 1828. The Sunday school
movement acquainted him with Anglican Evangelical activists
such as Orange leader Robert Jocelyn, third Earl of Roden,
and with Henry Cooke. McComb and Cooke served on the
Brown Square school's fundraising committee even after
McComb abandoned teaching for bookselling.

Cooke (1788?–1868), like McComb, came from County
Londonderry, son of a small farmer near Maghera. In the late
1790s Cooke's family faced intimidation because of their
hostility to the United Irishmen; this underlay Henry's abiding
political conservatism. After attending Glasgow University
Cooke was ordained to the Presbyterian ministry in 1808. He
was minister of Donegore (County Antrim) 1811–18, Killyleagh
(County Down) 1818–29, and May Street, Belfast (1829–67).
At Killyleagh Cooke became pre-eminent champion of
Trinitarian orthodoxy among Presbyterians. Between 1822
and 1829 his confrontations with the Unitarian minority (led

by Henry Montgomery, minister of Dunmurry) culminated in
the Synod's compelling ordinands to sign the Westminster
Confession of Faith; the Non-Subscribing dissidents seceded.
Cooke travelled throughout Ulster addressing public gather-
ings, displaying the eloquence and determination which led
admirers to call him the Presbyterian Athanasius; McComb
always thought Cooke the modern John Knox.[1] Cooke's
opponents countered with accusations of unscrupulous arrogance and self-righteous self-dramatisation.[2] The present text,
with Cooke's blunt challenges to O'Connell, self-presentation
as potential martyr, and warnings of the eternal damnation in
store for liars, can support both views.

In 1828 McComb became a bookseller and publisher,
offering "increased circulation to a sound religious literature",
including Sunday School Society publications. From 1829 he
published the *Orthodox Presbyterian*, a monthly (co-edited by
Cooke) defending the Synod majority against the Belfast
Liberal daily *Northern Whig* and the Non-Subscribing monthly
Bible Christian. McComb rapidly achieved business success; the
Belfast Linenhall Library has over 120 titles published by him
(mostly religious). McComb also published a tourist guide to
the Belfast area combining first-hand accounts of the battle of
Ballynahinch, and a moving ballad by McComb on rebel
heroine Betsy Gray, with reflections on the insurgents' folly
and the benefits of the Union.[3]

From 1840 he published *McComb's Presbyterian Almanac*,
containing verses by McComb, lists of Presbyterian ministers,
and accounts of Presbyterian progress in Scotland, America,
and the Continent, with missionary activities among Indians,
Jews, and Irish Roman Catholics. His verses rallied support
for Presbyterian overseas missions. He attended the departure
of the first Irish Presbyterian missionaries to India after the
Orthodox and Seceder Synods united in 1840. Cooke led the
prayers; McComb compared the scene to the departure of St
Paul and drew sketches of the missionaries in the Mission
Board's minute-book.[4] McComb's discernment of a Vatican
conspiracy behind O'Connell's visit to Belfast reflects his view

of the growing confidence and social status of nineteenth-century Ulster Presbyterianism as part of a global conflict with Popery.

Under the Whig governments of the 1830s, McComb joined Cooke in denouncing the newly instituted National Schools for "mutilating scripture" and allowing priests to supervise the religious education of Catholic pupils.[5] On 30 October 1834 Cooke and Roden addressed a rally on the Hillsborough estate of the Marquess of Downshire; Cooke "proclaimed the banns of marriage" between the Anglican and Presbyterian churches, defending the Conservative Party and Established Church as bulwarks against Catholicism. (Downshire (d.1847) and his son and successor Lord Hillsborough (d.1868), prominent in *The Repealer Repulsed,* flaunted their Tory-Evangelical paternalism; they worked with Cooke, who regarded them as friends.) Cooke was a committee-member of the Belfast Conservative organisation.

This alliance experienced internal tensions. Lord John George Beresford, Church of Ireland Archbishop of Armagh, surreptitiously backed a lawsuit where an Anglican successfully denied bigamy, claiming his first marriage (to a Presbyterian) was invalid because celebrated by a Presbyterian minister. The implied denigration of Presbyterian orders and Presbyterian marriages provoked uproar; Peel's government eventually validated Presbyterian marriages in August 1844. (McComb became Belfast's first Registrar of Marriages in 1845.)

Despite Cooke's efforts, Peel's government refused to allow Church of Scotland congregations to abolish the nomination of ministers to congregations by aristocratic patrons. This provoked the secession of the Scottish Free Church in May 1843. The Irish Presbyterian Church allied with the new body; Cooke spoke at its first assembly; and McComb wrote verses recalling the struggle of the Covenanters against the Stuarts. Many Irish Presbyterians turned fiercely against the Conservatives; Cooke avoided the General Assembly for some years rather than change his political allegiance. Cooke's influence was further shaken when he opposed the Ulster Tenant Right agitation of the 1850s (which saw Lord Downshire (formerly Hillsborough) chased from a public platform by discontented tenants). The aged Cooke was venerated as an elder states-man of the Presbyterian Church, but not its political leader. His physically feeble denuciation of Gladstone's disestablish-ment proposals at a new Hillsborough meeting on 30 October 1867, and a manifesto in support of Conservatism and Church Establishment issued from his deathbed during the general election of 1868, failed to turn the political tide.

McComb was extensively involved with Belfast charitable institutions; he was a founder, and first treasurer, of the Ulster Institution for the Education of the Deaf and Dumb and the Blind. (When Queen Victoria visited Belfast in 1849 she avoided the Institution because of its aggressively Protestant ethos.)[6] McComb taught blind children until a few months before his death.

From his early twenties McComb published verse in local newspapers; his first book, a verse lament for the harper Denis O'Neill, appeared in 1817. *The Voice of a Year, or Recollections of 1848* (1849) is a millennialist celebration of the downfall of the French monarchy and the expulsion of Pius IX from Rome, equated with the opening of the fourth seal in the Book of Revelation. McComb's *Poetical Works* appeared in 1864. He was called "the laureate of the Church"; his verse—in standard English and received literary forms – proved less enduring than the Rhyming Weavers.

McComb retired in 1864, but remained active in church affairs. He provided information to Cooke's son-in-law and biographer J. L. Porter after his hero died in December 1868. McComb may be one of the reporters who recalled being so enraptured by Cooke's extemporaneous eloquence that they threw down their pens and found neither they nor Cooke could recall what had been said.[7] William McComb died on 13 September 1873 at Colin View Terrace, Belfast. *McComb's Almanac* survived until 1884.

In 1842, after a service by Cooke in Carrickfergus for the bicentenary of the first Ulster presbytery, McComb composed a poem summarising the worldview he shared with his mentor. McComb contrasts the small group of 1642 with the 500 ministers and 4,000 elders of 1842, celebrates Presbyterian missionaries, and concludes:

> Two hundred years ago, the hand of massacre was nigh;
> And far and wide o'er Erin's land was heard the midnight cry;
> Now Presbyterian Ulster rests, in happiness and peace
> While crimes in distant provinces from year to year increase;
> O Lord! Their bondage quickly turn, as streams in South that flow,
> For Popery is the same it was two hundred years ago.[8]

The Repealer Repulsed

After his post-Emancipation calls for repeal of the Act of Union, O'Connell placed the issue in abeyance to secure "justice for Ireland" from the Whig government. After 1835 the Melbourne Government's dependence on O'Connellite support produced a sympathetic Dublin Castle administration and an influx of Catholics and Liberals into civil service positions. Major Irish reforms were, however, watered down by the Tory-dominated House of Lords and conservative elements within the Whig government. By 1839–40 the government tottered before a revitalised Conservative party; only Queen Victoria's influence retained them in office.

Whig divisions were exasperated when the Conservative frontbencher Lord Stanley put forward a restrictive Irish Registration Bill. As Whig Chief Secretary for Ireland (1830–3) Stanley had proved a capable administrator and an enemy of O'Connell, who called him "Scorpion Stanley". Despite his defection to the Tories over sequestration of Church of Ireland property, Stanley retained sympathisers on the government benches.[9] The Irish voting system, which had not been fundamentally revised by the Reform Acts for fear of strengthening O'Connell, was notoriously badly administered. Many conservative Whigs supported Stanley's measure; it would have

reduced still further a property-based franchise which, because
of Irish poverty, left the Irish electorate considerably smaller
than its British counterpart. O'Connell hoped reawakening
Repeal might extract further concessions and mobilise
electoral support.

Reforms secured by the Whig–O'Connellite alliance
included the 1838 Municipal Corporations Bill, abolishing
most Irish borough corporations (Protestant-dominated, often
corrupt and self-selecting) and giving major urban centres
new corporations with an extended franchise. In Belfast, the
forthcoming municipal elections inspired the *Vindicator*, a bi-
weekly Belfast Catholic paper founded in 1839 and owned
and managed until 1842 by Charles Gavan Duffy. The
Vindicator argued that Reformers could win a majority on the
new Belfast Corporation if they united; it suggested Liberals
should nominate two Catholics as aldermen and eight as
councillors. (*The Repealer Repulsed* sneers that there are too few
respectable Catholics for this and asks if "Hercules Street
fleshers" will be recruited.) While the *Vindicator* did not spare
Conservatives (Orange violence was highlighted, Cooke was
accused of aspiring to a bishopric) its fiercest artillery was
reserved for Belfast Liberals.

The *Northern Whig* accused the *Vindicator* of sectarianism. The
Vindicator called O'Connell's opponents "mongrels" ashamed
of being Irish; if they were foreigners they should return to
their country. The *Whig* accused the *Vindicator* of telling Ulster
Protestants to leave Ireland; the *Vindicator* claimed it had
meant "mongrels" were Irish and must acknowledge the fact.
It accused "the *Mongrel*" of conscious falsehood.[10] O'Connell
endorsed the *Vindicator's* attacks on the *Whig*, but demurred
when it denounced the radical *Newry Examiner*.[11]

Gavan Duffy's verbal savagery reflected bitterness at
Protestant privilege and officially tolerated Orange violence
he witnessed as a young man in Monaghan; before meeting
Thomas Davis he was "a nationalist of the school of Rory
O'Moore". This bitterness haunts his ballad on the 1641 Rising,
"The Muster of the North", which attracted similar accusations

to the "mongrel" editorial. The fact that McComb pointed to Catholic as well as Protestant Liberals criticising the *Vindicator* indicates a recurring theme of nineteenth-century Belfast nationalism: conflict between accommodationist Catholic and Liberal elites and populists trying to mobilise poorer Belfast Catholics and align them with nationwide nationalist movements.[12] (McComb satirises the *Vindicator*'s appeal to a plebeian audience, with four impoverished Catholics contributing a penny each for a single copy. *The Repealer Repulsed* cost two shillings.)

In this context of attempted mobilisation Duffy and his allies invited O'Connell to Belfast. After securing O'Connell's reluctant agreement in December 1840, the *Vindicator* promoted the visit as a historic event. Liberals were offered tickets for a Reform dinner to be addressed by O'Connell the evening before the main meeting, and given the choice of dividing Reformers in face of the Tory foe or apparently endorsing Repeal. The *Vindicator* proclaimed that O'Connell's audience would delight in the oratory which charmed Westminster; the smallest child present would enchant his grandchildren with memories of O'Connell. At this point, on 5 January 1841, Cooke publicly challenged O'Connell to debate Repeal.

Cooke's challenge reflected a period where public speaking served as a form of popular entertainment and spokesmen for rival churches staged public disputes to prove their creed's superiority through argument. The debate in Dublin between Fr. Tom Maguire and Rev. Richard Pope in April 1827 attracted nationwide attention.[13] The Presbyterian subscription controversy revolved around oratorical duels between Cooke and Montgomery. Much turned on Cooke's ability to reply extemporaneously before the Synod of Ulster to detailed accusations of hypocrisy from Montgomery, and his unanticipated appearance at a public meeting convoked by Montgomery amidst mutual accusations of Sabbath-breaking.

Cooke's challenge also incorporates an after-echo of the duelling tradition. Cooke and his allies repeatedly use metaphors of the duel, even the cockfight ("the craven at once

lowered his wing"). In February 1841 when the Orange
Anglican clergyman Tresham Gregg challenged Cooke to
debate Protestant attitudes to the National School system,
Cooke imitated duelling practice in submitting the dispute to
a board of honour consisting of clergymen from both churches.
(The board decided that Protestant unity dictated Cooke
should not debate Gregg.)[14] The duelling code implied that
those who passively accepted insults were unworthy to belong
to the ruling elite; O'Connell's refusal of Cooke's challenge
was similarly presented as implying unfitness for citizenship.
At a subsequent Conservative meeting on 22 January and a
dinner on the 23rd (organised by the Belfast Tory political
"fixer", John Bates), Cooke heaped insults on O'Connell with
the skill and ferocity of a practised stand-up comedian,
incorporating audience responses and encores into his speech.

   The Repealer Repulsed forms an intrinsic part of Cooke's
attempt to discredit O'Connell. An extensive report of the
Conservative gathering is preceded by a burlesque account of
O'Connell's refusal of the challenge and his experiences in
Belfast from his arrival on 16 January to his departure by ship
from Donaghadee on the 19th, and followed by responses to
O'Connellite apologias and satirical ballads and dialect commentary on the visit. McComb imitates the Tory journalism of
Blackwood's Magazine, snobbish, allusive, parading literary learning, burlesquing opponents in mock-epic terms, using dialect
to ridicule the alleged plebeianism of the Repealers and assert
its own common sense. *The Repealer Repulsed* shows a talent for
parody unexpressed in McComb's formal literary productions.

   Gary Owens has described how O'Connell's mass meetings used pageantry to convey their political message and
give a sense of participation to those who could not hear
the speeches.[15] McComb employs the opposite process.
O'Connell's magniloquent rhetoric is deconstructed with
relentless literalism. The decorations of the hall where
O'Connell spoke, with their messages of ancient glory and
contemporary greatness, are ridiculed as shoddy tinsel; the
hall itself is dismissed as a ramshackle construction designed

for Punch and Judy shows. The social hierarchy present at the Conservative rally addressed by Cooke is lovingly detailed; the middle-class audiences at O'Connell's private functions are dismissed as the sweepings of the streets, with the "beautiful and good" female participants ridiculed as maidservants or barelegged Hercules Street traders. O'Connell used vituperation to hearten followers by humiliating their socially superior enemies; here the same device was used against him. Cooke's speech and McComb's commentary form a compendium of insults habitually flung at O'Connell and his "tail" of MPs; even the hostile cartoons of John Doyle are cited. At a lower level of society, hostile crowds burned O'Connell in effigy, compared Derrynane to the new workhouses as an abode of beggars, cheered Ellen Courtenay, and mocked the "Big Beggarman" by holding out pennies to him on forked sticks.[16]

O'Connell's refusal to debate Cooke reflected unwillingness to elevate his rival's stature. (The *Vindicator* mocked the suggestion that the great Westminster orator should bandy insults with a provincial bigot, and replied to Cooke's description of O'Connell as "a great bad man with a great bad cause" by calling "Thersites Cooke . . . a little bad man with a little bad cause".)[17] The principal motive, however, appears to have been the potential for uncontrollable violence and disorder. The *Vindicator* pointed to the likely result of opposing and excited crowds in a confined space for hours of heated debate.[18] O'Connellite demonstrations depended on ability to control public space by weight of numbers; a large opposing crowd threatened catastrophe.

Planned ceremonial welcomes for O'Connell in border towns were hastily abandoned for fear of violence. (*The Repealer Repulsed* represents these plans as military preparations justifying the assembly of loyalist crowds.) Serious fears were entertained that O'Connell might be lynched en route. O'Connell's travelling on 16 January, two days before the time announced, under the name of the Dublin ventriloquist C. E. Charles, is mocked by McComb as abject cowardice. Repealers celebrated it as a master-stratagem to defeat plots against the hero's life,[19] but it formed a sad contrast to the triumphant entries which normally preceded O'Connell's rallies. As it was, the visit produced extensive rioting. The *Vindicator* accused Cooke and his allies of condoning attacks on Catholic houses and businesses (including the *Vindicator* offices). Cooke retorted that Catholics also rioted; McComb displayed in his shop a large stone hurled into a Protestant house. The contrast between McComb's accounts of the two meetings drives home the lesson that the Anti-Repealers controlled Belfast's public space; O'Connell's meeting in Donegall Square was reduced to a bear-garden, while Cooke and the Conservatives congregated in peace.[20]

The Repealer Repulsed contains one of the earliest statements of the economic case for Ulster Unionism, with Cooke's often-quoted ascription of Belfast's industrial progress to the Union—"Look on Belfast, and be a Repealer if you can". Cooke's primary argument, however, was religious, in keeping with his view that the intervention of ministers of religion in politics could only be justified when religion itself was at stake. Even his economic argument linked Belfast's prosperity to "the genii of Protestantism and Liberty". O'Connell's visit tried to present Protestant Liberals with the choice of endorsing Repeal or being blamed for dividing Reformers in the face of the Tory onslaught: Cooke repeatedly informs his Liberal townsmen that their only safety lay in Toryism and tries to reinforce the Anglican–Presbyterian alliance by presenting Repeal as the latest threat from a perennially persecuting Catholicism. The anti-tithe violence of the early 1830s and the violence directed by Archbishop McHale against Protestant proselytisers in Connacht were assimilated to imagery of Catholic aggression and Protestant martyrdom—Bloody Mary and the 1641 massacres, the Siege of Derry and the barn at Scullabogue. The Whig adminstration was presented as a new "Catholic ascendancy" from which an historic deliverance was at hand in the form of a Conservative government. The Hillsborough rally of 1834 was consciously evoked by Downshire, Hillsborough, and Cooke; a representative of

Archbishop Beresford joined Cooke in renewing the "banns" proclaimed in 1834.

More secular political and economic arguments came from the Belfast Conservative MP Emerson Tennent, principal intermediary between Cooke and Peel. Tennent argued that access to the British market allowed Irish manufacturers to benefit from economies of scale, and that an independent Ireland would lack leverage in concluding trade agreements with foreign powers. (Tennent also argued that Belgium's separation from Holland at the behest of "priests and patriots" was economically disastrous, and that O'Connell's hostility to the Corn Laws showed him sacrificing Irish grain producers to weaken the Union.)

The Repealer Repulsed is sometimes called a foundation text of Ulster Unionism. Cooke and McComb gesture towards an Ulster particularism which presents the Northern province as a Protestant promised land of peace and prosperity amidst Irish violence and chaos (though delegates at the Conservative meeting came from Sligo, Leitrim, Longford and Louth as well as nine-county Ulster, and Cooke—who conducted extensive missionary work in Munster—saw Ulster not as a separate unit but as the "anchor" binding Ireland to Britain.)

Some of the arguments employed on both sides were deployed as long as the Union lasted. During the debates on the Third Home Rule Bill, nationalists still pointed to the relatively high reported crime and illegitimacy rates of industrial Belfast as proof that Ulster Protestants were morally inferior to rural Southern Catholics; Ulster Unionists claimed the Catholic minority were responsible for these statistics and depicted north-east Ulster as a Protestant island of peace and modernity menaced by violent and superstitious Catholic anarchs. O'Connell's allegation that the Union impoverished Ireland through overtaxation would be re-echoed by writers like Tom Kettle; Unionists would point to Belfast. Protestants would point to Catholic complaints of political and economic discrimination and the violent silencing of Protestant missionaries by Catholic mobs as proof of an impending Catholic

ascendancy; Catholics would follow O'Connell in quoting
suitably chosen Protestant writers as proof of historic Irish
Catholic tolerance and declare that Unionist hostility to a
Catholic-dominated Irish parliament logically implied the
virtual repeal of Catholic Emancipation. At the same time,
the element of historical continuity should not be overstated.
The boasts, recorded by McComb, that Cooke's triumph
marked a turning point in Irish history, the confident predic-
tions that the impending Conservative government would end
"Popish Ascendancy" proved hollow. Even the Conservatives
could not rule Ireland without concessions to Catholic
opinion; divisions between Presbyterian and Anglican, tenant
and landlord, persisted. Despite its deferential elements, the
Ulster Unionism which developed in the 1880s and subsequent decades was made possible by the gradual dismantling
of many social and religious institutions which Cooke defended.
Cooke's philippics do have something in common with the
oratorical flytings of Ian Paisley; but Cooke's sharp-edged
defence of social hierarchies inhabited a world remote from
Paisley's Ballymena-accented ridicule of the "fur-coat brigade".

Nevertheless, the memory of "O'Connell-quelling Cooke"
played its part in subsequent Ulster politics. J. L. Porter
inflated the importance of the encounter by associating it with
O'Connell's monster meetings of 1843 and implying that
Cooke's challenge had indeed fulfilled its author's boast that
it would precipitate O'Connell's downfall. Presbyterian
Unionists celebrating the Cooke centenary during the Parnell
era, twentieth-century fundamentalists mourning the betrayal
of political and religious orthodoxy by political and clerical
elites, looked to Cooke as defender inseparably of Union and
orthodoxy. Many nationalist commentators retorted by presenting Cooke as sole explanation for Ulster Presbyterian
"abandonment" of the United Irish legacy.

The visit to Belfast figures much less prominently in
O'Connell's biographies than in those of Cooke. O'Connell
appears to have seen the visit in retrospect as a failure, rushed
on him by overenthusiastic local activists and providing an

embarrassing display of Repeal weakness in Belfast.[21] It was not the last time he would be troubled by Gavan Duffy. During the great Repeal campaign of 1842–3 no monster meetings were held north of Dundalk for fear of provoking sectarian violence. The careful organisation and electoral sharp practice of the Belfast Conservatives won them all forty seats when the new Corporation was elected in 1842; no Liberal won a seat until August 1855, and no Catholic until the Liberal Bernard Hughes was elected in November 1855.[22]

The Repealer Repulsed, with its contemporary allusions and mock-heroic tone, was a self-conscious "instant book", participating in an ongoing debate and offering a first draft of the history it recounts. McComb's claims to rank with the great ancient and modern historians were written with tongue in cheek; but in fact *The Repealer Repulsed* is frequently drawn on by historians of nineteenth-century Belfast politics and Irish evangelicalism. It remains a valuable insight into the contested construction of political Protestantism, and the struggle of nineteenth-century Irish controversialists to control the future by articulating rival visions of the past.

NOTES

I wish to acknowledge the help and advice of Jonathan Bardon, Paul Bew, Sean Connolly, Alvin Jackson, and Peter Jupp.

1 E.g. William McComb, *Poetic Works* (Belfast, 1861), pp. 180–1 "To the Rev. Dr. Cooke with a Portrait of John Knox". The standard biographies of Cooke are the official life, J. L. Porter, *Life and Times of Henry Cooke, D.D., LL.D.* (3rd edition, Belfast, 1875) and R. Finlay Holmes, *Henry Cooke* (Belfast, 1981).
2 Rev. John A. Crozier, *Life of the Rev. Henry Montgomery* (London, 1875).
3 William McComb, *McComb's Guide to Belfast and the Adjacent Counties of Antrim and Down, with an account of the Battle of Ballynahinch* (Belfast, 1861).
4 Robert Jeffrey, *The Indian Mission of the Irish Presbyterian Church: A History of Fifty years of Work in Kathiawar and Gujarat* (London, 1890), pp. 40–2; R. H. Boyd, *Couriers of the Dawn: The Story of the Missionary Pioneers of the Irish Presbyterian Church* (Belfast, 1938).

5   Holmes, *Cooke*, p. 110.

6   Christine Kinealy and Gerard MacAtasney, *The Hidden Famine: Hunger, Poverty, and Sectarianism in Belfast* (London, 2000), pp. 178–9.

7   Porter, *Life and Times of Cooke*, pp. vii, 263–4.

8   McComb, *Poetic Works*, pp. 210–12. McComb's career is outlined in a DNB entry by Rev. Thomas Hamilton; *Belfast Newsletter* obituary 15 September 1873, p. 3; obituary in *McComb's Almanac* for 1874; entry in the forthcoming *Dictionary of Irish Biography*.

9   As 14th earl of Derby Stanley led the Conservative party after the fall of Peel in 1846; he was Prime Minister 1852, 1858–9, and 1866–8.

10 *Vindicator* 14, 25 November 1840.

11 O'Connell to Gavan Duffy 24 October 1840, *O'Connell Correspondence*, pp. 375–6.

12 A. C. Hepburn, *A Past Apart: Studies in the History of Catholic Belfast 1850–1950* (Belfast, 1996).

13 Proinnsios Ó Duigneain, *The Priest and the Protestant Woman: The Trial of Rev. Thomas Maguire, P.P., December 1827* (Dublin, 1997).

14 Porter, *Life and Times of Cooke*, pp. 321–3. For the duelling code see James Kelly, *That Damn'd Thing Called Honour: Duelling in Ireland 1570–1860* (Cork, 1995).

15 Gary Owens "Nationalism without words: Symbolism and ritual behaviour in the Repeal 'Monster Meetings' of 1843–5" in J. S. Donnelly and Kerby A. Miller (eds), *Irish Popular Culture 1650–1850* (Dublin, 1998), pp. 242–69. For the role of symbolism in the banquets held for elite audiences in association with the monster meetings, see pp. 257–9.

16 Compare the election crowd at Shrewsbury in June 1841 who held out pieces of meat on sticks to Disraeli with cries of "a bit of pork for the Jew". (Stanley Weintraub, *Disraeli: A Biography* (London, 1993), p. 197).

17 *Vindicator*, 27 January 1841. This post-visit editorial responds to Cooke's comparison of O'Connell's audience to the wild-beast shows formerly exhibited at the same location by suggesting that the comparison would be more aptly applied to the Orange rioters stirred up by Cooke, and that Cooke's own origins are lower than any of those whom he insults as a canaille. It ridicules Cooke's presentation of "fat parsons . . . who directed the wholesale murders at Newtonbarry and Rathcormick, because the people would not pay [tithes] for a religion of which they conscientiously disapproved". After suggesting that Cooke "would make a very good scare-crow in a barley-field, for we are sure no bird would alight within sight of . . . his cadaverous and harpy-like countenance" and hoping he will never become a bishop "It would undo all that St Patrick has done for us, for if the serpents saw one of their own number enthroned, they would forthwith return to Ireland" the *Vindicator* concludes by predicting that O'Connell will soon return to "pour forth the golden stream of his eloquence in Belfast".

18 *Vindicator*, 9 January 1841.
19 Morgan O'Connell to O'Connell, *O'Connell Correspondence* letter 2799 vol. VI, pp. 8–9.
20 The dynamics of O'Connellite crowds are discussed in Maura Murphy "'Of One Mind?' O'Connellite Crowds in the 1830s and 1840s" in Peter Jupp and Eoin Magennis (eds), *Crowds in Ireland c.1720–1920* (London, 2000), pp. 139–72. The pro-Cooke crowds fit the pattern described by Mark Harrison's *Crowds in History* (see Peter Jupp and Eoin Magennis, "Introduction: Crowds in Ireland, *c.*1720–1920" in Jupp and Magennis *Crowds in Ireland*, pp. 1–42) of crowds gathering within a context shaped by local elites. I thank Peter Jupp for discussing this point with me.
21 O'Connell to P. V. Fitzpatrick, 26 January 1841 in *O'Connell Correspondence*, vol. VI, letter 2802.
22 Hughes set up his own bakery after being dismissed by his employers for attending O'Connell's meeting. He was a personal friend of Cooke and antagonised some co-religionists by supporting the Cooke statue in 1874. Jack Magee *Barney: Bernard Hughes of Belfast 1808–1878* (Belfast, 2001).

NOTE ON THE TEXT

The text of *The Repealer Repulsed* has been re-set from the Queen's University Belfast library copy. McComb's non-standard punctuation and spelling have been retained as far as possible, but some obvious misprints have been silently corrected.

THE REPEALER REPULSED

Look upon this Picture

and upon that

PUBLISHED by WM. McCOMB. BELFAST

Price 2.0.

THE REPEALER REPULSED!

A CORRECT NARRATIVE

OF

THE RISE AND PROGRESS

OF THE

REPEAL INVASION OF ULSTER:

DR. COOKE'S CHALLENGE

AND

MR. O'CONNELL'S

DECLINATURE, TACTICS, AND FLIGHT.

WITH

APPROPRIATE POETICAL AND PICTORIAL ILLUSTRATIONS,

ALSO,

AN AUTHENTIC REPORT

OF THE

GREAT CONSERVATIVE DEMONSTRATIONS,

IN BELFAST,

ON THE 21st AND 23d OF JANUARY, 1841.

"Belfast is the seat of the greatest criminality in Ireland."—Mr. O'CONNELL, *out of Belfast,*
"I love the black North." "The lovely and the good of Belfast."—
Mr. O'CONNELL, *in Belfast.*

BELFAST:
WILLIAM M'COMB, 1, HIGH-STREET;
DUBLIN, W. CURRY, JUN., AND CO., J. ROBERTSON; DERRY, MRS. CAMPBELL;
EDINBURGH, J. JOHNSTONE, JAS. GALL AND SONS; GLASGOW, WM. COLLINS,
D. BRYCE; LONDON, NISBET AND CO.; MANCHESTER, GALT
AND ANDERSON; LIVERPOOL, J. PERRIS.

1841.

THE CHALLENGE

Your proposed Repeal Meeting, in
Belfast, shall be a Discussion, between your-
self & your humble Servant.
Subject — The advantages, or disadvantages of a
Repeal of the Union to Ireland.
And, now, Mr. O'Connell, let me speak a word
plainly to you. You cannot avoid this dis-
=cussion. I am the Man you have so often
reviled behind his back, can you do less
than meet him face to face?

H. COOKE.

ERIN *directing the attention of* BRITANNIA *and*
CALEDONIA *to Dr. Cooke's challenge*

THE CIRCUMSTANCES under which the late Repeal visit of Mr. O'Connell to the North has been made, are so peculiar, and the event itself constitutes so important an era in the modern history of Ireland, that an explanatory introduction is essentially requisite, before we proceed to a statement of the details, which it is the object of our publication to furnish. Some newspapers have compared O'Connell's mission, to the hostile invasion of Belfast, by Sir Phelim O'Neill, during the rebellion of 1641, and which terminated in his signal discomfiture at Lisburn, then called Lisnagarvey; but this is, in many respects, a forced comparison. O'Connell is not a man of war in the personal acceptation of the term, and whatever may be his general delinquencies, martial daring would be unjustly reckoned amongst their number. In this respect, he cannot be fairly classed with the chieftain of Benburb;[1] and we must, therefore, seek amongst the records of other Anti-British movements, for a character or characters, with whose mischievous activities the recent agitation tour of O'Connell to this part of Ireland, may be properly brought into comparison.

On Wednesday, the 11th of October, in the year 1791, the celebrated Theobald Wolfe Tone, made his first entry into Belfast, and it is a circumstance worth noting, that on the following day, Thursday, October 12, he was introduced to, and dined with W. Sinclair, Esq., own brother to the identical chairman of the Repeal Meeting, which was lately held, by substitution, in the vicinity of the Royal Hotel, of which meeting, a detailed report shall, in its proper place, be laid before our readers. In the mean time, it is important to observe, that, Tone did not visit "*Blefescu*", as he hierographically denominates Belfast, in the character of a revolutionist—far from it—he came merely as the paid Secretary of the

"Catholic Committee" in Dublin, and as the accredited agent
of "peaceful and constitutional agitation" in the North.[2] But
history has recorded the ultimate effects of his ostensibly
tranquil mission, and that reader must be deplorably wanting
in the attribute of perspicacity, who does not immediately
recognize the parallelism between his professions, and those of
O'Connell, on the occasion which we have chiefly in view.
This allowance, however, must be made, that when a case of
extremity had arisen, Tone proved himself to be a soldier—
his prototype from Kerry does not advance any claim to a
character so respectable. The main point to be observed
is, that both were salaried missionaries of Irish Roman
Catholicism, and that both affected devotion to objects strictly
constitutional, while the career of the one is now no longer
concealed, but stands broadly prominent in his own autobio-
graphical sketches, and the other habitually exhorts his min-
ions to "*strike the blow*", reminding them, with more of Scotch
caution, than of Milesian chivalry, that it must be done by
"*themselves*".[3]

    The attempted introduction of the Repeal agitation into
Ulster, unfolds a system of curious, and on general principles,
not very explicable policy. When Mr. O'Connell, some years
ago, in Drogheda, toasted the "Immortal memory", in a
tumbler-full of actual Boyne water, it was easy to see that his
object was to conciliate even the most ultra classes of
Protestants, by practically shewing that he could, if necessary,
assume for the time all the external symbols of confirmed
orangeism.[4] This was a policy which we can understand—its
aims were patent to the humblest capacity—but of the system
finally adopted, an explanation must be sought amongst the
hidden archives of the Vatican, since fallible wisdom is scarcely
adequate to its rational exposition. That Repeal is essentially
a Roman Catholic interest, no one can doubt—its object and
intended effect are to give Irish Roman Catholics an ascendant preponderance in the councils of the state; and, of course,
to depress Protestants, in a civil point of view, to the level of
their numbers, as compared with the bulk of the general

population. The demand for household, and even for universal suffrage, which is concurrent with the agitation of Repeal, abundantly proves that the advocates of the latter measure, look mainly to the counting of heads in their contemplated re-organization of Ireland, as a kingdom, distinct from, though nominally dependent upon, Great Britain. If a numerical majority is to rule the destinies of this country, without any counteracting influence arising from comparative property, or the expediencies necessarily generated by imperial, as distin-guished from, while it is not opposed to, local interests, then is it evident that Roman Catholicism must triumph in the exclusive ascendancy of its professors, and, that Protestantism must suffer in proportion. We are not now arguing an abstract point—we are simply reasoning from an acknow-ledged fact—and the inevitable conclusion is, that Roman Catholics are the only religious party in this country, who could possibly be invested with superior power and importance, in consequence of a Repeal of the Legislative Union between Great Britain and Ireland—just, because, they constitute the more numerous class of the community. It is then quite consistent with human nature in its selfish aspects, that Roman Catholics should seek for their own corporate ele-vation; but equally consistent, is it with equity and justice that the adherents of a different, and, as they themselves believe, a purer faith, while they accord to their opponents their fair share of social and civil privileges, should, nevertheless, have an ultimate regard to their own self-protection, and should hesitate before confiding implicitly in the mercy of a system, which punishes dissent with an eternity of exclusion from covenanted mercy; and, which through the medium of a secular interference, has been the first to consecrate virtual murder under the abused name of Christianity. Too much has sometimes been made of the intolerant character of the Romish system, but taking the lowest possible ground, that even scepticism can indicate, namely—that all ascendant sects are naturally prone to exclusiveness, still an unanswerable argument is furnished against the adoption of a measure,

which, in the nature of things, *must* have the effect of
establishing in this country a Roman Catholic ascendancy.

The policy of the Court of Rome has been usually distinguished for its deep subtlety, and its flexible adaptation to
contingent circumstances, and whenever a seemingly desperate
measure has been resorted to, a secret agency has been
generally at work, preparing the way for the expected issue;
but, in the case of the late invasion of the North, it is impossible for human sagacity to discover the calculations on which
the conclave had depended. Possibly the prudential arrangements sketched at head-quarters were over-ruled by the
violence, and we may add, providential indiscretion of local
coteries. Be this as it may, the following is a correct historical
sketch of the mode in which the conversion of Ulster to the
doctrine of Repeal has been attempted, after the jesuitical
Boyne-water drinking farce, already alluded to, had failed in
producing its anticipated effects.

We pass over a number of political scenes that were
successively enacted, all of which proved, that, while the
Northerns were actuated, and would abide, by principle, not
even the most Radical amongst them (we refer of course to
men of intelligence), could be cajoled into a participation in
the Repeal movement; and the celebrated Corn Exchange
scene of "Sharman, my jewel",[5] effectually put an end to
Mr. O'Connell's hopes, if indeed he ever seriously entertained
such hopes, of converting the men of the North to his
insidious purposes. A new, and considering that the policy
had emanated from Rome, a most extraordinary plan was
resolved upon—it was no less than that of endeavouring to
proselytize Ulster to Roman Catholicism, and, failing this
primary object, to make the Roman Catholic community
greater bigots than even the natural tendencies of their
religion, and their habitual association with Protestants, had
previously allowed them to be. An exclusive system of
education had, many years before, given sanction to the
principle, and its application to other subjects was a matter of
no consequent difficulty.

In Belfast itself, and in the Counties adjacent to it, the friendly intercourse which subsisted between Roman Catholics and Protestants had rendered the former generally disinclined to the disturbance of amicable relations, in whose benefits both parties equally participated, while the educated, intelligent Roman Catholics looked with secret, and frequently with unconcealed disgust, upon the more gross absurdities of the creed to which they had been attached by the accident of birth alone. This, in the estimation of the Roman Catholic Priesthood, was an evil of no common magnitude, for whose prevention a remedy must be instantly devised, and this remedy was found in the establishment of a newspaper called the *Vindicator*. The wary and politic Dr. Crolly had been elevated to the Roman Catholic Primacy,[6] and a set of half-fledged Maynooth Priests succeeded to the direction of the machinery, which, for many years, he had plied with consummate dexterity. Charged equally with the bigotry, the proverbial ignorance, and the consequent self-importance of Maynooth, these worthies hit upon the notable device of inflaming the sectarian passions of their own religious adherents, while they scrupled not to insult the faith of all who differed from them, until at length they arrived at such a pitch of audacity, as to lay down the principle of *numbers* as the measure of civic representation under the New Corporation Act—exactly as we have shewn that they want to do under the more extended scheme of a Repeal of the Union. Roman Catholics, whether qualified or not, must be appointed to municipal dignities, on the sole ground of their being Roman Catholics; and though it would have been difficult for them to find, amongst their whole body, so many individuals of respectability as would have been equal to the number of posts demanded, yet even a Hercules-street "flesher"[7] must not be refused, should his election be necessary to the completion of the list selected by the Priests. These, and similar indications of an aggressive spirit, quickly awakened the slumbering faculties of all classes of Protestant society. It was instantly seen, that, unless the insolent intolerance of the Maynooth upstarts were checked

with some effect, the worst feelings of sectarian animosity
would be aroused, and that our peaceable community must
soon present the appearance of that most lamentable of all
judicial inflictions, under which "every man's hand is set
against his neighbour".

But our readers are not to suppose that political aggression
was the attempt primarily made. No; the direct inculcation of
Popery, as a system of orthodox infallibility, and the denunciation of Protestantism, as the foulest of heresies, were the
precursors, both of the municipal sectarianism first proposed,
and of the Repeal agitation by which it was subsequently, but
for a time hesitatingly followed. O'Connell, in his letter to the
Wesleyan Methodists,[8] adopted about the same time a new
character, and, concurrently with the *Vindicator*, appeared as a
virulent assailant of Protestantism in general. At this period he
was in London, and must have been acting under the spiritual
control of Dr. Wiseman, the Vicar Apostolic; and hence we
infer, that the sectarian crusade adverted to, must have been
part and parcel of a general system, though its working may,
in particular districts, have fallen into the hands of persons,
who, like their Scriptural class-fellow, cast about only "fire-
brands, arrows, and death, to themselves as well as their
neighbours, while they imagine that they are only engaging in
a piece of harmless, and possibly beneficial "sport" to their
ecclesiastical mother.

The appearance of Mr. O'Connell in the new, and for
a professed patriot, unnatural character of a "loathsome
Theologue", produced an universal sensation, and many
liberal Protestants, who, in despite of his previous inconsis-
tencies, still felt a lingering regard for his political fame, were
desirous of attributing his conduct, in this instance, to one of
those cometic aberrations to which great minds are said to be
occasionally subject. The men who thought so were quickly
made sensible of their error, as the sectarian Priests of the
Vindicator knew their man better, and accordingly they increased
in the violence of their tone, and the arrogance of their assump-
tions, until a large body of the educated and respectable

portion of the Roman Catholics themselves became so thoroughly disgusted with the exclusive journalism of the *Vindicator*, that they drew up and signed a respectful, but firm PROTEST, against the intolerant doctrines which had been put forth. They had lived—many of them from infancy—amongst Protestants, and they knew that the latter had never, in private life, made any distinction between them and other classes of citizens, while they recollected that the passing of the Emancipation Act of 1829 had been effected mainly by Protestant exertion; so that, in addition to its gross impolicy, the course protested against was attended with the aggravating accompaniment of ingratitude. The PROTEST, and especially the respectability of the signatures attached to it, threw the sacerdotal clique into confusion, and agencies of the most extraordinary description were resorted to, in order to compel individuals to withdraw their names—"enormous lying" was, in some cases, not spared, and the terrors of the Priest's spiritual cut-whip were held out in others; but, though partial secessions occurred, the better part of the Protestors remained firm to their original purpose. Dr. Denvir, the Roman Catholic Bishop, then came forward, and, in no very indirect terms, added to the cause of the priestly exclusives all the weight and sanction of his Episcopal authority, so as to identify the *Church* with the policy of the *Vindicator*, in its two-fold character of Anti-Protestant rancour and Roman Catholic aggrandizement.

All this time the question of Repeal itself was studiously kept in the back-ground, and the system of daily assault on the Protestant faith which we have described, and which, from the striking facts already adduced, was evidently not the effect of mere accident, was kept up with increased vigour. What benefit to their cause the contrivers of that system could have expected from its operation, we may safely defy human ingenuity to discover. It was calculated to alarm and disgust Protestants of all religious and political creeds; and it had this effect to a degree scarcely equalled in the records of public opinion. Yet this was the preparatory ground-work upon which Mr. O'Connell, and his partizans, had resolved to

erect, in Ulster, the imperishable temple of Repeal. The plan
was notably devised, and it exhibited, in its every development, the genius of some mighty architect, whose fame ought
to be transmitted to all futurity. The plan was, first, to insult
us and our religion, without distinction of sect or party;
secondly, to attempt the putting of our necks under the feet of
the Roman Catholics, even when the latter are in a local
minority; and, lastly, to call upon us, in no very humble tone,
to join them in the promotion of a scheme for exalting them
to the dignity of a permanent national ascendancy! If *they*
exhibited, and the *Church*, patronized, such a spirit as this,
when, in regard to Belfast at least, Roman Catholics constitute
an insignificant, uninfluential minority, what would they not
do, supposing them to have in their own hands the uncon-
trolled direction of the national councils? We had nearly
forgotten to state, that Mr. O'Connell himself openly participated in the *Vindicator's* policy; and, lest the PROTEST above
referred to should, in any way, shake the confidence of the
Roman Catholics in that "very useful journal", as Dr. Denvir
had called it, Mr. O'Connell took the trouble of writing a
special letter to the "useful journal", in which he not only
made common cause with the sectarian faction here, but gave
additional proofs of his own zeal on its behalf, by blackguarding
Protestantism in general, through all the moods and tenses of
the most vituperative oratory which he could command, in
the exercise of his recently assumed function of a "loathsome
Theologue". Let this important fact be distinctly recollected,
as it forms the concluding link in a chain of evidence, resistless
as demonstration itself, as to the ulterior intentions of the
Repealers—intentions which the parties themselves had not
the sagacity to hide—and they must, consequently, now stand
permanently convicted upon their own recorded testimony.

Occasionally, during the course of last Summer, the
Repeal doctrine was quietly hinted in the *Vindicator*; but, when
the way was supposed to have been nearly opened, that doctrine was directly propounded, in the shape of communications
from "English Gentlemen" and others; and lastly came its

direct advocacy. Besides abusing our religion, O'Connell himself was, at intervals, preparing the Northern soil for the reception of the "good seed" about to be cast into it, by bestowing upon the people of Belfast especially, all the foul epithets to be found in his copious vocabulary. Such were the spiritual and moral arrangements that were made for our conversion to the great national cause of Repeal—and they were, in every respect, worthy of that cause; though we must acknowledge, with a becoming regard to truth, that it is seldom the devil has shown himself to be so great a blockhead as he proved to be in this instance.

It having now been resolved upon, in solemn conclave, to throw aside the reserve previously manifested, and to declare at once for Repeal, the work was vigorously set about, and the agents employed were admirably suited to their vocation. The Priests wrote in proportion to their knowledge of English, and their acquaintance with the questions which they pretended to discuss, while the tavern meetings, frequently rendered necessary by the critical posture of affairs, had the double effect of promoting the cause of national independence, and of ministering to the equal necessities of arid clerics and thirsty laics, whose "zeal" had literally dried them up. In consequence of remonstrances which had been privately forwarded from a certain high quarter, against the impolicy of the *Vindicator's* sectarianism, the manifestation of which was regarded as premature under circumstances to be shortly expected, a tone approaching to religious conciliation was adopted—and, in truth, it was now most painfully manifest that the original system had not only failed, but had, in addition, done unexpected mischief. Sectarian exclusiveness was ostensibly repudiated; and feelers were put out, for the purpose of ascertaining the extent to which the instinctive recollections of the past could be obliterated from the public mind.

Not long after the close of the Parliamentary Session in August last, Mr. O'Connell announced his intention of making Provincial "progresses" throughout Ireland, for the purpose of organizing his favorite agitation against the Legislative Union;

and the distant hope of a Repeal demonstration in Belfast,
presented irresistible charms to the ardent imaginations of
certain aspirants after distinction amongst the Roman
Catholic body of this town. The thought of being brought
into personal communication, and probably personal contact
with the "Liberator", was a temptation of no common power,
and then the possibility of his consecrating some hitherto
unknown domicile, by the acceptance of its hospitable protection, either by night or day, added transcendentalism to the
prospect, and bade utter defiance to the icy suggestions of
prudence. The wiser heads amongst the party deprecated this
project, and protracted were the discussions which ensued;
but at length, the juniors so far prevailed, as to have the
decision of the matter left to Mr. O'Connell himself, and
communications on the subject of his visiting Belfast, were
accordingly made to him. He knew the North better than to
be rash in giving an affirmative answer; and in the meantime,
the prudential section of the Repealers, who were sufficiently
aware of the real weakness of their party, did not fail to put
Mr. O'Connell in possession of their sentiments and their
fears. For a considerable time he demurred to the proposal of
the *Vindicatorial* Consistory, but their upstart vanity impelled
them only to renewed urgency on this account, and accordingly at a meeting held in the "Victoria News-Room" (*Vindicator*
office) on Saturday, October 17, 1840, it was arranged, that a
deputation should meet Mr. O'Connell at the dinner to be
given to him in Drogheda, on the following Monday, and
should formally invite him to Belfast. It is to be presumed,
that the deputation fulfilled their Mission, since in the Report
of Mr. O'Connell's speech at the Drogheda dinner, he is
made to say—"If the Belfast Repealers wish my attendance, I
will attend—if they prove themselves *worthy* of our co-operation,
we will co-operate with them." Indifferent comfort this!—
especially when taken in connexion with the two dilatory,
and almost tantalizing postponements which followed.
Mr. O'Connell spent from the 19th day of October, till the
4th of December, in deliberating whether the Belfast Repealers

were or were not "*worthy*" of the honour of his co-operation—
being a period of rather more than a fortnight—and on the
day last mentioned, he wrote to Charles M'Alister, esq.,
Druggist, Belfast, the most extraordinary letter that has ever
been penned, in reply to an invitation to any dinner public or
private. From an Editorial analysis of this unique production,
published at the time in the *Belfast News-letter*, we take the
following curious particulars:—

1. Mr. O'Connell, after reproaching himself for the *delay*
which had occurred in forwarding his reply to the Belfast invitation,
expressed his fears, that in consequence of the delay, a public dinner
could *not* be had.

2. He would accept a dinner, if arrangements for it could possibly
be made.

3. He would rather have *no* dinner, but would prefer addressing
a public meeting.

4. Enemies were in the way, a bigoted press at work, and then
to quote his own words—"It is still more lamentable, that your estimable and excellent Assistant Barrister, has had occasion to describe
the *state of* CRIME *in your town, as* EXCEEDING ENORMOUSLY *that of* ANY
OTHER TOWN IN *Ireland*." He had his personal fears, it seems.

5. Again, Mr. O'Connell urged the inexpediency of a public dinner, unless effective arrangements could be made, and he concluded,
by informing Charles M'Alister, Esq., that on the 19th instant, he
would write to him again.

The same number of the *Vindicator*, which contained
this letter, contained also an announcement, that the dinner
arrangements, as originally proposed, would go on, and
consequently, Mr. O'Connell was pledged to attend. At first,
it had been given out as a "St. Patrick's Orphan Charity"
dinner, in the expectation that some considerable number of
Protestants might be tempted to associate themselves with
Mr. O'Connell at the festive board, especially, as the object
was to be ostensibly a benevolent one—the question of Repeal
being *burked*[9] for the occasion. This trap was intended chiefly

to catch the Liberal section of the Protestant community, but it signally failed, and then the scheme was reverted to, of trying a *Reform* dinner on general principles, without committing any individual either to Repeal, or to any other plan of organic change. Loud were the appeals made to Liberals of all classes on the necessity of Union, and the oblivion of all minor points of internal difference, and tedious were the disquisitions supplied by the priests on the public services rendered to Ireland, by O'Connell, and the more than doubtful sincerity of that nominal Irishman, who would not hail his advent to the Northern Metropolis, with "shouts of high acclaim". This device also failed to accomplish its end, and then the *Vindicator* gentry turned round upon the Protestant Liberals, with a fury that was absolutely rabid— every man who should refuse to attend the O'Connell festival, was denounced as being *no* Irishman, but a *"mongrel"*, or a bigotted descendant of John Knox, or some *"foundling of nature"*, who had derived his origin from *"a fifer in Cromwell's army"*. Ireland, it was boldly declared, rejected all such characters, and with the fierce tones of an Indian war-whoop, they were peremptorily ordered to begone to their " *own country*". A broad, unconcealed intimation was held forth, that the descendants of all English and Scotch settlers in Ireland, who would not tie themselves to the tail of Mr. O'Connell, ought to be expelled from our "sacred island", in common with the herd of reptiles driven into the sea, by the miraculous agency of our patron Saint, while the enjoyment of all the riches of the soil, and of all the natural beauties of Irish scenery, should be left exclusively to the offspring of Milesius, and to the "foreign" minority, who might fraternise with their cause, thus purchasing the privilege of being last devoured by a dereliction of all honourable principle. This was out-speaking with a vengeance, the purport of which, idiotism itself, could scarcely mistake; but we return to our regular narrative.

Although Mr. O'Connell, in his first letter, had promised to write to his respectable correspondent in Belfast, on the

19th of December, yet, as in the former case, he took nearly a fortnight longer before he could make up his mind as to the ultimate *worthiness* of his Northern admirers. In a letter dated December 30, and addressed to Charles M'Alister, Esq., he at length informed him of the extreme satisfaction which he felt in accepting the invitation to a public dinner in Belfast, where he would be on the 18th of January, in full time to make himself acquainted with the arrangements. He had been informed that the dinner would take place in the evening, that the Repeal movement would be held on the following day (Tuesday) and that arrangements had been made by a number of ladies for a soirée, to which Mr. O'Connell was invited, and which was to take place on the evening of the day last mentioned. In reference to this additional compliment, he said, in the letter under review, "I am proud to be allowed to pay my respects to the lovely and good of your town". Before this period, Belfast had been the most enormously *criminal* town in all Ireland; now, it appeared that there were *some* "lovely" and "*good*" ones in it, who, like the five "righteous men" in the Scripture history, had sufficient influence to save a whole city from judicial condemnation. The tone of this letter, too, was essentially different from that of the previous communication: every thing now must be conciliation and kindness—no driving of "*mongrels*" into the sea with "kail stocks"—no offensive exhibition must take place, for neither in "matter nor in *manner*" ought the opponents of Repeal to have any cause of complaint against its adherents. The moderation, thus affected, came, however, too late to be useful, as nineteen-twentieths of the "*criminal*" respectability of Belfast had determined to give no countenance to the affair in any shape.

This letter, as we have said, was dated on the 30th of December, and appeared in the *Vindicator* of January 2; but, at the meeting of the Repeal Association, in Dublin, on the 27th, Mr. O'Connell had ostentatiously proclaimed his triumphal journey towards the North, and, after particularizing (amidst cries of "God speed you") the 17th of January as the day upon which he would leave the metropolis for Belfast, he added "I wish I could collect in my pocket handkerchief all the cheers I will get until I pass by the Linen-Hall there, and I am much mistaken if they do not get a re-echo when I go there." (Cheers and laughter.) This did not look like a wish or an intention to avoid every thing that might be unpalatable in "matter or *manner*" to the parties opposed to him. He wrote, moreover, a letter to Dr. Blake, the Roman Catholic Bishop of Dromore, announcing the very hour of the day at which he would pass through Drogheda, Dundalk, and Newry, respectively, at each of which places triumphal processions were arranged to meet and accompany him on his progress; and it was in this style that he originally proposed to march to the "peaceful agitation" of the North. It is needless to add, that apprehensions of the most serious nature were universally entertained by all who wished well to the tranquillity of society; and it would appear from the event, that Mr. O'Connell himself was not long in discovering the perilous nature of the experiment which his inherent love of popular display had prompted him to suggest. Within three short days, a "change came o'er the spirit of his dream".

It may be necessary to mention that, in the letter last quoted, Mr. O'Connell carefully limited his stay here in the following terms, viz.: "I should hope to be able to sail for Glasgow on the night of the 19th or early on the 20th; if not, my better way may be to return to Dublin on the 20th, and go hence that night to Liverpool." A vague report, as will afterwards appear, had reached him, relative to Dr. Cooke's probable intention of inviting him to a public discussion, all opportunity for which it was determined to preclude, under the convenient plea of engagements contracted beforehand.

On Saturday, the 2nd of January, Mr. O'Connell's definitive acceptance of the Repeal invitation to a dinner in Belfast appeared in the *Vindicator*, as we have already intimated. On the following Tuesday, an authorized announcement of Dr. Cooke's intention to challenge him was published in the *Ulster Times*, and the challenge itself came forth, in an official form, in the *Chronicle* of the following morning (Wednesday). We are thus particular in noting dates because in some of the newspaper discussions which ensued considerable stress was laid upon the circumstance of time. The annexed is a copy of the learned Doctor's challenge:—

TO DANIEL O'CONNELL, ESQ., M.P.

Belfast, 5th January, 1841.

sir,—So long as you confined your *Repeal Agitation* to the South of Ireland, no man *dared* to meet you. But this want of *daring* was not want of *courage*—it was the mere shrinking of gentlemen from such rude and ungenerous treatment as you furnished to your *quondam protégé and friend*, Mr. Sharman Crawford, when, in the simplicity of confidence, he allowed himself to be inveigled to the *Corn-Exchange*, where a *fact* was turned aside by a *jest*, and an *argument* replied to by an *insult*.

But when you *invade* Ulster, and unfurl the flag of *Repeal*, you will find yourself in a new climate. And as there never yet was a man who could equal you in "putting off or on" to suit his company, I do expect to find you in Belfast as innocent and well-mannered a gentle-man, as anyone could desire in a summer day. And were I sure that you would never return to your *original nature*, and abuse Belfast, *when you had fairly got out of it*, as lately you did—when, echoing the eructations of a bilious Barrister, you pronounced it one of "*the most criminal towns in the kingdom*";—and, were I sure you would not affirm that "*from Carrickfergus to Cape Clear*", you were received, not only with-out opposition, but with eyes of admiration and shouts of applause— were I sure on all these points, I must confess I should shrink, as others have done, from venturing or offering to come into conflict with you. But, so far from being sure that you will not do these things, I am fully convinced that they are just the very things you would do. You will "*blarney*" Belfast so long as you are in sight of it, and it will be in your vocabulary a "*great city*" of the "*lovely and the good*"; but, once over the border, it will again shrink into "*a village*" (you recollect that) and the "*lovely and the good*" town will again become "*the most criminal*

THE CHALLENGE.

in the kingdom". And I know, that were you to enter and pass through Ulster in unimpeded triumph, your organs, that at first proclaimed your *invasion* as "the most signal triumph ever achieved over bigotry", but who, on hearing of the possibility of your being met in argument, have lately drawn in their horns, and begun to inculcate *peace* (rare apostles they of peace who have called Mr. O'Connell into Ulster to proclaim it)—were you once fairly out of town, full well I know they would soon be at their "*triumphs*" once more, and the North and the South would ring with the "*hullabaloo*" of your unexampled victories; and as for yourself, I do equally well know you would dare to tell the British Parliament that *Repeal* was the very lifepulse of the country, and that "*The sturdy Presbyterians of Belfast*" had received you with all their hearts as its mighty organ, the people with "*morning shouts*", the gentlemen with *dinners*, and the "lovely and the good" with *oceans of evening tea!*

Now it is just because I know you would attempt all this, and more, that I, by God's help, will attempt to prevent you; and that, Mr. O'Connell, not in your own favourite style of "*Sharman my jewelling*", but in calm, deliberate, and logical argument. And to this decision I, perhaps, should never have arrived, but that, being challenged *by one of your own entertainers*, to meet you and discuss *Repeal*; and acting upon a principle that I have long adopted, *that* "*a jest has always some earnest in it*", I replied, "I *would* meet you", and hoped by God's blessing, on a good cause, literally *to make an example of you.* And, this, I said, in no vain confidence in my own poor abilities, but, literally, and plain truth to speak, because I believe you are a great bad man, engaged in a great bad cause—and as easily foiled by a weak man, armed with a good cause, as Goliah, the Giant of Gath, was discomfited by the stripling David, with no weapon but a sling and two pebbles from the brook.

I propose, accordingly, the following plan for your consideration:—

1. Your proposed *Repeal meeting* in Belfast, instead of a meeting for harangues, "*all on the one side*", shall be a discussion between *yourself and your humble servant.*

2. The meeting shall be managed by a committee, composed equally of your friends and mine.

3. Tickets (*free*) shall be issued under their common authority—
one-half to your friends—*one-half* to mine.

4. Subject—The advantages or disadvantages of a *Repeal of the
Union* to Ireland—in its bearing on agriculture, manufactures,
general trade, safety of the present settlement of all property, and the
protection of civil and religious liberty.

5. Each speaker to confine himself, as far as possible, to two hour
speeches, but no absolute limit beyond the feeling of the speaker;
but, if the opener of the discussion occupies three hours, he shall
forfeit his right of reply.

6. The meeting to be governed by two chairmen, one chosen by
each discussionist.

And, now, Mr. O'Connell, let me speak a word very plainly to
you. *You cannot avoid this discussion.* I am the man   you have so often
reviled *behind his back*—can you do less than meet him *face to face*? You
can not pronounce me too ignoble for your argument, when you did
not judge me too obscure for your abuse. Turn the matter as you
will you can find no excuse or evasion. Let your friends hint that it
may *endanger the peace.* The time to have thought of that was, *when they
invited you to make an experiment upon our Northern patience.* But, in point
of fact, Mr. O'Connell, the discussion will be the surest mode to
preserve the peace, which your presence can never once endanger.
Even the recollection of all your recent abuse of "*our village*", our
"most criminal village in the kingdom", could not provoke us to
more than *a legal morceau*, which I have provided for your feasts, viz.
the STATISTICS OF NORTHERN CRIME, in which, by reference to the
records of *county gaols* and *local prisons*, I purpose to trace upwards,
both before *you and the empire*, the streams of crime, and inundate the
really guilty with the polluted waters they have muddied and
embittered at their fountain heads.

Nor think, Mr. O'Connell, to evade me by saying—"Ah! *The
loathsome Theologue* means to drag me into a religious controversy—
and, as it suits my present tactics *to forget all I said about his religion last
year*, so I can make that my excuse for refusing to meet him." No, no,
this will never do—I will not leave you this pitiful loop-hole—I
pledge myself *to avoid every purely theological topic*, and to confine myself

exclusively to *subjects of political economy and jurisprudence*: and, if your church have embodied these subjects in the tomes of her theology, her decretals, extravagants, and bulls, that is no fault of mine. As a lawyer, you know that this mixture took place when Popes were Emperors, when Cardinals were prime ministers, when priests were counsellors, and monks scriveners. Another secret let me whisper to you—if you refuse this discussion, the ghost of it will haunt you on the benches of St. Stephens'. I grant you that, to prostrate me, could gain you little credit, but to shrink from me, under any pretence, would ensure you the greater disgrace. You profess to be able, if they would   but hear you, to convince the *Conservatives* of the mischiefs of the Union. You never before had such an offer of a Conservative audience. Prove then your sincerity, by appearing before them.

I have only now to add, for the satisfaction of the public, that, as I have written you a *private letter* to Dublin by this evening's post; and as that letter will reach you on the morning of the 6th, before you set out for *Mullingar*, where, I perceive, you are to be on the 7th— having thus given you timely and sufficient notice, I beg to crave your reply on the 9th, or 10th at *farthest:* and that, for two reasons— I wish the public to have timely notice of your intentions; and, in case you do not accede to my proposal, I have other public duties on hand that would call me to Scotland for a few days, and so render our meeting impossible.

I have the honour to be, both for truth and peace's sake, your faithful servant,

H.Cooke

p.s.—So far as the public are concerned, I beg to remind them, that I have written to Mr. O'Connell on the 5th instant, and that if I do not receive his answer on or before the 11th, I do not purpose to meet him in discussion; and the reasonableness of this limitation will, I hope, be acknowledged.

It is impossible to describe the state of consternation and dismay into which the appearance of this admirably written letter threw the Repealers, whose plans were now entirely disconcerted. On the other hand, the exultation of the friends of British connexion was great in proportion; and it is only justice towards the Liberal Protestants to say, that the great body of them were, in regard to the learned Doctor's championship on this question, quite as enthusiastic as were the Conservatives. Even the *Northern Whig* hailed the appearance of Dr. Cooke in the field as an auspicious event, likely, in its moral consequences, to give a quietus to the Repeal agitation in Ulster; while the *Chronicle*, generally neutral on public questions, took a decisive part on the present occasion. The *News-Letter*, in anticipation of the subterfuges to which recourse would be had by the Repealers for an avoidance of the proposed controversy, accompanied its publication of Dr. Cooke's letter with an Editorial article embodying and removing by anticipation, almost every possible excuse that could be alleged. The following is a copy of the article in question:—

We need information on the Repeal question, and must have it, and, in order to prevent disappointments, in regard to Mr. O'Connell's coming here at all, we beg leave to enter our protest against the occurrence of all and sundry of the following casualties, that is to say—

1. We protest against Mr. O'Connell taking a *cold* at Mullingar or elsewhere.

2. We protest against his carriage breaking down under any circumstances.

3. Most emphatically do we protest against the unexpected sickness or sudden death of any relative or connexion of Mr. O'Connell, within the forty-seventh degree of consanguinity.

4. We protest against every other accident whatever, *minus* an earthquake, which may possibly render his arrival in Belfast physically impossible on the day promised.

5. We protest against the slippery state of the roads being alleged as an excuse, so long as there is a smith in the kingdom to put into the horse's shoes a few extra "frost nails".

6. We protest against any urgent business arising, *ad interim*, in the universal world, which may prevent the Liberator from fulfilling his purpose of coming to Belfast.

Having now, as we conceive, by our varied protests, secured Dan's arrival amongst us, we go on still farther to protest against a series of possible excuses which may be alleged, for the purpose of avoiding a meeting with Dr. Cooke, and

1. We protest against Dan's dying in the *interim* on any account.

2. We protest against the supposition that a single Anti-Repealer, be he Orangeman or not, will apply to him a single epithet, much less treat him to a mouthful of mud.

3. We protest against the allegation that the *peace* would be endangered, as we will guarantee the orderly conduct of the Unionist portion of the audience. If any individual of this class shall misbehave, we engage that he shall be forthwith bundled neck and crop out of the place, by his own party, without the intervention of a policeman.

4. We protest against the supposition of Dr. Cooke's private letter to Mr. O'Connell not having been received previously to the departure of the latter gentleman for Mullingar. This town is distant from Dublin exactly 39 miles, and the Dublin Post-office is open at seven o'clock in the morning, so that no plea can be founded on the circumstances alluded to. It is not credible that O'Connell would leave Dublin before the delivery of the mail; but even if he had, there is a daily post between Dublin and Mullingar.

5. We protest against discussions in general being objected to, as Mr. O'Connell once did before in the case of Dr. O'Sullivan.[10] The bearer of the message was politely shewn to the door, and no formal answer returned. The excuse was, that Theology was in question, but in the present case politics alone are concerned.

6. We farther protest against the refusal of a public discussion. Our protest rests on the grounds distinctly set forth in one of Mr. O'Connell's own letters, in which "Protestants, Presbyterians, and even Orangemen" were invited to attend the Repeal meeting. He never could mean that they should implicitly swallow his statements without making their own objections. And this is exactly what

Dr. Cooke's meeting with him will effect. If he did not intend to
convince our judgments, by listening to, and answering our conscien-
tious objections, we are entitled to ask in his own style—

> What are you after, Daniel, my jewel,
> What brought you here, O'Connell, my man?

7. We protest against Mr. O'Connell's pleading his engagement
at Leeds as a pretext for skulking away on this occasion. He
avowedly expects no justice from British legislation; and what are the
interests of Leeds, at which he is to be only a subordinate actor, as
compared with the interests of all Ireland?

8. We protest against all mere humbugs that may be resorted to
in order to avoid a fair discussion of the question. O'Connell comes
to convert us to his Repeal agitation, and he must consequently hear
us in our own vindication before he can expect us to tie ourselves to
his tail. We cannot all speak at once, and Dr. Cooke being our common representative, so far as the Repeal is concerned, *must* be heard
if there is to be a public meeting at all.—If it is to be a private
meeting or a Ribbon Lodge, or any thing of that sort, why we shall
not trouble our heads about it; but, in other circumstances, we will
in the name of Protestants of all political denominations *insist* upon
a calm, rational, deliberate investigation of the whole matter. It may
be that we are all *wrong* in our opposition to Repeal, and what we
want is a fair opportunity of being set *right*. Would it not be a grand
triumph for O'Connell to bring over the North to his cause, and is
any sacrifice too great for the attainment of such an object?—*Belfast
News-Letter, January 8.*

Intense curiosity now existed in the public mind, in
reference to the answer which Mr. O'Connell would give to
Dr. Cooke's letter; and, accordingly, the appearance of the
Vindicator of Saturday (the 9th of January), was awaited with
some interest, as being likely to afford a shadow of the
"coming event". The *Vindicator* did appear, and declared it to
be *impossible* that Mr. O'Connell should *condescend* to meet
Dr. Cooke; but, amidst the ridicule and derision of the whole
Anti-Repeal community, and to the utter confusion and dis-

comfiture of even the ordinary herd of Repealers themselves, who are neither the most intelligent nor the most sensitive of mortals, the organ of the clique authoritatively stated, that they had in readiness "*a Hercules-Street Artizan!*" alias, a BUTCHER!! who was ready to accept the offered challenge!!! This substitution was so palpably ludicrous as to afford materials for incessant laughter to the universal public, including the Repealers themselves, who made a deplorable figure by generally laughing "on the wrong side of their mouths". Deep dissatisfaction prevailed amongst the mass of Repealers, and many curious anecdotes might be related in this respect, were it consistent with the objects of our publication to enter upon a topic so discursive. The individual to whom fame had originally pointed as the "*artizan*", who was to employ his cleaver upon Dr. Cooke's arguments, was, we believe, not a little indignant at the office assigned to him, and would have settled his account rather smartly with the authors of that report had they been immediately tangible.

As a mere sample of the bitter disappointment which prevailed amongst the great bulk of the "rent-payers", and of the recriminatory conversations which consequently took place, the following dialogue, the scene of which is laid in Ann-street, on the forenoon of Saturday, the 9th of January, is extracted from the *Belfast News-Letter* of the 12th. The Editor introduces it with an apology for the vulgarisms and oaths which it contains; but to expunge these would have deprived the conversation of its reality as a picture of actual life:—

TERRY *loquitur*, SHAKING HANDS—

"Morra, Barney,—how *are* ye man, every inch iv ye,—an' how's Katty an' the childre?"

"All bravely, glory be to God; and how are ye yerself, Terry? An' Molshie, the crathur—how's *she* getting' an?"

"Troth only middlin', poor sowl—this weather's hard an her, but still she buffs Harry, surprizin'ly. Where have yez been this a way?"

"Troth, I've been over the way there, gettin' the *Alligathor* of this mornin'. Pat an' Mike, an' Briney an' mysilf clubbed our pennies a-piece, an' here's the paper."

"Och, it's the *Vindicator* ye mane."

"To be sure it is, but the sorra wan o' me can get my tongue about the word this could weather, till I've put in a frast nail or two."

"Well, what's the news?"

"Tare an' ounty, man a live, is that all ye know about it? Hasn't Cooke challenged Dan?"

"Don't I know all *that*; but is Dan to meet him?"

"No, in sowl, but the *Alli-* the *Vindicator* I mane—says, that Lanty, the Harcklis-street boy, ye know, has challenged Cooke in Dan's place, an may be *he* won't do for him. The *Vindicator* says he'll welt the—out of him."

"Arrah, botheration! Is it fun ye're makin'"

"No, by the frost—there's the paper, an' there it is, in black an' white, afore yez."

(Reads). "Big tare an ounthers, an' *that* won't do for me by any manner o' manes. What for didn't some of the clargy take up the cudgels, an' not make *gomases* iv themselves wid sich an *amadhaun* as Lanty. By the powers iv Moll Kelly, the pass is sowld upon us, an' that's all about it. The Prispitearin blaggards 'ill have a purty while's laughin' at us. *Manam go Dhia.*"

"Tundher an' turf, Terry, what is it ye're afther.—*Manam an dioul*, if I don't think you're cracked or turnin' heretic yerself."

"The devil a morsal iv it, Barney—but blud an' ages, man, who can stan' to see us made fools an' asses iv, an' mocked at every corner by them blastit intherlopin' blackmouths an' swaddlers,[11] an' us not havin' a word to say for ourselves? I heerd about Lanty, but thought it all a joke. It was started in Tim B-g-n's back kitchen the other night over a go of grog; but who on arth would hae thought our own people sich asses as to expose us this a way afore the town? By my s-w-l, if I had some iv them by the ear I'd warm it for them comfortably, so I would—for makin' game iv us, for sorra hap'orth its else, betune you an' me."

"Whisht, Terry—man alive—don't ye see that sconsin' luckin' blaggard listenin' to us every word we say? Come acrass here to Jack's and I'll trate ye to half a one—the weather's cowld. (Whispering.) To blazes wid the rascal—he'll tell every word he has heerd, as sure as a gun's iron. How wud it do to mark him to grace with the laste taste in life iv a snow-ball?"

"Come along, Barney; never mind—we'll take the half-ones in the name iv goodness, an' say no more about it; only we're fairly—upon—that's the God's truth, an' every body knows it. If Dan disn't take the consate out iv Cooke afore lavin' this, tattheration to the farthin' iv *my* money he sees for a twel'month iv Sundays to come. To stick Lanty in for id, 's a mortial humbug, so it is, an' I won't stan' it; an', more be token, I don't care a traneen if all the yellow bellies in Belfast heerd what I'm sayin'. The cause iv ould Ireland to be dam-nified bekase Dan won't stan' by us, an' us workin' the nails aff our fingers to make up the Rint! To Darrynane wid him back again, if the dacent spark's not in him, says Barney O'Rourke; an' for Lanty, the worst I wish him is, more sinse nor to let his silf be made a worl's wondher iv, unless he's ped for it; an' then every mortial crathur till his taste, as the Heelan' man said when he kissed the cow."

"Thrue for ye, Barney—an' if Dan shud be bate, what the d-l do we pay him for but batin'? I was ax'd to take a ticket this mornin'; but no, by de hokey, says I, isn't it the man that gets the money that thrates! If he shakes the nonsense out iv Cooke, an' clears our correcthur, I'm his man; but to Peg Trantum's back parlour wid him, if he disn't."* [Exeunt—Barney in a passion.]

In the *Commercial Chronicle* of Monday, the 11th of January, the following letter appeared from the Rev. Daniel M'Afee, Wesleyan Minister, of Donegall-Square Chapel:—

---

* *Peg Trantum's* is a public house, said, by the vulgar, to be situated half-way between h-ll and purgatory; so that there is more bitterness in Barney's execration than might at first appear.

TO DANIEL O'CONNELL, ESQ., M.P.

Belfast, 5th January, 1841

SIR,—Were a gentleman to leave this country in debt to a merchant or a banker, there would be nothing extraordinary, if, on his return from America or the Continent, the creditor should demand payment, and, in case of default, hand him over first to a bailiff, and then to the Sheriff of the County. You are deeply in my debt. The public at large are witnesses. You were furnished with the items in seven letters, dated from 8th of Aug., 1839, till Jan., the 11th, 1840. On the 11th instant, then, you will be exactly twelve calendar months in my debt. It is rather remarkable that this should be the very date in which the Rev. Dr. Cooke demands payment of his bill! How strangely things occur; both are now pressing for payment, because we are aware you have got *quantum sufficit* of the tribute to pay you for your self-styled patriotism, and, in common honesty, you should now discharge all out-standing debts. No doubt it must startle you a little to find your old creditors coming upon you at such an eventful crisis. I fear greatly, however, that the worthy Doctor and myself will come off at a dead loss, as it is likely some Jesuit or other will strike the docket of bankruptcy against you, confine you in Limbo, and thus prevent the possibility of a legal arrest on the 18th inst., the day appointed for your visit to this "most immoral town in the kingdom". Come, however, you must—you are confidently expected—you are announced in all the newspapers, and placarded on every wall about town, as president of the grand *soiree* to be given by the ladies. Ulster is now in commotion—the cry of *Repale* is up— "the beloved Blackfeet and Whitefeet", the midsummer pilgrims to Lough Derrig and Struile Wells,[12] will pour into this great emporium of the North just to catch a glance of your burly figure, and see you shoulder the Ulster Protestants to one side as you swagger down the streets. From M'Swine's gun,[13] in the county of Donegal, to the Cushendall glens, and from Malin Well to Lake Sheelin, in the extremity of Cavan, the grey-coated boys will come furnished, each with his shillelah, and stand ready to cry out at your bidding, "hurrah for *repale!*" And then consider the trouble and expense

connected with the evening party—the cost of the splendid room—
the hire of tea tackle—the price of grapes, wine and confectionary—
the disappointment of the priests, their nieces, and the pretty servant
girls, who, for once in their lives, will show off for ladies of the first
quality at the *swarry*. Why, Sir, you *must* come—the disappointment
would be tremendous—you will prevent an immensity of mockery,
and, at the same time, excite more attention than any or all of the
gentry in Batty's Circus. To complete the matter, do bring O'Sullivan,
the family piper,[14] along, as he is excellent on that instrument. He
can play "No King but Charley", for the party, it being your favourite air, especially on Sunday evenings. Old Orpheus on his harp
charmed the trees and the stones from their places; but what is the
harp compared to the pipes, especially when treason and Repeal are
in the sound? Besides all this, the Protestants of all denominations
are expecting you; Churchmen, Presbyterians, Wesleyans, Baptists,
and Independents, and even the very Friends themselves are won-
dering if "thou wilt come". I am expecting you, and Dr. Cooke has
given you a *cead mille falteagh*. Never did any man enter Ulster before
under more favourable auspices. High and low, rich and poor, the
nobleman and the beggar, the clergy and the laity, are all of one
mind, and say—"Come, Mr. O'Connell, come." But stop, Sir, and
let us glance at the work before you. What is the preparation for it,
and what will be the result? Count the cost before you move one
inch out of the way, and consider well what you have to perform.

1. Above all things you must take care of *your sanctity*—not *your
person*. Here there is no man will shoot, stab, or insult you—Antrim
is not like Tipperary. Ministers here do not conceal murders, as they
have no confessional. You need have no fear for any thing but your
piety, as this is "the most immoral town in the kingdom". There are
fewer persons here who worship a piece of bread, pray to the Virgin
Mary, go to Peter Dens' Confessional,[15] dread Purgatory, seek for
Extreme Unction, renounce the Bible and follow the *ignis fatuus* [will
o' the wisp] of tradition, than in any other large town or city in
Ireland, and hence there is less *piety* and more of rational and
scriptural religion! Take care, therefore, of yourself. Confess for a
week forward before you set out—double your devotions every day,

and thus have a week's surplus of merit on your hand; and, above all things, bring a bottle of holy water in your pocket, and a holy scapular round your neck, to preserve you from the immoral infection of this Protestant atmosphere. Thus you may enter into Belfast fortified against immorality. Protestant truth will not be able to infringe on your popish falsehoods, nor open, manly, Protestant candour on your jesuitical and shuffling intrigues. You can then blow hot or cold, blarney or abuse, praise or blame, assert or deny, keep faith or break it, sing a psalm or a song; but never chaunt a palinode where you have inflicted an injury or uttered a well-known misrepresentation. So much for the tools; now let us glance at the work.

2. When you arrive here you *must* meet Dr. Cooke. There is no alternative but stay away altogether, or meet your antagonist face to face. No apology will avail.—Read a capital article in the *News-Letter* of to-day, hemming you in on every side. You must neither take a sore throat at Mullingar, sprain your ancle on the frost, take ill with gout or toothache, or, returning home, say you did not receive the Doctor's letter in time, complain of the shortness of the notice, plan another meeting for yourself, dread a breach of the peace; nor, above all, affect to despise or treat with silent contempt the letter of Dr. Cooke. You cannot do this. He stands on too high a pedestal for your low scorn to reach him. Protestant Ulster will shake her sides with laughter, and screw the muscles of her sober face in stern contempt at your refusal in *any form whatever*. Your party, chop-fallen, will hang the under-lip—the swaggering priest will become as pale as his apostolic cravat—the throat of Repeal will be cut in the jugular (or juggler's) vein, and the very life-blood of blustering, bubbling, blarneying humbug will flow, as it were, into the Lagan, along with rotten turnips and dead cats. You may then wander around the walls of Darrynane Abbey with Tom o' Bedlam's song in your mouth—

> "I'll mount upon the dog star,
> And there pursue the morning;
> I'll chase the moon till it be noon,
> And make her quit her horning.

I'll scan the icy mountains,
To shun all female gipsies;
And play at bowls with sun and moon,
And scare them with eclipses.

The stars pull'd from their orbs, too,
I'll cram them in my budget;
And if I'm not a *roaring boy*,
I'll leave the world to judge it."[16]

3. On arriving here, you *must prove* that Repeal will be a *benefit* to the country—that the glorious days of Brian Boroihme, when champions rode to battle on a *sugaun*, without saddle or stirrups,[17] were nothing to what Ireland shall then be—that the priests will build no more splendid chapels to exalt their religion, and that from the pence of those who are starving in mud-huts. You must prove, Sir, that there will be less corruption among a parliament of Papists, that in the old one of Protestants—that the union has had an influence in lessening instead of increasing trade in Ireland—that the state of agriculture will be better then than now—that manufactures will spring up under your fostering care, and that you will never be suspected of taking a bribe in relation to the working inmates of those commercial prisons, as it is thought you did in the factory question in England.[18] You must prove, Sir, that Belfast, which has far more than doubled its population, and increased its trade six fold since the Union, would have been a better town without it, and will rise into far greater importance if Repeal took place—it might not be amiss for you to show, that as Popery increases immorality will decrease in Belfast, because the opinion is generally entertained that the greatest number of delinquents belong to your infallible Church, though they are a very minor party in town.—Above all, you *must demonstrate*, and that as clearly as the 47th proposition of Euclid—that, in case of Repeal, you do not want *ascendency* for your Church—that she is not "Mystery, Babylon the Great"—that she never had a principle of arrogance which led her to trample on the necks of Kings, and place the spiritual above the secular power in states; that if this were the case, at one time, as all history testifies, how came she to *resign*

this arrogant pretension and still *remain infallible*, "unchangeable and unchanged"? You *must demonstrate* also, that Protestants shall have liberty of conscience; that Ribbon societies shall cease; that we are to have no more assassinations and systematic murders; that Protestant life as well as Protestant property shall be secure; that under the *mild* sway of such an incarnation of arrogance and impudent pretensions, as are embodied in John of Tuam,[19] we are to have liberty to worship God in peace, and shall have no dread of another massacre such as that in 1641. You are to *demonstrate* to us that we are to have no more paid political harlequins, who, under pretence of patriotism, disturb the country, drain away the resources of the starving peasantry, and thus form a tribute for the support of the greatest national humbugger in the wide world. Now, Sir, if you *demonstrate* all this, you may come to Belfast, and we will believe you and join with you; but mark! It must be clear, sound *demonstration*; we will take *no vows*, listen to *no promises*, heed *no oaths*; all these will be useless to heretics like us. We know their value. Dr. M'Ghee has demonstrated this before the nation;[20] away then with these cobwebs, and let us now have *demonstration*.

4. On your coming here, in order to gain all parties and unite them in one cry for Repeal, see what you have to do. To gain the Presbyterians you must put down Dr. Cooke! To gain the Churchmen you must answer the charges of Dr. M'Ghee. To gain the Wesleyans you must publicly and decidedly recant the open, barefaced falsehoods which you uttered respecting the Rev. John Wesley—you must acknowledge Father O'Leary to be guilty of forgery, and that you still stand with your feet in his trap. To gain my approbation, for one, you must answer my letters; you must prove that many Popes have not been infallible monsters of iniquity—you must confess that Belfast never possessed a viler culprit, with all its immorality, than some of those holy fathers—and that a priest has a power of turning one of the half-penny cakes, which shall be handed round at the soiree, into the body and blood, soul and divinity of the Saviour of the world! Lastly, in order to gain the thinking portion of the "*finest pisantry*", belonging to our communion in the North, you must say something about the case of *Shanahan*, stated at large in my letter to your son Maurice. You recollect how he voted for your interest— how he, a Roman Catholic, was ruined for the good of the

Church— how he repaired to Darrynane Abbey with a document stating the fact, and signed by 22 of your most respectable adherents in Tralee, with Dr. M'Ennery's name, the Vicar-General of the Popish diocese, at the head of the list—and you recollect, also, how you wrote at the bottom of the paper, "I should consent to have all my family excluded from Parliament, and myself, also, sooner than have applications made to me for money in this shape." This docu- ment I saw, with your ruthless reply. Now, Sir, will you explain this? Do condescend to give a *taste* of explanation. The tribute, I under- stand, is withheld here until you arrive. Do justice to poor Shanahan. I appeal to the Treasurers. Let them retain Shanahan's share, at least what he had contributed before he was ruined by false promises. The sum can be easily transmitted. His address is, "Mr. William Shanahan, Ardfert, Kerry". The poor fellow will still take it as a matter of *right*, and though he will never forgive your cruel and ungrateful treatment, it will go to shew that there is some little honour and retributive justice subsisting even among beggars.—I remain yours, &c.

DANIEL M'AFEE. [21]

Belfast, Jan. 9, 1841.

The "*Hercules-street Artizan*" had turned out to be a blunder so egregious, that its contrivers themselves were heartily ashamed of it, and were soon glad to drop all reference to a topic so little calculated to supply gratifying recollections. The answer of O'Connell himself became the principal subject of curiosity, and that answer was given at a Repeal meeting, held in Dublin, on the 9th, as reported in the Dublin *Monitor* of the same evening. After a speech, *de omnibus rebus*, Mr. O'Connell proceeded, in the following classic terms, to descant upon Dr. Cooke's challenge:

"I must soon be upon my road for Cork; I am sorry for this, as it would amuse me to have some leisure to reply to my friend Bully Cooke, the cock of the North. He is a comical fellow; he invites me to a conference, and the mode he takes of conveying that invitation is by writing me the most insulting letter he could possibly pen. What a way of coaxing me to do the thing. (Laughter.) Why he'd coax the birds off the bushes. (Laughter.) I admire the talent exhibited in his letter. There is a good deal of talent in it. It amused me exceedingly when I read it, and I read it over twice for the pure pleasure of seeing what a clever cock of the North he was. (Laughter.) But, Sir, it came upon me by surprise. I mentioned to a friend of mine—by the way of asking an advice, as people do when they have made up their own minds on the subject—the contents of this letter; and my friend, who understood me to say, that not only was the challenge given, but that I had accepted it, said to me, 'my judgment is this: I think he was a fool for sending the challenge and you are a fool for accepting it.' (Laughter.) Oh no, said I, now stop a while, you are mistaken, neither of us are fools. There is more wit about the anger of Daddy Cooke than you imagine. It is a mere plan of his, for when does he send to me? On Wednesday morning when I was going off to Westmeath—(hear, hear)—I got a letter on that morning, signed, I thought, 'John Cooke'. I won't say positively what the signature was, but it was challenging me to a political discussion. It was not half the length of the document that appeared in the newspapers, nor the one-tenth part of it; but, when I saw the signature, I recollected that I had read an authorised contradiction in the *Ulster Times*, that Dr. Cooke had any such intention as that of challenging me;—that is, he told them he would not, and yet he afterwards did so. Why, he told a lie in his own person, in the first instance; for the authorised contradiction was authorised by him, and it was as if he signed the contradiction one day, and denied the next day his having done so. (Cheers.) I am in the habit of throwing into the fire every anonymous letter I receive –every letter without a signature in it goes, and those I conceive to bear fictitious signatures in they go also,—(laughter)—so it was with the document I speak of. I had read about five lines of it over when I flung it into the fire—I am sorry for it; for had I thought it was of value, I would have kept it as a curiosity; but, even had I preserved it, of what use would his challenge have been, for I was going that morning to Westmeath? That day, I could do nothing—the next day I could do nothing, for I was engaged at the meeting and dinner at Mullingar. The day after I could do nothing, for I had to come right to town in time for this day's meeting of the Association. To-morrow I will be in Kilkenny or Carlow, and go on to Fermoy, and the next day attend the Munster meeting in Cork; then, on the 13th, I have to be in Dungarvan; on the 14th, I have to come up to attend the great reform meeting on the following day, the 15th; on the Saturday morning, a meeting of this Association; on the 18th and 19th, I must be in Belfast; on the 21st, by means of railways, I will arrive in Leeds—remain there until the 22d; on the 23d, I must be at Leicester; and on the 25th, be in London—(long cheers)—so that by that calculation, my worthy cock of the north— (laughter)—knows I could not comply with his letter, and therefore he sends it to me. Now, let him crow as much as he pleases—I consent to it. He is entitled to the benefit of his trick, and as it was a good trick, why let him have the benefit of it. He throws out in his letter an excuse that he is a theologian, but would introduce no questions of theology. Now I tell him this—I am not a bit afraid of him on questions of theology. (Cheering.) That is his trade though it is not mine; but I challenge him to this—let him assail my religion in one of the Belfast newspapers, and if he does not get an answer, let him write me down any name he pleases. (Loud and continued cheers and laughter.) But I won't contend with him, nor am I such a blockhead as to take up a political question with him. (Hear, hear.) I have no notion to give him that advantage, which would be this—he is at the head of the Presbyterians of Ulster, and if I was to go argue politics with him, it would be admitting that I was an antagonist of theirs in politics. (Cheers.) I am placed by my education and convictions, it is true, in a difference of religious tenets with the Presbyterians, as they are to mine; but I am no antagonist in politics with them; on the contrary, I am most desirous to

serve the Presbyterians in every way in my power—(hear)—
and if, in my present struggle, I succeed, it will be as much for
their benefit as for that of the Roman Catholics. (Cheers.) Oh,
no, Daddy Cooke, I will not gratify your trick.—(laughter)—
but if this motive was not in my way, and if it did not compel
me to reject your challenge, I would reply to you, and say to
you, you come upon me in a hurry; you will be so good as to
remember, when this question was before Parliament, that in
my opening speech I occupied the House for five hours."

MR. REYNOLDS—"Five hours and a-half." (Cheers.)

MR. O'CONNELL—"Aye, five hours and a-half, for a
man that had his watch out counting time got tired of the
occupation. (Laughter.) You ought to remember, I would say,
that Mr. Spring Rice replied to me in a speech of six hours;[22]
and I wish to know how, in one day, the cock of the north and
I could battle it out—go through the entire of the business? I
would have an advantage. I am accustomed to fasting and he
is not. (Laughter.) Small blame to him." (Roars of laughter.)[23]

It may well be supposed that the publication of this worse
than bungling explanation, couched, as it was, in terms of
blackguardism, which would have been tolerated in no society
except that of the Corn-Exchange,[24] neither satisfied the public
mind nor allayed the excitement which had been progres-
sively growing up. On the contrary, the sympathetic contagion
rapidly spread throughout the country districts; and, whilst
the Repealers durst neither pit their champion against his
opponent, nor recede from the embarrassing dilemma in
which they had placed him, they struggled, with enfeebled
energies and with palpably hesitating councils, against the overwhelming torrent of public opinion which had already begun
to set in. Though considerable progress had been made in
fitting up the Pavilion, at the lower end of Chichester-street,
for the purposes of the intended dinner, yet, in the sporting
world, bets were freely offered that the Liberator would not
attend, and that the Committee and their friends would have
the consolation of dining "alone in their glory". In these

THE ERUCTATIONS OF A BILIOUS BARRISTER or "A second Daniel come to judgment."

pitiable circumstances a crumb of comfort was unexpectedly
ministered to them from a quarter which roused the just
resentment of the respectable portion of the community, while
it struck all classes with astonishment. Who, in the moment of
their distress, should come in to "heeze up" the hopes of the
Repealers, "but Andrew and his cutty gun", in the person of
John Gibson, Esq., Assistant Barrister for the County of
Antrim—the "estimable and excellent" individual a short time
previously eulogised by Mr. O'Connell. In reference to the
use which the latter gentleman, in his first letter to Charles
M'Alister, Esq., had made of Mr. Gibson's observations at a
former Quarter Sessions, to the effect that Belfast was the *most
criminal town in Ireland*, Dr. Cooke, in his challenge, censured
this statement as the effusion of a "bilious Barrister". On
Tuesday, the 12th of January, Mr. Gibson opened the Sessions
here, as usual, with an address to the Grand Jury, and in this
address he thought it consistent with his public duty, and with
the gravity and dignity belonging to his official situation on
the Bench, to make an attack upon Dr. Cooke, in language
which we forbear to characterise. Lest we should be accused
of partiality, we copy the *Vindicator's* report of the observations
which fell from his Worship on the occasion mentioned.
According to this friendly journal the Barrister said:—

"On the one hand, the observations made from this place
may possibly, to the prolific mind of a great national leader,
suggest appropriate materials for retaliation against that place,
where he may have thought the most extensive manufactories
of vituperation against himself, and those who think with him,
are carried on. On the other hand, the same observations
may, to a *ferocious* divine, writhing under the pangs of tortured
vanity, suggest a fit foundation for coarser sarcasm against the
individual who did not happen to be sufficiently enlightened
to discover that all must be peace and innocence, and bliss,
within the influence of the sanctimonious belligerent. It does
appear to me, gentlemen, that there would be about as much
justice of holding me responsible for the dexterity of the
orator as for the vulgarity of the priest."

This was strange language for a judicial functionary, officially engaged in the administration of public justice, to employ in regard to a private individual, who was not sisted before his court, and against whom no charge had been preferred; but, strange as it may seem, the fact that it *was* used, is corroborated by the reports of the *News-Letter* and the *Whig*, both of which agree with the above extract, almost *verbum verbo*. The *Chronicle* report, too, with the exception of one word, which *does not improve the case*, is in substance the same. This explanatory statement is necessary to a correct understanding of allusions to the circumstance above detailed, which will occur in the subsequent portion of our narrative— but to return—

Dr. Cooke, as may be supposed, lost no time in replying to the extraordinary speech of Mr. O'Connell, delivered on the 9th instant, so soon as it was ascertained to have been correctly reported, in so far as Mr. O'Connell's silence in regard to it, could be taken as corroboration. Accordingly the following letter shortly afterwards appeared in the newspapers:—

TO DANIEL O'CONNELL, ESQ., M.P.

Belfast, 14th January, 1841.

"It is a mere plan of his; for when does he send to me? On Wednesday morning when I was going off to Westmeath. (Hear, hear.) I got a letter on that morning, signed, I thought, "John Cooke"; I won't say positively what the signature was, but it was challenging me to a political discussion. When I saw *the signature*, I RECOLLECTED that I had seen an AUTHORIZED CONTRADICTION in the *Ulster Times*, that *Dr. Cooke* had any such intention as that of challenging me:— that is, *he told them he would not*, and yet he afterwards did so. (Hear, hear.) Why, HE TOLD A LIE in his own person, in the first instance, for the AUTHORIZED CONTRADICTION was *authorized by him*, and it was *as if he signed the contradiction* one day, and *denied* the next his having done so."—*Dublin Monitor's* Report of a Speech, delivered on the 7th, and *uncontradicted* by Mr. O'Connell, 14th January, 1841.

Mr. O'Connell, I pity you; indeed I do. And believe me, if I know my own heart, I can adopt the words of the poet, and say, my "*pity is allied to love*". Yet do not mistake me—it is not *the love of approbation*—for that were to merge the blackness of your sin in the brightness of your talents. But it is the love of *forgiveness* for all the slander you have been tempted to utter against *me*, and of prayer, that God would forgive you for all the falsehoods you have been tempted to utter against *your own soul*. And here, let me remind you, Mr. O'Connell, of the solemn sentence of our Lord, "What is a man profited, if he should gain the whole world, and lose his own soul?" or what would a man give in exchange for his soul? And now, Mr. O'Connell, do not, I beseech you, throw *this* letter into the fire; the terrible remedy I propose to administer to you may be your *turning point* for eternity.

First, then, Mr. O'Connell, you have my entire pardon for all the uncivil epithets you have bestowed upon me. For, surely, if you, *as a gentleman*, can *use* them, I *as a Christian*, am much more bound to *forgive them*. Secondly, Mr. O'Connell, I forgive you for unceremoniously calling me a *liar*. But while I do so, I feel at liberty, nay, bound to defend myself against the foul imputation, and to warn you against the *deadly sin* (your own church being the judge) into which you have plunged.

Hear me, Mr. O'Connell, and hear me, ye misguided people, who are said so loudly to have *cheered* him when I stood indicted before you on this foul charge of *lying!* Were I guilty, what is my deserving? I must skulk into bye-paths to hide my dishonoured head. I dare not look into the faces of my beloved ones, lest they should be reading the guilty records of a husband's or a father's dishonour—I dare not meet my friends, lest they should shun me on the streets—I dare not ascend the pulpit, the tribunal of truth, nor open the Bible, lest the lightnings of its page should smite me. Ah! Mr. O'Connell, yours is a profession that too often draws its glory from making "the worse appear the better cause", and you may consider it but a mere "trick of your trade", so unceremoniously to accuse me of *deliberate lying*. And had you so accused me in a court of law, when you were a *mere advocate for another*, I could have *pitied* the sad necessity that, in the world's opinion, though surely not in God's approval, gave sanction

to *conventional falsehood*. But when you accuse me in a case where you
are not *advocate*, but defendant—above all, when you accuse me in a
case where you profess to be a *Christian*, a ready champion of your
Church's doctrine, and a tried practitioner in her self-imposed aus-
terities,—surely, then, I am entitled to summon you into court, and
to indict you before God and your country. And now—to vary but
a little the language of a distinguished ornament of your own profession—"I will tie you down to the ring of *falsehood*, and I will bait you
at it, till your testimony shall cease to produce a verdict against me,
though human nature were as corrupt in my readers as in yourself".

I entreat you, then, Mr. O'Connell, to look back upon the *motto*
prefixed to this letter, and to read again your accusation against me.
And, now, stand up—rather *look up*, if you can. Look higher—look
up to God who sees your heart, and to whom you and I must give
an account of every *idle word*—and hear me.

1. In what *number* of the *Ulster Times* did you ever read any
authorized statement that I would not challenge you?

What do you answer, Mr. O'Connell? Pardon me if I am compelled to give a tongue to your silence.

MR. O'CONNELL *(for once in life apparently in perturbation)* replies, I
cannot exactly tell in what number I saw it; but, as I have *said it*, the
people will believe it. So, hurrah for *old Ireland, Repeal, and the Parliament
in College Green!* (Loud cheers.) Ah! Mr. O'Connell, Mr. O'Connell—
pardon me, when I feel that in a case so solemn, I approach the
burlesque. But, Sir, I must "hold the mirror up to nature"; and
there, Sir, in that ephemeral shout, which you purchased *at the expense
of an everlasting falsehood—everlasting,* if not washed out by the drops of
mercy—I say, Sir, in the purchase of that *ephemeral shout* lies at once
the mystery of your long-lived popularity, but the seal and the
earnest of your approaching and inevitable degradation.

YOU TOLD A LIE! Yes, and you *knew* it when you told it. But your
popularity was at stake, and—I shudder to write it—but—let
conscience finish the sentence.

Was it Mirabeau who boasted that he had ruled over *eleven millions*
of Frenchmen? You, Mr. O'Connell, have boasted of ruling or
representing *eight millions* of Irishmen. Yet he was an idol but of *four*

years: you have enjoyed the popular *apotheosis* of twenty. *But your days are numbered.* Had you met me like a man, the chivalry—nay, perhaps, the condescension—of the act had insured you, in any event, against a diminution of honours. But to skulk from the conflict beneath the meanness of a *falsehood!* Ah! It will pursue you like your shadow—it will haunt your very dreams—like the spirit of the murdered, it will "sit heavy" on the soul of your eloquence, and the whisper of my humble name—of the man whom you abused and belied *behind his back*, but whom you dared not to encounter *face to face*—will drown in the ear of conscience the loudest shouts of that momentary popularity which you purchased at the expense of every honest man's respect—and, what is worse, at the expense of your own.

I do ask you, Mr. O'Connell, when you said you had read in the *Ulster Times* my *authorized* disclaimer of any intention to challenge you—did you believe it yourself? And can you produce this moment *one man in all Ireland* that will say *he believes* you?

Perhaps you will plead that your *memory* deceived you. Take care, however, it was not your *imagination*. And remember there are those to whom a *good memory* is a most valuable appendage. After all, I should not be surprised if your *memory* were failing, as I perceive your *eyesight* is nearly gone, having mistaken my signature for "John Cooke". And as you have not condescended to favour me with a reply, so that I might feel at liberty to favour you again with my autograph for your future direction, I recommend you to purchase *M'Comb's Belfast Almanack*,* in which my signature may be found, that you may explain to your friends by what process of perverted or defective vision you came to a mistake so inconvenient for your reputation.

You say I played a "trick" upon you, and that I took you by "surprise"; you calculate your *cometic* motions to prove you have not "time" to meet me, and you talk of your "five hours spent" in Parliament, and of your wonderful powers of "fasting". In the North we call this *fudge*—pray how do you call it? What will they call it in Belfast, where you will have the *whole* 19th instant without a single

---

* [A correct likeness of Dr. Cooke, with his autograph, is to be seen in *M'Comb's Belfast Almanack* for 1841.—ED.]

thing to do but *sight-seeing* from *ten* in the morning till *soirée* time at *seven* in the evening? Don't say a word about the necessary parenthesis of a dinner. You know you could "fast"; and, as for myself, I dare make no boast of either my inclinations or capacities in that line, but when I cry hunger or weariness, it will be time enough to boast of yourself and to taunt me. Here, Mr. O'Connell, you had nine good hours, of which—be it remembered—I gave you your will. Freely should I have given you five, and contented myself with four. Within that time I do believe that by God's blessing, I should "*have made an example of you*"; but you have saved me the trouble, for by the public utterance of a *notorious falsehood*, you have "*made an example of yourself*".

You conclude your pitiable subterfuge by offering to encounter me in a *theological* discussion; and theology, you say is my *trade*. This is a miserable *ruse* that would disgrace any other man; but it got you another shout from the "groundlings", which you hailed as the presage of my certain discomfiture. I do not wonder, Sir, that you call my *theology* a *trade*. A man accustomed to sell *truth* for a puff of applause can never believe a man less venal than himself. I allow you, therefore, to assume the full benefit of the *sarcasm*; but not the benefit of the *bravado* with which it is trumpeted. *I take you at your word.* I am ready to impugn, in the newspapers, the sectarian and heretic doctrines of your church, upon one simple condition, for the reasonableness of which I appeal to the good sense of the public and to your own sense of shame.

The reason of my demanding a condition is this:

1. You stated, in Dublin, that you *recollected* having read, in the *Ulster Times*, what never was *written, printed,* or *spoken* by me; and the gulls shouted.

2. You stated I had told *one lie* on one day, and *another lie* on the next; and the gulls shouted again.

Now, if, by producing the *Ulster Times* in which your statement is contained you prove that *I told a lie*, and that you *told no lie,*—then, I confess, I am unworthy to meet you, and only wonder at your humility in condescending to challenge me. But if you have defamed me, and disgraced yourself, while I also might assert your utter unworthiness of notice, I shall overlook it as something in the way of

your "*trade*", and barely require to conduct our discussion on such
terms as shall shield me from your *genteel talent of invention*. To protect
myself, therefore, from the exercise of this talent, my proposal is this:
you obtain me, in one or more of your own papers—say the *Register*
and some other—one, two, or more columns per week, fortnight, or
as you please. You take for defence as much as I am allowed for
attack; and thus, by God's blessing, I trust to open both your eyes,
and the eyes of the multitude that shout after you, to the errors and
heresies that disfigure your theology, and the disloyalties and the
cruelties that disgrace your jurisprudence.

For yourself, Mr. O'Connell, and all who "*trade*" upon the
deception of the multitude, while I feel the pity due to the *men*, I
cannot, and should not, repress the righteous indignation due to the
religious or political *cheats*. For your country's sake and your own, I
would you had a better "*trade*". I am not yet so old as you but I have
some knowledge of "what is in man", both from observation and the
word of God; and of this I can assure you, while I warn you—that
the man who even makes a jest of truth, or delivers himself from a
dilemma by means of a lie, were he as cunning as the father of it,
will yet be caught in his own snare, and hopelessly overwhelmed in
the pit he has digged for others. And, further, let me tell you from
the same sources—never yet was there a man who employed his
power of popularity, not to enlighten reason, but to inflame the passions of his country, that did not sooner or later, kindle a fire that he
could not extinguish, and perish in the flames of his own raising.
Beware, Mr. O'Connell! Your expedition to Belfast perils the peace
of the kingdom. You won't discuss with me, forsooth, because I am
a PRESBYTERIAN, and you are not politically opposed to PRESBY-
TERIANS. I tell you, little for your comfort, Mr. O'Connell, there is
not, to my knowledge, a *Presbyterian Repealer* in Ulster—and I bless
God that I can proclaim the glorious news to the empire. Minor
political differences there may be amongst us; but in opposition to
you and Repeal, we present an united and indissoluble front. Had you
agreed to discuss with me calmly the question of Repeal *the Ulster
Presbyterians*, in common with their *brother Protestants*, would have
listened as calmly. I pay them no compliment when I say, they are
a thinking people, and they *see clearly through you*. They see you can

declaim, but dare not argue; and they see you want to overawe the Government, and to terrify the North by processions of physical force. But again, I say, beware! If the peace of the country be disturbed, and if, notwithstanding all the salutary precautions of Government, Belfast becomes another Bristol,[25] and property and life be sacrificed to the insatiable Moloch of your vanity—upon your head and upon your conscience let all the guilt descend. The very men who, in their folly, called for you, are standing like the fabled wizard terrified at the apparition their own incantations have conjured up; and, believe me, I do truly read your own mind, when I tell you, you would give a month of the *Repeal Rent* that you had never promised your fatal visit to Belfast. Mark me, Mr. O'Connell, I am not speaking out of vanity, but I tell you, you will never recover the blow inflicted by *a Presbyterian*. You have begun to fall before them, and so sure as ever Haman fell before Israel,[26] so sure will you continue to fall—unless you cast off your vanity, and repent of your sins—which may God grant, I do most sincerely and humbly pray. For peace and the truth's sake,

I remain, your obedient servant,

H. COOKE.

It may be added, that the *Ulster Times* formally contradicted the statement of Mr. O'Connell, relative to the publication of the alleged authorised paragraph, and offered to place its files at the disposal of any one desirous of investigating the matter. This proposition was scarcely necessary, as every reader of our local newspapers knew perfectly well, that no such paragraph as that described had ever appeared, and it was therefore, *physically impossible* that Mr. O'Connell *could ever have read it.*

In the mean time, in conformity to Mr. O'Connell's published announcements, the prevailing impression was, that he intended to carry out the mad experiment of having processions along his line of march, at least as far as Newry, in which town, preparations were actually made for his reception upon a grand scale. It was well understood, that if a procession were formed in Newry, scarcely any influence

whatever could have restrained the mob from accompanying
Mr. O'Connell on his way to Banbridge, and in this event,
a counter array would inevitably have been formed to stop
the invading cortege. Had a hostile collision between the two
parties taken place, no human foresight can calculate the
terrible consequences which might have ensued—Ulster, and
probably the whole of Ireland, would at this moment have
been a scene of butchery and bloodshed, such as has not been
known in Irish history during the last two centuries. Horrible
as were the scenes of 1798, they were but as feathers in the
balance, when compared with the still more murderous
results, which a miraculous interposition of Providence alone
could have stayed, in the event of O'Connell's having
attempted to carry out his original programme of a mob
procession towards Belfast. All the military in Ulster could not
have kept the two parties asunder, and, while we feel grateful
to divine Providence for the issue, we almost tremble at a
retrospect of the dangers from which, as a nation, we have
happily escaped.

The authorities at Dublin Castle seem to have had tolerably correct information, respecting the state of public feeling
here, and the consequent necessity of taking prompt measures
for the public safety.

The 99th Regiment, in two detachments of 400 men each,
was sent down from Dublin in steamers specially engaged for
that purpose by order of the authorities at the castle. A
considerable reinforcement of the Enniskillen Dragoons was,
also, marched from Dundalk to Belfast; and a large body of
Artillery, with four pieces of cannon, arrived from Charlemont,
a day or two previous to the Repeal exhibition. These forces,
in addition to the local garrison of Belfast, constituted a military array of more than 2,000 men, including cavalry; and our
town presented, for a time, all the external phenomena of a
besieged city. Extraordinary reinforcements of Police, under
the direction of Captain Flinter, arrived, to aid the local
Constabulary, if necessary, in the preservation of the public
peace; and our hitherto tranquil community wore a gloomy

aspect of bustle, confusion, and threatening preparation, unequalled during the last twenty-five years. Strong bodies of Military and Police were, also, stationed in Banbridge, Dromore, and the intermediate towns on the expected line of O'Connell's march, so as to be ready for action in the event of any emergency arising. Nor were these precautions altogether superfluous, as the threatened invasion of Down, by the frieze coats from the Louth and Jonesborough mountains, and the "redshanks" from the classic regions of Killeavy and Forkhill; the latter, consecrated in story by deeds of darkness and of blood, inferior only in tragic celebrity to Wild Goose Lodge,[27] had spread throughout the rural districts of Down, and the adjacent parts of Antrim, a noiseless, but deep and desperate excitement, which expended not itself in words—action would have been its characteristic, had the rumoured procession made its appearance. The newspaper organs of Repeal afterwards found it convenient to represent the matter as a conspiracy to assassinate Mr. O'Connell personally, but no assertion can be more false than this—it is a libel upon the Protestant community of the North, as there is not an agitator belonging to the Repeal brotherhood who might not, with entire safety, perambulate the country, not only without molestation but without insult. It was the intimation of a procession which created the danger; and so determined were the Repealers upon their physical-force display, that the *Newry Examiner*, one of Mr. O'Connell's own organs, exultingly announced the fact, that his arrival in Lisburn would be hailed by 4,000 sons of the Church, all marshalled in triumphal array! Is it any wonder, then, that the Protestant party felt alarmed, and were prepared, if requisite, to take measures for their own protection? In Dromore an immense crowd, accordingly, assembled on Monday, at the time when Mr. O'Connell's carriage was expected to pass, and several figures, denominated by the populace as his effigies, were hanged and burnt, with expressions of the utmost contempt. Similar excitement prevailed in Hillsborough, and in Lisburn the hostile assemblage were, if possible, more numerous and more determined in their resolution than at either of the places we have named. Placards, of which the following are copies, had been previously issued, and their effect was in the highest degree exciting. The 4,000 Repealers would have cut a sorry figure had they been so insane as to shew themselves in formal array. Here are the placards referred to:—

"O'CONNELL'S INSULT TO THE NORTH!"

PROTESTANTS!—A singular coincidence seems to occur at this time—exactly two centuries have elapsed since Phelim O'Neill, of notoriety, made rapid strides to overthrow all that bore the name of Protestant, in the North of Ireland, until he was signally defeated by a few of Lord Conway's troops, in Castle-street, Lisburn. And once more our hitherto peaceful and quiet town is likely to be disturbed by a second Phelim, who possesses a few of the talents, but wants the courage, of his predecessor. Now, we, *Protestants of Down and Antrim,* will be the last to offend the laws of our country, or offer an insult to the public peace; but this we avow, if there be any unusual excitement caused by the entrance of Mr. O'Connell into town, or any thing in the shape of a procession to disturb the public peace. And, further if there be any insult offered to even a school-boy, by any of his *Kailrunt*[28] *Infantry,* we will treat them to a *thunder of Northern Repeal,* that will astonish the brewers of treason and sedition, to put to rout his *darlint pisintry.*

"Protestants of Down and Antrim! Shew your loyalty to your Sovereign and your cause, by attending, on Monday, the 18th instant, in the Market-Square, at 12 o'clock, to assist the small remnant of her Majesty's troops, if necessary, and see the defamer of the glorious character of Protestant Ulster pass through in peace, the same way that other travellers do, upon more important matters than Repeal.
"*God save the Queen!*"

"HURRAH FOR REPEAL!

"On Monday next, being the day appointed for the Big Beggarman's visit to the North, Joseph Jelly, Comptroller-General of the Lisnegarvy paupers, begs to state, that a procession of Dan's peculiar fraternity will meet their illustrious brother, at 'Darrynane the younger', their future residence, on the Hillsborough road. It is expected that *all* who know the advantages to be derived from the trade, by a Repeal of the law prohibiting the exercise of calling on the Union, will join heart and hand in welcoming their esteemed friend, 'Dan, the Prince of Paupers.'" [29]

At Lisburn, as well as at Dromore, an effigy, intended to represent Mr. O'Connell, was borne along in solemn procession, so soon as it was ascertained that the original had passed through in disguise. This effigy was suspended to a tree, and, after hanging there the usual time, flames were observed to burst from its mouth, till the whole body of the image was gradually consumed, amidst the shouts and exultations of the multitude, who afterwards bore away the shapeless head in triumph. It was, however, distinctly understood, that, if O'Connell had come through Lisburn, as a private individual, without any ostentation or public display, no injury would have been attempted beyond the harmless accompaniment of a full chorus of groans and hisses; but when the degree in which his newspaper organs had roused the passions of the people is considered, it is, perhaps, fortunate that the experiment was timeously abandoned. We now approach

THE ADVENT

"THE Devil first saw, as he thought, the mail,
    Its coachman and his coat;
  So instead of a pistol he cock'd his tail,
    And seized him by the throat;
  'Aha', quoth he, 'what have we here—
    'Tis a new barouche and an ancient peer!'
  So he set him on his box again,
    And bade him have no fear."—BYRON.[30]

AT five o'clock, on the morning of Saturday, January 16, 1841,
Mr. O'Connell started from Dublin in a private carriage, in
company with his nephew, Mr. Charles O'Connell,[31] Tom
Steele, the renowned Pacificator of Clare,[32] and Dillon Browne,
M.P. for the County of Mayo,[33] all armed with blunderbusses,
pistols, and other implements of war, in order to be prepared
for any adverse contingency that might arise along the road.
The parties travelled under fictitious names, and so secretly
was the expedition conducted, that, though in accordance with
an engagement solemnly contracted at the Corn-Exchange a
week before, the "pocket handkerchief full of cheers" was
duly discharged at the Linen-hall here, on the arrival of the
cortege—yet not a solitary echo responded to its contents. In
fact, the "boys" of Drogheda, Dundalk, and Newry, had been
prudently disappointed of their expected turn out, and the
Liberator quietly crept into our town about six o'clock in the
evening, and took up his residence at the Royal Hotel,
Donegall-place, without so much as a welcoming peal of
"marrow-bones and cleavers" from the musical "artizans" of
Hercules-street. For this prudential self-denial we are far from
blaming O'Connell—it was judicious, and would have
merited our praise, had it not been preceded by empty
boastings, relative to the popular ovation with which his entry
would be greeted. The expected display had been found
impracticable and vain, and necessity was therefore turned
into the semblance of a virtue. O'Connell literally stole into
our town "as a thief in the night". As Mr. O'Connell has
generally made it a point to observe, with regularity, the
forms prescribed by the Roman Catholic Church, the upper
portions of Donegall-street, together with the adjacent streets,
were filled, on Sunday forenoon, with crowds of idle spectators, anxious to catch a view of the Liberator going to Mass,
at the Chapel in Donegall-street;[34] but their curiosity was
destined to disappointment. He remained in his hotel during
the day, but, like the vanquished Peris in the Oriental fable,
who, when taken captive and confined in iron cages by the
Dives, were regaled by their companions with the choicest

odours,[35] a special Mass was said in the hotel for behoof of
our hero of the spoiled procession. How the remainder of the
day was spent, we know not, and have no right to inquire; but
in the evening a meeting was held in the Victoria News-room
(*Vindicator* office), at which orations were delivered amidst tremendous shouts of applause. We presume that the exercises of
the evening were not devotional, inasmuch as it is not the
custom of ordinary Christians to vociferate during sermon—
to stamp on the floor till a whole neighbourhood is alarmed—
or to address the preacher with "bravo, my buck, go on"—
"hear, hear, hurroo, ould Ireland for ever", "three cheers for
the Liberator", &c. Equally unusual is it for Christians, who
have assembled on a Sabbath night for religious purposes, to
address each other in under-tones to the following effect—"d-
yer sowl for a whelp, ye've nearly tramped the toe aff me". We
conclude, then, that it was a Sabbath profanation meeting; it
was, consequently, no inappropriate introduction to the agitation scenes about to be publicly enacted on the two following
days—and this naturally brings us to

THE EXHIBITION
PART I.—THE LEVEE.

" But yester-eve, so motionless around,
  So mute was the wide plain, that not a sound
  But the far torrent, or the locust bird
  Hunting among the thickets could be heard.
  Yet hark! What discords now of every kind,
  Shouts, laughs and screams are revelling in the wind,
  The neigh of cavalry"—MOORE.

BRIGHT rose the sun at the appointed hour on Monday,
the 18th day of January, in the year one thousand eight
hundred and forty-one; clear was the sky, glittering and hard
the frost, and winter smiled as propitiously as winter could be
expected to do, upon the preparations which were in busy

progress at the Pavilion, in Chichester-street. Up rose Daniel
O'Connell—up rose Tom Steele, whose first care was to
ascertain the trustworthiness of his pike, and last, though not
least, up rose Dillon Browne, whose first orisons having been
duly made for the safety of his hair-trigger "bulldogs",[36] he
instituted a formal inspection of their working order, before
entrusting himself to the society of the "lovely and good", by
whom the portals of the Royal Hotel were about to be speedily
thronged. Up rose the Repealers, male and female—up rose
the Military and Police, while the din of arms, and the enli-
vening notes of martial music pealed in all directions, and
were borne by the breeze in softened harmony through the
far extending vallies of the Lagan, in which responsive echoes
were awakened, which had lain voiceless amongst the hills
since the days of Cuchullin. We have said that we knew not
how Mr. O'Connell had spent the residue of Sunday, after
private Mass, but this statement is not characterized by our
accustomed accuracy in regard to matters of fact. The truth
is, it was dedicated to the holding of a sort of Levèe, at which,
numbers of the "people" attended, and had the distinguished
honour of shaking hands with the Liberator. The forenoon of
Monday was spent in a similar style of "popularization", as a
late Repealer of some notoriety would have called it, and curious were many of the scenes which occurred. Mr. O'Connell
made himself agreeable to all, and certainly did the honors
with all the dignified suavity of a regularly bred courtier, while,
by way of giving effect to his frequent sallies of Irish humour,
he studiously retained his rich Kerry brogue. The blunt vale-
diction of an old "*artizan*" of Hercules-street—"God bless you,
Dan", was well received; and the exclamation of the Liberator
after saluting a lady, and then admiring her healthy condition—"why, my dear, you look as well as if you had been
fed upon Munster potatoes", elicited boundless admiration.

On this day, too, at half-past twelve o'clock, a deputation
from the Trades of Belfast, headed by Mr. Charles Bradley,
Mr. Owen Kerr, &c., waited, by appointment, upon Mr.
O'Connell, at the Royal Hotel, and presented him with a

congratulatory address in the name of the whole body, in which address they announced themselves as decided Repealers. Mr. O'Connell received them in a green figured dressing-gown and black cap, and, in reply, delivered to them a semi-ethical discourse on the necessity and advantages of political moderation, as the parties, he said, appeared to be "too angry with the Orangemen", while, on the question of Repeal, he was gratified to find that their hearts were in the right place. These formalities being over, Mr. O'Connell heartily shook hands with the delegates individually, many of whom, as the *Northern Whig* remarks, "must have afforded him considerable amusement by the blunt cordiality of their greetings, such as "give me your hand, Dan"; "here's a hand, Dan, my boy, with a heart in it", &c., &c. But those who court popular favour must not shrink from the occasional realization of their own theories of republican equality, else the magic secret of their power were gone for ever, though, at the conclusion of the farce, they may, like Wilkes of "forty-five" notoriety, confidentially whisper in the ears of friends, that, at no period of their political lives, were they their own partizans.[37]

No sooner was it known in Belfast that a number of individuals, professing to represent the various Trades, had presented to Mr. O'Connell the address above described, than the most indignant excitement generally prevailed, and counter resolutions were immediately adopted and published by overwhelming majorities of the several Trades alleged to have been represented. The Printers, the Bookbinders, the Bootmakers, &c, &c, all disclaimed the act which had been done in their names by "self-appointed" individuals, so that the *ruse* which had been adopted had the unexpected effect of bringing forth strong Anti-Repeal declarations from influential bodies of industrious and respectable workmen, whose sentiments might have remained unexpressed, had an abuse so unwarrantable not been made of their names; and, in the respect alluded to, the occurrence which we have noticed was singularly propitious. But these are merely preliminary scenes, and we must hasten to the proper business of the day.

"Nae man can tether time or tide,
  The hour approaches, Tam maun ride."[38]

PART II.—THE DINNER.

"THEN horn for horn they stretch and strive—
  Deil tak' the hindmost—on they drive,
  Till all their weel swalled kytes belyve
  Are bent like drums."—BURNS.[39]

DURING the whole of Monday Mr. O'Connell stirred not abroad, and did not so much as shew himself to the boyish crowds who, during the day, occasionally assembled in the neighbourhood of the Royal Hotel in the hope of catching a glimpse of one so renowned in agitation history, until about four o'clock in the afternoon, when he appeared at one of the windows, and exhorted the parties to betake themselves in quietness to their several residences. Six o'clock was the hour appointed for dinner, and this preparatory oration was consequently brief; but, before detailing the after-dinner proceedings, it is necessary that we should describe the *locale* of the scene, and the appearance which it presented to the eye of a disinterested spectator.

The Pavilion, in which the entertainment took place, was the old Victoria Theatre (Chichester-street), fitted up with wood-work for the occasion, and certainly, in point of internal arrangement and temporary decorations, it did no discredit to the taste of the parties who had charge of the business, as they made the most of the materials which had been placed at their command. The principal table was situated at the north-west of the building, while, at right angles to it, ten tables, each calculated to accommodate one hundred persons, were extended towards the opposite extremity. Side galleries for the accommodation of ladies had been erected, while the orchestra was placed in that quarter which immediately fronted the chair. The external covering of the gallery had a rather elegant and even rich appearance, but the depending curtains were, if not orange, at least of a colour which bore to it an exceedingly near resemblance, while the fringes might have been taken indifferently for a gentle blue, or a still more mitigated green. Behind the chair were two female figures crowning O'Connell with what seemed to be, and most probably had been intended for, a wreath of laurel, while on either side were banners exhibiting national devices, one of which was a figure of Erin, with a harp encircled with shamrocks; but so coarse was the workmanship, that, if the truth must be told, poor Erin had more of the bloated exterior of a shebeen house-keeper than of the angelic idealism naturally associated with a personification of the "Emerald Isle". Another emblematical representation of the same subject was placed in front of the orchestra, with a wolf-dog reposing at the lady's feet, and near it was a landscape sketch of Darrynane Abbey, while the mottos on these, and several other illustrative decorations, were occasionally ill-spelled. On one side of the gallery was placed a cast of her Majesty Queen Victoria— on the other, a bust of Prince Albert, while similar likenesses of O'Connell and Napoleon Bonaparte adorned the front of the orchestral department, in addition to the decorations already noticed. The room was lighted by several rich-looking lustres, while a profusion of party-coloured lamps, tastefully arranged, at intervals, amongst festoonings of laurel and other evergreens, imparted to the scene a truly picturesque effect. Considering their relative insignificance, as a party, the Repealers had exerted themselves in order to bring off the affair in a manner as creditable to their cause as circumstances permitted. Shortly before seven o'clock, Mr. O'Connell entered the room in company with a number of gentlemen, and immediately took his seat at the principal table. Robert M'Dowell, Esq., (the only Liberal Protestant who could be prevailed upon to accept the situation), took the chair amidst loud cheering, and, as no blessing was thought necessary on the occasion, the assemblage fell to work without a moment's delay, and it is only justice to add, that, during a good half-hour,

at least, "no slackness there was found". On the right of the
chair were the following gentlemen, besides Mr. O'Connell,
viz.:— John Sinclaire, Esq., ; John Martin, Esq., jun.,
(Killileagh);[40] Thomas Steele, Esq., (the Pacificator); John
Wallace, Esq., (Attorney); Chas. M'Alister, Esq.; Edward
O'Rorke, Esq.; James Russell, Esq.; Chas. O'Connell, Esq.
On the left were Dr. Denvir; Owen and Alexander M'Mullen,
Esqrs. (Castlewellan); Alderman Smith (Drogheda); Robert
Boyd, Esq.; John M'Adam, Esq.; Dr. M'Laughlin, (Roman
Catholic Bishop of Derry); S. Carson, Esq.; Thomas
M'Conkey, Esq.; John Workman, Esq., &c, of Belfast. An
abundant array of Priests, from all parts of the country, was
in attendance, and a few (not exceeding half-a-dozen) Liberal
Protestants, whom curiosity alone had brought to the scene,
were to be found stealthily ensconced in the bye-holes and
hiding-places of the meeting, as if anxious to avoid popular
observation. On the other hand might be seen the scouts and
out-runners of the *Vindicator*, slyly fishing them out, and noting
their several identities with an accuracy which must have
caused to the parties concerned no slight uneasiness, as, with
the possible exception of the Chair himself, and two other
Protestant gentlemen who sat near him, one of who is not
now a resident in Belfast, not one of the Protestant remainder
ever was, or now is, a Repealer! We have said that the tables
were calculated for the accommodation of 1,000 persons, but
those on the extreme right and left of the Chairman were, in
a great measure, unoccupied, while the lower parts of several
others were thinly peopled, and, allowing 40 feeders to the
principal table, the whole dinner party could not have
exceeded 840, or, at the most, 900. We say nothing as to the
quality of the bulk of the company, and equally imperative is
our silence in regard to the "galaxy of beauty" by which the
upper boxes were adorned. Some of the dresses exhibited
were certainly showy enough, and did no discredit to the
artistical talents of their makers; but beyond this candid
acknowledgment our information does not enable us to go.
Indeed, were our abilities in this regard superior to what they

really are, we would hesitate ere we employed them, when the power of the sex, as described by the Lady in Hudibras, is taken into account.

> "We make and execute all laws,
>   Can judge the judges and the cause,
>   Prescribe all rules of right and wrong,
>   To the long robe and the longer tongue.
>
> * * * * * *
>
>   We rule in every public meeting,
>   And make men do what we judge fitting,
>   Are magistrates in all great towns,
>   Where men do nothing but wear gowns."

We must, therefore, wear our "gown" and hold our peace, unless we would covet, as we do not, a renewed exhibition of the Cromwellian scene, in which

> "The oyster women locked their fish up,
>   And trudged away to cry—No Bishop."[41]

We have already intimated that the Repealers did not think their dinner worth the invocation of a divine blessing, and, of course, they could not be expected to take the trouble of returning thanks to the Divine Being for it. Accordingly, after no thanks whatever had been returned, and the cloth removed, the following loyal and constitutional toasts were given from the Chair, viz.:—

"The Queen", "Prince Albert", "The Princess Royal", "The Duke of Sussex, and the rest of the Royal Family resident in England", "Lord Melbourne and Her Majesty's Ministers", &c., &c. At length came the toast of the evening, "The Health of Daniel O'Connell, Esq., M.P.", which was received with tremendous cheering, and waving of handkerchiefs. It is impossible for us to record every thing said by Mr. O'Connell in the speech which followed, and we shall, therefore, confine our attention to a number of the most important passages. He began by professing himself lost in admiration at the enthusiasm of the assemblage, and emphatically asked—is this Ulster? Why the enthusiasm of the warm Southern heart is nothing to yours—here, if you once warm, you'll never grow cool. (Laughter, and cries of "get on the table". Mr. O'Connell accordingly got on the table, and proceeded.) What I want to know is, why I did not come sooner amongst you, for I never met men after my own heart till I came here. (Cheers.) Will they call this—have they ever called this the "Black North"? To me it is the bright and brilliant North, (pointing to the ladies' gallery,) no North contains such stars as these.—This galaxy of beauty would ornament any region upon earth. I am bound to admit, that there is a factitious appearance given to our present meeting, not so much from the zeal and energy of our friends, as the craft and activity of our enemies—from the boxing buffoon of a Divine (laughter), up to the truculent threatening of the worst instrument of faction, and a slight bit of hypocrisy amongst it. (Laughter.) Mr. O'Connell then went on to repudiate in strong terms, the idea of his having come to invade Ulster—he denied that Dr. Montgomery and the Belfast Reformers had been badly treated at the Reform Meeting lately held in Dublin and he characterised, as untrue, the charge that he (Mr. O'Connell) had ever calumniated the inhabitants of Belfast. He then referred to the danger to which he had exposed, not only his person, but his life, in opposing the Trades' combinations in Dublin, when he found them tending to produce criminality,[42] and he added—when coming here, you know I did not flatter any of you before I arrived; but, on the contrary, perhaps I was not only indiscreet, but worse, in taking up the Assistant Barrister's charge of criminality, but I allude to it, to show that I am not flattering the Reformers of Belfast. I am incapable of it, but I owe it to them, and to myself, to state, that I never included them all in my censure, and, at present, wish to exclude them from censure of any kind—(hear, hear)—I wish to wipe out the old score completely; and here I am now offering

Reformers of every class in Ulster to forget the past—to look
upon what has occurred as a dream at best, and to join with
me, heart and hand, in the struggle for Old Ireland. (Cheers.)
Let those refuse me who choose—at least I will have cleansed
my heart, and cleansed my conscience—if I have given blows,
I have received them—I forgive my share—am sorry for what
others suffered, and I cast open the door for all to perfect
reconciliation. (Cheers.) Mr. O'Connell next proceeded to
deny the charge of sectarianism, which had been preferred
against him, and, in doing so, said—there never was a man
more calumniated than I have been, or, at all events, more
abused; but, whether it be abuse or calumny—there is one
ting certain, that I have never been charged, either by friend
or foe, with one single sentence reflecting on the spirit of
bigotry or fanaticism in the religion of another. (Hear.) On no
other occasion before was I charged, even by the most virulent calumniator, or my deadliest foe, with one word of bigotry,
for the entire tenor of my speeches has been the reverse,
emanating, as they did, from my heart and judgment. I never
allowed a thought of bigotry or of animosity to my fellow man,
on account of his religion, to pass through my mind. (Hear.)
This fact, he said, he wished to proclaim to the men who had
assembled that day, to bar his way on the Queen's high road;
and he proceeded to narrate the services which he had done
for Orangemen, even after their own party had deserted their
cause. The Corporation Officers of Dublin, instead of applying
to the *Recorder*, or Dr. Lefroy, had come to him,[43] and even
the Deputy Grand Master of the Grand Orange Lodge, Sir
A.B. King, who would have been left to starve in misery, but
for his (Mr. O'Connell's) exertions,[44] and he added—I would
go one hundred miles to meet an Orangeman if I could serve
him, and I would do as much for an Orangeman, as I would
for a Catholic. Mr. O'Connell then read a warm letter of
acknowledgment from Sir A. B. King, and proceeded to say,
in reference to the Northern Orangemen—"I laugh at their
opposing my progress, on the ground that that progress was
entered into or conceived, in the spirit of religious or sectarian

bigotry, or with the intention of insulting any sect or party. (Cheers.) I leave such objects to the *Cookes* of a festivity of a different description from this." (Laughter and cheers.) Again, he said—"I have lived but for the promotion of freedom— unrestrained freedom of conscience to all classes and sects of the human family—I have lived but to be the advocate of civil and religious liberty all over the world—I have lived only for the advocacy of those exalted objects, and I have not, I think, lived in vain. I have not assumed the attitude of the gladiator, however, nor of the ferocious Divine". (Laughter and cheers.) "I hail the amalgamation of Protestants, Presbyterians, and Catholics. The principle that directs such an union, has been the principle on which all the acts of my life have been founded." (Cheers.) Mr. O'Connell then instituted a comparison between the English constituencies and the Irish, considered in reference to population, and he argued that Ireland was inadequately represented. In regard to Dr. Cooke's challenge, he said, he was ready to give him not two, but six, and even twenty-six hours, if he wished, on any subject connected with civil or religious liberty. (Cheers.) After a lengthened review of the "transition state" of society on the Continent and in America, as compared with a former period, the hon. and learned gentleman sat down, amidst prolonged cheering, and rounds of the Kentish fire,[45] which after some time were suppressed through the interference of Dr. Denvir.

The following toasts were given from the chair, and were duly responded to—"The Right Rev. Dr. Denvir and the Catholic Hierarchy of Ireland"; "Right Rev. Dr. M'Laughlin, Catholic Bishop of Derry"; "Civil and Religious Liberty". "The clergy of all religious denominations who have honoured us this evening with their presence", (there being no clergy of any denomination, but one, in attendance, the Rev. George Crolly,[46] Roman Catholic Curate, replied in a speech of tedious magnitude, which was brought to a premature close, in consequence, it was understood, of a hint privately conveyed to the Rev. gentleman from Mr. O'Connell.) "R. D. Browne, Esq., M.P. for Mayo". (Here Mr. Edward Campbell rose and asked Mr. O'Connell, whether, since he had given his son John to all Ireland, he would not give Dillon Browne to Belfast? Mr. O'Connell was understood to reply, that Dillon Browne was just such a man as Belfast wanted.) (Cheers.) "Mr. John O'Connell", "William Sharman Crawford, Esq., and Vote by Ballot", "Thomas Steele, Esq.," "Alderman Smith", "John Sinclaire, Esq. and the Volunteers, of '82", &c. The principal speakers, after Mr. O'Connell, were, Dr. Denvir, Dr. M'Laughlin, Rev. D. Curoe, Charles G. Duffy, Esq., R. D. Browne, Esq., M.P., &c. The party broke up about two o'clock in the morning.

PART III.—THE REPEAL MEETING—ITS PRELIMINARIES AND ADJUNCTS.

> "FY, let us a' to the 'Royal',
>   For there will be bickerin' there,
>   For Daniel's light horse are to muster,
>   An' O, how the heroes will swear!
>   An' there will be Daniel, commander,
>   An' Tammie the battle to win;
>   Like brothers they'll stand by each other,
>   Sae knit in alliance and kin".
>   An' there will be black-nebbit Johnnie,
>   The tongue o' the trump to them a';
>   An' he getna h— for his haddin'
>   The deil gets nae justice ava'
>   An' there will be Mayo's blithe birkie,
>   A boy nae sae black at the bane,
>   But as for his fine nabob fortune
>   We'll e'en let the subject alane".
>   *Burns's Heron Ballads*, No. 2.[47]

MONDAY night passed away tranquilly, in consequence of the admirable disposition of the Military and Police forces, and Tuesday arrived with all its bustling preparation for the important drama which yet remained to be enacted. Strangers, from all parts of the country poured into town, influenced, for the most part, by curiosity to hear Mr. O'Connell's far-famed oratory. Accordingly, at an early hour in the forenoon, the neighbourhood of the Pavilion was literally besieged by crowds anxious to obtain admission, but no disorder of any kind ensued.

The leading Protestant Liberals having heard of Mr. O'Connell's conciliatory overture in his speech of Monday night, resolved to send a Deputation to the Royal Hotel, to wait upon him, for the purpose of explaining the reasons of their refusal to honour him with their company at dinner. A long conference took place between the parties, of which an official account was afterwards published in the *Whig*, by the gentlemen who composed the Deputation; and, as this is a document of some importance, we make no apology for its insertion. After a few introductory remarks, the Deputation, addressing the *Northern Whig*, proceeded to say—

"It was necessary, in courtesy to Mr. O'Connell, and in justice to our own feelings, that the reasons which prevented us from joining on the present occasion, in giving that gentleman a hospitable reception to our town, should be distinctly explained. These reasons were stated to be two-fold:—First—because the dinner was in our judgment a portion of the demonstration in favour of Repeal, which the greater number of us could not conscientiously attend. Mr. O'Connell, with perfect frankness and courtesy, admitted that this was substantially the fact. The second reason was of a less general nature, and although it originated in the very dissen- sions, which it was our object to heal, our case would have been incomplete had it not been distinctly stated, inasmuch as some of our number were not so unfavourable to Repeal, as to have allowed that consideration, alone, to keep them back from welcoming Mr. O'Connell as a distinguished Reformer. This reason was, that Mr. O'Connell's visit had been princi- pally brought about by, and turned to the account of a small party, who, to the best of our judgment, but without imputing to them any improper motive whatever, had acted injudiciously as regarded the cause of Reform, by exhibiting an apparently sectarian spirit, and by what we felt as an offensive tone, and unjustifiable attacks, directed against the Liberal Protestants of Belfast, and against such of the Catholics also as did not concur in their views. As an illustration of the sectarian spirit which was thus unhappily introduced among us, the demand put forward at one time for a certain number of civic officers, &c., from the Catholic body, was particularly specified, and Mr. O'Connell immediately observed that *he* could not be accused of countenancing this proceeding, as he had taken an early opportunity, in a letter to the Right Rev. Dr. Blake, strongly to *condemn* any such principle of selection. It was stated, however, in explanation of the feelings of the gentlemen present, that by his neglect of the plain and temperate statement of the Editor of the *Whig*, 'with respect to the original ground of dispute, and by the tone of his letters to the *Vindicator*', and speeches on several occasions, he appeared to us to have descended from the high ground to which he had been called as an *arbitrator* of our disputes, in order to make himself a *party* to them; insomuch that his visit to Belfast was considered in the light of an attempt to strengthen one division of Reformers against the rest.

"Mr. O'Connell referred, on this subject, to the hostility shown to him by the *Whig*, notwithstanding his wishes and attempts to be of service to the proprietor, at considerable personal sacrifice. We endeavoured to show him the strong provocation which the *Whig* had received on several occasions; and further called his attention to the fact, that, if the *Whig* had been occasionally too persevering and acrimonious in controversy as many among us felt that it had, at least it had always advocated the broad principles of civil and religious liberty, without a tinge of sectarianism, in which respect it perfectly expressed our sentiments. Mr. O'Connell was reminded, also, that the Reformers of Belfast, of all classes, had given, on all occasions, proofs of zeal and sincerity, had made sacrifices, and gained results, which ought to have exempted them from his censure, if it did not secure them his approbation. It was on this part of the subject, that a Catholic gentleman took occasion to refer to the subscriptions of Catholics and Protestants to the expenses of the last election, as noticed in your paragraph, but it was expressly stated, and confirmed by every one present, that the Catholics of Belfast contributed liberally in full proportion to their means, and that our only object was to shew what the Protestant Liberals *had done*, and not in the least degree to insinuate a doubt of what we all acknowledged and admired, the honest, fervid, and liberal patriotism of the Catholic body. All this part of the conversation was merely explanatory of our feelings and views on the subject of his visit to Belfast, and of the entertainment given in his honour. Our main object, however, as already stated, was, not to recall the misfortunes and misunder-standings of the past, but to avert their recurrence for the future. For this purpose, we conceived it necessary, on the one hand, that the tone and the temper, which had not only divided Catholics from Protestants, but Catholics from Catholics also (as was evinced by the fact, that several of our most respectable Catholic fellow-townsmen were present and concurring), should be abandoned; that, on the other hand, we were convinced that the *Whig* would be as willing for con-ciliation, and as well disposed, in Mr. O'Connell's own language, to forget and forgive the blows they had given and received, and as ready to abandon all unnecessary recurrence to past grievances, as we were ourselves; and that we trusted Mr. O'Connell would exert his great influence in the right direction, to bring about this desirable end. He was assured, that he was quite misinformed, if he had been led to believe that he had any personal enemies among the Liberal party here; and that, on the contrary, it was painful to us to have been compelled to hold back from contributing to his hospit-able reception; and that, had the circumstances permitted it, with honour or consistency, as regarded our feelings and principles, we would cordially have joined in welcoming to Belfast, a man, to whose distinguished public services in the cause of liberty and humanity, we all felt ourselves deeply indebted.

"Mr. O'Connell's manner, throughout, was distinguished by courtesy and conviviality. He declared, with much warmth, that this interview and conversation, with so many of the Liberal inhabitants of Belfast, had given him the highest gratification, and that he trusted it would tend to produce the effect which we had in view. He expressed himself as being willing and anxious to receive such information and sugges- tions as we might be able to afford; and, although he did not at the moment see precisely in what manner he could best promote our praiseworthy object, yet he desired us to be con- vinced, that he was as deeply impressed with the importance of union among Reformers, and as decidedly opposed to all sectarianism as ourselves; and he finally assured us, in a most impressive and energetic manner, that whatever he found he *could* do, to promote the permanent union of the Liberal party in Belfast, he *would*.

> ROBERT JAMES TENNENT.
> ROBERT GRIMSHAW.
> JAMES MACNAMARA.

Belfast, 22nd January, 1841.[48]

With all due respect to the authors of this document, we may take leave to remark, that it is far more fulsomely complimentary towards the Agitator than we would have expected, from the character of the men whose names are attached to it; but we have no right to quarrel with their taste. The great value of this document is the *official* proof which it contains, not only upon Liberal Protestant, but upon Roman Catholic authority, of the sectarian exclusiveness attempted by the Repeal clique in Belfast, as detailed in the introductory portions of our narrative. Mr. Macnamara, one of the gentlemen, who signed the above paper, is himself a respectable Roman Catholic.

It is time that we should return to the Pavilion, in order to chronicle the doings that took place therein—and here it must be observed, that the admission of the public was regulated by tickets varying in price from 6*d* to 2*s* 6*d* each—the sixpenny audience being located in the body of the house, the shilling payers being treated to the gallery, while the half-crown men were politely shown to the platform. About 11 o'clock the public were let in gradually, and in half-an-hour the body of the house was tolerably filled, the galleries crowded, and the platform rather sparingly furnished. Twelve o'clock came, but with it came not Mr. O'Connell, and considerable uneasiness began now to be manifested at this delay. Half-past twelve, and still no Mr. O'Connell—the Priests, some score of whom were rambling about the platform, might be seen anxiously scrutinizing the mass of faces before them, for the purpose of scanning their political character, and it was evident, from the suppressed bustle that prevailed, and the frequent consultations which took place, that it was feared too many Anti-Repealers had got inside the walls. It was quietly whispered, too, that Dr. Cooke was about to make his appearance, and the faces of the clerical group wore a curious expression of dismay, not unmixed with hope, that by some dexterous *coup de main*, the dreaded result might be avoided. In the mean time an alarm was got up that the galleries were sinking, and scores of individuals hastily quitted their places, paid for extra-platform tickets, and placed themselves, as they imagined, beyond the reach of danger. The impatience of the crowd at Mr. O'Connell's delay momentarily increased; and though it was impossible to guess with precision the relative strength of the two parties, yet it was very evident that the Anti-Repealers had mustered in no inconsiderable numbers. In order to make sure of the matter, an individual mounted upon the left side of the platform and unfurled a green banner, on which was inscribed in large characters the word "REPEAL". At sight of this emblem the Repealers shouted vociferously, while the Unionists maintained a steady silence; and, to any one who could command a view of the assemblage, it was plain that the parties were nearly equally divided, or, if any difference existed, that it was not in favour of the Repealers. This experiment decided the future movements of the day, and in a short time afterwards the public were respectfully informed that Mr. O'Connell was not to be expected in the Pavilion at all, but that he would address the meeting from the balcony at the Royal Hotel. The looks of those who had paid doubly for their tickets were amusing subjects for a painter's study. A distinguished authority says—

> "Doubtless the pleasure is as great,
>   Of being cheated as to cheat;"[49]

but our friends of the rueful countenances thought very differently. They applied for their money to him who "had the bag"—but there was no money to be returned. They demanded their tickets—but these could not be had; and an angry tempest was on the point of breaking forth, when one of the "leaders" volunteered to procure for the disappointed parties places at the Hotel, equivalent to those of which they had been deprived by the adjournment. They confidingly followed him; but he dexterously effected his own entrée into the privileged quarter, leaving his dupes outside to enjoy the luxury of the streets, and the pleasant companionship of the "greasy nations" of Hercules-street and Smithfield.

> "There's nought here but Repealer's filth,
>   Repealer's scab and hunger;
>   If Providence has sent us here,
>   'Twas surely in an anger",

was the exclamation of one of the disappointed.

The crowd having now collected around the balcony of the Hotel, fronting the Linen-hall, Mr. O'Connell soon made his appearance outside, surrounded, as Wolfe Tone would say, by the "old set"; viz.—Dr. Denvir, Dr. M'Laughlin, the Messrs. M'Mullan, from Castlewellan, John O'Dougherty, Esq., Killygordon, (County Donegall), Robert M'Dowell, Esq., John Sinclair, Esq., (formerly of Belfast, now of Ballintrae,

in Ayrshire), John M'Kittrick, Esq., Woollendraper, (Newtownards), Charles M'Alister, Esq., (Belfast), Surgeon Lynch,
Tom Steele, Dillon Browne, and Priests innumerable. The
day, though frosty, was clear, and, upon the whole, extremely
fine for the season. John Sinclaire, Esq., was called to the
chair, which he occupied with becoming dignity, and did not
swear half-a-dozen oaths during the whole proceedings. This
fact we are prepared to certify, should any doubt be expressed
on the subject.

The appearance of the principal personages upon the
platform was the signal for uproarious applause on the part of
the Repealers, and for corresponding disapprobation from
the rest of the assemblage. Yells, hisses, groans, cheers, and
exclamations of all descriptions were blended together in the
most strange confusion imaginable; so that the building of
Babel, or the unearthly noises which "vexed the ear of chaos
and old night",[50] could scarcely have been worse. To think of
hearing a single word that Mr. O'Connell, or any one else
actually said, was a physical impossibility, except, perhaps, to
some of the newspaper reporters, who placed their note-books
upon Mr. O'Connell's back, amidst entreaties that they would
not press too hard, lest they should throw him over amongst
the crowd, while they were occasionally obliged to ask, over
his shoulder—"what's that?"—when they had lost, amidst the
confusion, the purport of his oration. At one period there might
have been, in front of the platform and around the Linenhall,
about 8,000 or 9,000 persons, but, upon an average, there
were not more than five thousand in attendance during the
day, and of these about one-third were Repealers, the
remainder being partly composed of persons whose curiosity
had prompted them to hear the speeches, and the rest of
sturdy Anti-Repealers, who spared not their voices on the
occasion. On one of the trees inside the Linen-hall, and
directly fronting Mr. O'Connell, was placed a large placard,
bearing, in conspicuous characters, the title—"DR. COOKE's
CHALLENGE";[51] while many of the exclamations uttered by
the mob were ludicrously characteristic—"Ha, Dan, there's

Dr. Cooke coming"—"No Pope"—"No Surrender"—"Come down out of that, ye big beggarman, till we shake hands with ye"—"Three cheers for Ellen Courtenay"[52]—responded to by—"put out the Ballymacarret weavers; go home to your sowens, ye scarecrows"[53]—"Dan O'Connell for ever"—"Hurrah for Repeal", &c. In regard to the numbers present we may mention, that the space occupied by the crowd has since been carefully measured, and it has been ascertained, mathematically, that it could not possibly have contained more than the extreme calculation already assigned, and we have been liberal in our estimate rather than otherwise.

In the way above stated, newspaper reports of Mr. O'Connell's speech were obtained, but, in reference to the bulk of the meeting, the whole affair was absolutely dumb show, as not a syllable could be heard at the distance of a yard from the spot, on which Mr. O'Connell stood. The following is taken from the *Northern Whig:*—

Mr. O'Connell rose, and, throwing off his green cloak, displayed a surtout of Repeal frieze,[54] with a white velvet collar, and Repeal buttons. He was received with deafening shouts of applause, mingled with those discordant yells, from the rere of the crowd, which had prevailed incessantly from the speakers mounting the platform. When a degree of silence had been obtained, the hon. Gentleman addressed the assemblage, as follows:— Gentlemen, I came here today prepared to address you in a much narrower compass than that in which you are now met. (Cheers.) I feel that some apology is due to those who assembled in the Pavilion where the entertainment took place, last night, for the delay which has been occasioned to them, by the change in the place of meeting to-day. The reason why the meeting of to-day is held in a different place from that originally intended is, that it was considered, that the multitude who would congregate would be far too large to allow us to show the triumph of Repeal, in Belfast, by confining them in so limited a compass as the walls of the Pavilion. (Loud cheers.) I have here, in my hand, a memorandum taken from the ancient history of the North of Ireland. (Hear, hear.) I have a series of resolutions, passed at a time when Irish liberty was in a flourishing state.—(Hear, hear.) The first were agreed to on the 15th of February, 1782, at the convention held in Dungannon[55]—Colonel W. Irvine in the chair—a meeting at which the principal part of the nobility, gentry, landed proprietors, and respectable merchants of the Province, were present. The resolutions are as follow:—

"Resolved.—That we hold the right of private judgment, in matters of religion, to be equally sacred in others as in ourselves.

"Resolved, therefore,—That as men and Irishmen, as Christians, and as Protestants, we rejoice in the relaxation of the Penal Laws against our Roman Catholic fellow-subjects; and that we conceive the measure to be fraught with the happiest consequences to the union and prosperity of the people of Ireland.

These resolutions, gentlemen, were passed at a meeting such as I have described, with but two dissenting voices. (Cheering.) I shall read for you one resolution more,—a resolution passed in the town of Belfast, on the 7th of March, 1782, at a meeting held in the Town-house,—Thomas Sinclaire, Esq., in the chair. [The hon. Gentleman here pointed to the venerable Chairman, seated on his left; and gave occasion to a renewed burst of cheering.] The resolution is to this effect:—

"Resolved unanimously,—That if any Irishman has been, or shall be, hardy enough to assert, directly or indirectly, that any body of men, other than the King, Lords, and Commons of Ireland, had, have, or ought to have, a right to make laws to bind this realm, in any case whatsoever, every such man insults the majesty of the King of Ireland, the dignity of its Parliament, and the whole body of its people; is an enemy to this kingdom, and ought to be reprobated as such, by every friend of Ireland.

"Resolved unanimously,—That it be, and it is hereby, most earnestly recommended to all the inhabitants of this Province, to assemble in their several towns and parishes, to deliberate on those matters, and, in case they shall approve thereof, to enter into similar resolutions; as we are fully convinced, that nothing is now wanting to establish and secure the freedom and prosperity of Ireland, but the *avowed union of its people.*

Yes, gentlemen, these were the resolutions passed in your town, and by your ancestors, before the passing of the Union. (Cheers and hooting.) The first resolution I read to you was adopted at one of the greatest meetings of Reformers ever held in this Province. (Hear.) And the crowds whom I behold assembled before me, this day, prove, that the old spirit is yet alive in Ulster, and show the countless multitudes that belong to the Repeal spirit here. Even the clamour which is raised, to prevent those who speak from being heard distinctly, proves the strength of the Repealers here assembled. (Cheering.) That interested clamour, which you find it necessary to shout down, while you add to the difficulty of hearing my words— that clamour is a species of interruption which only proves the weakness of your opponents, and the vast number of the Repealers of Belfast. (Cheering and groaning.) I defy any man to call that Union a contract—I defy any one to call it any-thing else than an imposition practised upon the brave people of Ireland, by force and fraud—an imposition practised upon them at a time when they were weakened by broils and political dissensions—(hear, hear)—which had been fomented by the English themselves. (Hear, hear.) It would have delighted me to show you Sheriffs of counties calling meetings, in the absence of the people, those meetings being afterwards dispersed, at the point of the bayonet—to have shown you martial law in force—*Habeas Corpus* suspended, and the Jury-box empty—the prisons full—the scaffolds crowded—public opinion stifled—and the Union carried, in the presence of an overwhelming military force.—(Cheers.) I would have shewn you, that there were employed, in addition, for the purpose of effecting the Union, bribery and corruption, the most unpar-alleled. I would have shown you, that no less a sum than £1,275,000 was paid as the actual price of the Union, while

£3,000,000 was distributed, in sums of various amounts, as
pecuniary bribes. (Cries of "Hear, hear" and groaning.) That
noise which is created, in order to prevent the utterance of
those sentiments which I came here to deliver to you—to
stifle the advocacy of Repeal—will cause the cry of Repeal to
ring through Belfast. (Cheering.) All I wish now to intimate to
the sober, thinking people of Belfast is, the simple fact of the
fiscal robbery which has been perpetrated upon us, by the
Union. (Cheers and hooting.) [Here a person behind the line
of police, on the opposite side of the street, displayed a large
coloured placard, with the words, "DR. COOKE'S CHALLENGE",
printed in very conspicuous characters. A Constable tore it to
pieces, on which, Mr. O'Connell smiled, and called out—
"Never mind the bill—leave it with him."] There is not a
man, who is at all conversant with the history of the Union,
who does not know, that it was based on the grossest injustice.
(Hear.) At the time it was carried, the national debt of
England was £446,000,000—that of Ireland did not amount
to £20,000,000. (Hear and cheers.) The Irish Parliament,
while we were permitted to retain it, kept the debt within
£20,000,000; while the English Parliament, in its profligacy,
had allowed the nation to be involved in the amount of
£446,000,000. This was the extent of the national debt of
England, at the time of the Union—it was now upwards of
£800,000,000; and of this, Ireland was liable to one-half.
(Hear, hear.) The bargain, in fact, was the same as if one
merchant were to meet another on 'Change and say to him,
"I owe £446,000,—you £20,000; let us enter into partnership
and share the profits equally." What would the latter think of
the former's proposition? (A laugh.) That was the substance of
the financial agreement brought about by the Union, though
it has ever been most cunningly and carefully disguised. Lord
Castlereagh promised, at the time of the Union, that Ireland
should only be subjected to her own share in the debt.
England pays but five millions of taxation when, by right, she
should pay seventeen millions. If the bargain had been carried
out to the letter of the agreement, England should now be

paying, at the very least, ten or twelve millions more than she does at present. (Hear, hear.) This surplus for the past forty years, has amounted to, at least, four thousand millions. (Hear.) Never was there such wholesale plunder, never was there corruption and injustice so palpable, never was there such gigantic robbery, as was heartlessly perpetrated at the miscalled Union. (Great cheers.) The next giant grievance consequent on the Union is absenteeism. The drain of money out of the country, immediately subsequent to the Union, amounted to one million per annum; and, according to the latest calculation of the Railroad Commissioners, the drain of the country's wealth amounted to four millions annually. (Hear, hear and cheers.) Four millions, for forty years, amount to one hundred and sixty millions, which, added to the previous four hundred millions of debt, to which the country has been so unjustly subjected, will amount to five hundred and sixty millions. (Cheers.) This was monstrous.—(Hear.) Here is robbery unheard of. The next injustice inflicted on our country is that which regards the revenue. A surplus of two millions has annually found its way, in this department, from Ireland to the sister country. The coffers of England are enriched by our wealth, in this respect, as well as the others I have mentioned. Sum up all these different amounts, and then reflect on the extent of the annual exhaustion from our country, and the consequences of it. (Hear, and cheers.) How can the people expect to receive adequate wages for their labour under such a system? I promised last night to speak to you for two hours to-day, on Repeal. I could easily keep that promise, if you would only have patience with me. But you are not unlike the Irish bagpipes. (Laughter.) There is a grunt and a groan with you; and it generally happens that these grunts and groans drown the musical part of the entertainment. (Loud cheering and great laughter.) We have the music here near us, and the groaning and grunting is at a distance. In all my lifetime I have been playing second part to the drones, which is, of course, the musical part. (Laughter and cheers, mingled with great shouting.) There is a class of

Reformers who must soon be with me. They cannot become stationary. They must either advance or recede. They must become either Conservatives or Repealers. The different sects of Reformers in Belfast must go onward in the movement. I came hither to help them on. Those who are here the advocates of household suffrage and vote by ballot, must soon become Repealers; and we will receive them with a *cead mille failte*. (Cheers.) The Imperial Parliament will never attend to the interests of this country. The House of Lords is inimical to us, and in the House of Commons we have had *four* majorities in favour of Stanley's Bill. The Bill will come on again. "On, Stanley, on". (Hear, hear and cheering.) This will be the watchword at the opening of Parliament. It is argued against Repeal that we are anxious for Catholic ascendancy. I deny it. There is not a Protestant more opposed to Catholic ascendancy than I am. Three times the Catholic party have been in power since the Reformation. Three times it was the principles of the Government. Mary's persecutions contaminated religion, and injured the country. But I will read to you the following passage from a Protestant historian—"Taylor on the Civil Wars of Ireland":—

"The restoration of the old religion was effected without violence; no persecution of the Protestants was attempted; and several of the English who fled from the furious zeal of Mary's Inquisitors, found a safe retreat among the Catholics of Ireland. It is but justice to this maligned body to add, that, on three occasions of their obtaining the upper hand, they never injured a single person in life or limb, for professing a religion different from their own."[56]

The Learned Gentleman then proceeded to read, also, the following extracts from the Work of Mr. Wm. Parnell, a Protestant gentleman, in his Heretical Apology for the Catholics of Ireland:—[57]

"A still more striking proof, that the Irish Roman Catholics in Queen Mary's reign were very little infected with religious bigotry, may be drawn from their conduct towards the Protestants, when the Protestants were at their mercy. Were we to argue from the representations of the indelible character of the Catholic religion, as portrayed by its adversaries, we should have expected, that the Irish Catholics would have exercised every kind of persecution, which the double motives of zeal and retaliation could suggest. The Catholic laity, in all the impunity of triumphant bigotry, hunting the wretched heretics from their hiding places—the Catholic Clergy pouring out the libation of human blood at the shrine of the God of mercy, and acting before high heaven those scenes which make the angels weep."

"But on the contrary, though the religious feelings of the Irish Catholics, and their feelings as men, had been treated with very little ceremony during the two preceding reigns, they made a wise and moderate use of their ascendancy. They entertained no resentment for the past; they laid no plans for future dominion. Even Leland allows, that the only instance of Popish zeal was annulling grants which Archbishop Browne had made, to the injury of the See of Dublin, and certainly this step was fully as agreeable to the rules of law and equity as to Popish zeal. Such was the general spirit of toleration that many English families, friends to the Reformation, took refuge in Ireland, and there enjoyed their opinions and worship without molestation. The Irish Roman Catholics bigots! The Irish Roman Catholics are the only sect that ever resumed power, without exercising vengeance."

The learned gentleman then referred to the kind offices performed by the Catholic Corporation of Dublin to the men of Bristol at a former period. He proceeded to say, that as the House of Lords in a domestic legislature would be Conservative it would be absurd to apprehend religious ascendancy. The House of Commons would be popularly formed, and would pass popular measures, and there would be sufficient check on the possibility of a religious ascendancy. It was no sectarian conflict they were engaged in. It was a struggle for all creeds, and all Ireland in fact. (Cheers.) He repeated that the Repeal question ought to draw to its support every denomination of Christians, as it sought to reflect equal advantages and equal rights on every sect and party, both political and religious. Insult no man—let no illegal oath be taken—let no secret Society be formed amongst you—(hear, hear)—for no man will be considered a Repealer who violates the law in any respect. (Great shouting.) Remember that the motto of Repealers is, "That whoever violates the law strengthens the enemies of Ireland". Don't you think that some of the boys who are hooting here to-day would be very glad if you broke the law?—(great shouting)—instead of hooting they would be laughing at you, if you were violating the law, but don't interfere with them—don't insult them, but laugh heartily at them. (Laughter, and rounds of Kentish fire.) Yes, my friends, I did assist in achieving the great measure of political amelioration. (Hear, hear.) I assisted in obtaining Catholic Emancipation—(cheering)—and mark me, my friends, before we achieved that boon for our country, we obtained the emancipation of the Protestant Dissenters in England. (Great cheering, and hisses.) Our struggle for them had nothing sectarian in it—it was on the principle of freedom of conscience—and the feeling we were guided by was, that the man that interferes between his fellow-creature and his God, you may call him Protestant, Presbyterian, or Dissenter, or Catholic, as you please, but to me he is not a Christian at all. Join with me, then, in this peaceful agitation for the Repeal. (Great cheering and hissing.) Hurrah, then, for Repeal. (Loud cheering and hissing.) My duty, my friends, has been performed. I am amongst you, and when this demonstration has concluded, separate in peace and good order—go to your homes in the innocence as well as the merriment of children. Nothing can be more satisfactory than the manner in which the authorities have and continue to conduct themselves; and, in your names, my friends, I thank the Magistrates—(loud cheering)—peace and order have been preserved—the rights of freemen have not been infringed upon. 'Tis pleasant to see justice administered in that way. (Hear, hear.) I congratulate you on it, and it cheers me onward on my route. Now take my advice—the moment the chair is vacated, let every body go directly to his own home. (Hear, hear.) If any body tells you that he has hooted us to-day, take off your hat to him and bow. (Laughter and cheers.) Oh, yes, I do triumph in this spirit—I exult in the certainty of having so many peaceful and orderly Repealers, ready to assist their country in her need, by the performance of their duty to that country, and without the violation of any law whatsoever. (Cheering.) We will rally for old Ireland—the wise and the good of all sects and persuasions will struggle with us—and you will yet have your election here for Members for the Irish parliament. (Cheering and Kentish fire.) College Green will re-echo with the shout of emancipated millions. The fraternal force of liberty, presaging prosperity, will rise from Connemara to the Hill of Howth—will pass from Cape Clear to the Giant's Causeway; and the men of Belfast will gladden, in pleasing gratitude, as the joyous sound passes them; and there will not be a voice in Ireland more true to the country than that which shall proceed from the emancipated Irishmen of Belfast. (The Hon. and Learned Gentleman then retired, amidst cheering, hissing, and Kentish fire.)

Several Repeal resolutions were passed and Mr. Steele attempted a speech, but not one word of it reached the groundlings, amongst whom an incessant uproar prevailed, and the orator was at length compelled to sit down. Robert M'Dowell, Esq., was then called to the chair, and the usual formality of thanks to his predecessor having been gone through, the parties withdrew. During the meeting the Military and Police were so admirably placed as to keep the hostile mobs from coming into collision, while the vigilance and activity of the Magistracy were in every quarter unremitting. Popular excitement had now reached its height, and indications of mischief were on all sides observable.

PART IV.—THE SOIREE.

AFTER this day's *success* at the 'Royal',
With Sinclaire, M'Dowell, & Co.,
We'll end in the utmost of splendour,
And down to the Music-hall go;
When, in gallons of Bohea and Congou,
We'll drink all our sorrows away,
And the 'twinkling feet' of the *ladies*
Will welcome the break of the day.
Whack fal de ral, &c."—*Repeal Rhymes.*[58]

IT had been announced beforehand, that, on the evening
of Tuesday a Soirée, for the benefit of the St. Patrick's
Orphan Charity, would take place in the New Music Hall,
May-street, under the superintendence of a Committee of
Ladies, at which Mr. O'Connell would take the chair.
Accordingly, at a quarter before 7 o'clock, Mr. O'Connell,
accompanied by his friends Messrs. Steele, Browne, Drs.
Denvir and M'Laughlin, &c. entered the Hall by the private
door, and took their respective places on the platform. The
house was filled in every direction, and presented a striking
and animated appearance, which contrasted strongly with the
greasy mob amongst whom Mr. O'Connell had spent the
previous part of the day. The Hall was brilliantly lighted, and
large numbers of well dressed ladies were in attendance, while
a small, but efficient Band, which had been placed in the
gallery, tended in no slight degree to diversify and enliven the
enjoyments of the evening. This was, in reality, the only
popular exhibition on which Mr. O'Connell could look with
any feeling approaching to satisfaction since his arrival in the
North, and we will do the parties the justice to add that it had
been tastefully got up, and was most respectably conducted.
Between 300 and 400 individuals were present, of whom more
than one half were Ladies; but it were obviously a mistake to
set down the fair ones as Repealers; for, during the evening
when an incidental allusion chanced to be made which drew

forth the pocket-handkerchiefs of the political "angels", it was very observable that the latter constituted not more than one-sixth of the entire "galaxy of beauty"—the rest preserving a respectful silence. Tea and Coffee were served up in elegant style, after which Mr. O'Connell, in accordance with a previous arrangement, proceeded to introduce to the meeting a series of sentiments prepared for the occasion. In his introductory remarks he was frequently very happy, though his style of oratory was of a rather subdued cast, and he several times contrived to bring in, without any seemingly studied effort, a variety of well applied compliments to the fair sex. His correction of the lines—

> "Oh woman, in your hours of ease,
> Uncertain, coy, and hard to please",

by another couplet from the same author—

> "When pain and suffering wring the brow
> A ministering angel thou."

produced a simultaneous burst of applause. Again when incidentally alluding to the loss of his wife, he became so affected that he was compelled abruptly to sit down.[59]

The following are some of the sentiments given on this occasion—"The Queen", "The Princess Royal", "The Duchess of Kent", "the Ladies of the St. Patrick's Orphan Charity", &c. Towards the conclusion Mr. O'Connell proposed the health of the friends who had accompanied him on his way to Belfast, viz. Messrs. Steele, Brown, and Nicholas Markey. Mr. Brown returned thanks in appropriate terms acknowledging in the words of the Poet—

> "—if hearts that feel and eyes that smile
> Be the dearest gifts that heaven supplies,
> We never need leave our own green isle,
> For sensitive hearts and for sun-bright eyes."

The only other speakers of the evening were Dr. Denvir, and the Rev. G. Crolly, the former when proposing Mr. O'Connell's own health, and the latter in acknowledgment of that of the "Ladies of the St. Patrick's Orphan Charity".

Shortly after Nine o'clock, Mr. O'Connell, in company with his friends, retired through the private door already alluded to, and returned to his rooms in the Royal Hotel. The majority of the Company then withdrew to the lower room of the Music Hall, where dancing parties were immediately formed, and "many twinkling feet" kept up the hilarity of the occasion with no lack of spirit till a late or rather an early hour—

> "Qualis in Eurotae ripis aut per juga Cynthi,
> Exertec Diana Choros"[60]—

From the spirit of excitement which the Repeal meeting had created amongst the populace in the early part of the day, it became evident that the utmost vigilance of the authorities would be required, to avert the mischief which might be reasonably apprehended; and though no precautions were omitted, yet, towards dusk, immense multitudes of persons began to perambulate the streets, to break windows and commit other acts of violence. A dense mass of individuals congregated about the Music-hall, at an early period of the Soirée, smashed with stones several panes of glass, and one stone was thrown with such force as to cut right through the blind inside, dash to pieces several lamps of the splendid chandelier suspended from the centre of the ceiling, and falling upon a young lady slightly to injure her face. Other mischievous acts were also done, which every respectable member of society will reprobate, whatever may be the party from which they proceeded. A good deal of alarm existed for a short time, especially amongst the ladies; but the Police drew up in force about the Hall, and, in this quarter, no farther annoyance was experienced. We now approach

PART V.—THE RETREAT.

"DUNCAN he cam' gallopin', gallopin',
Arms an' legs a wallopin', wallopin'
Deil tak' the last, quo' Duncan M'Calapin,
Laird o' Tullyben, jo."

Scotch Song.

"Now, Johnnie Cope, be as good's your word,
An' try our fate wi' fire an' sword,
An' dinna tak' wing, like a frighten'd bird
That chas'd frae its nest i' the morning.

*   *   *   *   *

When Johnnie Cope to Dunbar came,
They spier'd at him—'whar's a' your men?'
'The de'il confound me gin I ken,
For I left them a' i' the morning.'"

Jacobite Relics.

During the greater part of Tuesday night, the mob
exercised their faculties with unwearied activity in the
breaking of windows; and when, through the intervention of
the authorities, aided by the Police, the work of destruction
was suppressed in one quarter, it was almost instantaneously
begun in another. The windows of several of the leading
Repealers were smashed, and considerable damage was done;
but the Repealers themselves had their mob, who attacked
the houses of their opponents, and, in one instance, the life of
a respectable lady, a member of Dr. Cooke's congregation,
was seriously endangered, in consequence of a brick bat,
which weighed 1lb. 14oz., having been thrown into her room.
After Mr. O'Connell's retirement from the Soirée, the Royal
Hotel was assailed, and, we regret to add, several vollies of
stones were thrown into the room in which Mr. O'Connell
was sitting amongst his friends. This occurrence, taken in
connection with the disturbed and highly dangerous state of

the town generally, induced Mr. Kerns, the proprietor of the Hotel, and "honest Tom Steele", to swear the following affidavit before the magistrates:—

COUNTY OF ANTRIM, *To wit.* The information of Thomas Steele, Esq., of the County of Care, who, being duly sworn, states, that he was, this evening, sitting in the room in which Daniel O'Connell, Esq., and his friends, have dined, for the last two days, when both windows were broken by stones, thrown from the streets; and many other windows of the hotel were broken, as informant heard and believes. Informant being under a decisive impression, that said stones were thrown by an Orange mob, with intent to murder said Daniel O'Connell, or to do him some bodily harm, claims, from the Magistrates of Belfast, the protection which ought to be afforded to the said Daniel O'Connell, under such circumstances, by granting a sufficient guard, for this night, and protection to the place of his embarkation.

Signed,

THOMAS STEELE.

Sworn before us, at Belfast, this 19th day of January, 1841.
Signed,

"Robert J. Tennent.	A. Chichester.
R. Grimshaw.	Thomas Verner, (Sovereign).
James Macnamara.	Walter Molony, (Resident Magistrate).
R. Coulson.	H. Brownrigg."

"The information of Charles Kerns, hotel-keeper of the town of Belfast, who, being duly sworn, states, that Daniel O'Connell, Esq., and his friends, have resided in his hotel, since their arrival, on the 16th January; that, on this evening, a riotous mob broke several windows in said hotel, and, particularly those of the room in which the said Daniel O'Connell usually dined.

Signed,

"CHARLES KERNS.

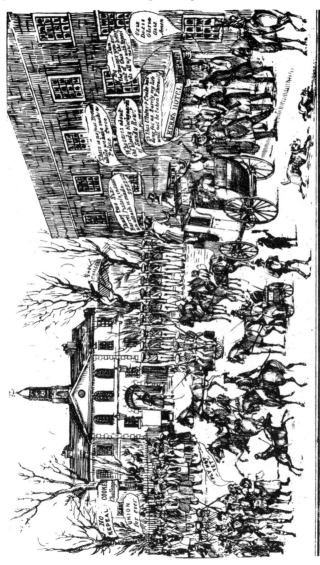

O'CONNELL'S *departure from Belfast or popularity of Repeal in Ulster.*

Sworn before us, at Belfast, this 19th day of January, 1841.
Signed,

"A. Chichester.	Robert J. Tennent.
Thomas Verner, (Sovereign).	R.Grimshaw.
Walter Molony, (Resident Magistrate).	James Macnamara.
H. Brownrigg.	R. Coulson."

In consequence of these applications, a guard was placed upon the Hotel during the remainder of the night, and a strong Police force, under Mr. Giveen, was ordered to escort Mr. O'Connell in the morning as far as Donaghadee.

A celebrated author has recorded his opinion, that

> "In all the art of war no feat
> Is nobler than a brave retreat;
> For those that run away and fly
> Take place, at least, of the enemy."[61]

In confirmation of this exalted sentiment we need not fatigue the patience of our readers with hacknied classical recollections about Xenophon and the "Ten Thousand", as we have at hand a modern instance, and one still more significantly appropriate. At the pavilion dinner one of the decorations was a bust of Napoleon placed in a niche adjoining that occupied by a similar bust of Mr. O'Connell, and one of the orators on that occasion instituted a flattering comparison between the originality of genius belonging to these two great characters, the one in the science of war, and the other in that of politics. Each in his own department discovered and applied, with tremendous effect, new powers whose existence had been scarcely suspected, until made patent through the medium of their gigantic achievements respectively. We accept this parallel, at the same time reminding its ingenious author, that Napoleon once, in the pride of imaginary conquest, went *"too far North"*—a piece of daring generalship in which his "parallel" is not likely to imitate his rashness—and the barren rock of St. Helena, became in the end his palace and his grave.

On Wednesday morning Mr. O'Connell left Belfast, and proceeded towards Donaghadee by Newtownards. When within a short distance of the last mentioned town, the funeral of the late Peter Johnston, Esq., was seen approaching in a long and solemn procession attended by a vast concourse of people. Our travellers were sadly frightened, as they mistook it for an insurgent band of Anti-Repealers, who probably intended to do bodily mischief to the "Liberator", and the uneasiness of the parties was manifested in no equivocal manner. At length the reality was discovered, and, the courage of the gallant band became reassured. No time, however, was lost in reaching Donaghadee with the least possible delay.

At Donaghadee itself a number of persons collected to view the strangers as articles of curiosity, and though a cry for repeal was attempted by one or two individuals, it signally failed. It is said that the friends of Mr. O'Connell, on entering the town, took care to exhibit their loaded pistols which were conspicuously stuck in their belts. They had no need of any such ostentatious precaution, as there are no Rockites in the North, and here at least no sun shines on "showers of gore from the upflashing steel of safe assassination". After breakfast Mr. O'Connell and his suite proceeded towards the Quay while a Highland piper, whether from accident or design we know not, actually struck up the well known lilt of "*We'll gang nae mair to yon toun*". From the deck of the steamer Mr. O'Connell briefly addressed the crowd, which lined the Quay, on the necessity and advantages of Tee-totalism.[62] This politic man-oeuvre brought him a number of parting cheers—then waving his cap, he bowed to his audience, bade farewell to the inhospitable regions of the North, and, aided by her Majesty' steam-packet, continued his retreat until he had reached in safety the rock-bound shores of Portpatrick. We now conclude this eventful history in terms of Lord Byron's characteristic farewell to Malta, which certainly embodies some of the reflections that must have arisen in the mind of our hero on getting clear of the North—

"Adieu, thou palace rarely entered,
    Adieu, ye mansions—where I've ventured,
    Adieu, ye cursed streets of stairs,
    (How surely he who mounts you swears!)
    Adieu, ye merchants ever failing,
    Adieu, thou mob for ever railing!

        *   *   *   *   *   *

Adieu, ye females fraught with graces,
    Adieu, red coats, and redder faces!

        *   *   *   *   *   *

I go, but God knows when or why,
    To smoky towns and cloudy sky,
    To things (the honest truth to say)
    As bad—but in a different way."

ADDENDUM.

The following resolutions which were unanimously agreed
to at a meeting of Students belonging to the Presbyterian
Church in Ireland, deserve a place in these pages, in
connexion with O'Connell's agitation visit to Ulster.

"1st, resolved—"That, understanding a declaration was made,
some time ago, by Mr. O'Connell, to the effect, that the Presbyterian
youth of Ulster would coincide with him on the question of Repeal,
but for the undue influence of Dr. Cooke, we, the Students of Belfast
Royal College, feel ourselves called upon, at the present time, so far
as we are concerned, publicly to repudiate the groundless assertion
of Mr. O'Connell; and, also, to profess our decided and conscien-
tious opposition to the political creed of this gentleman, believing
that it is inimical to Protestantism, and subversive of the best
interests of our country.

2nd, Resolved—"That, in common with the Protestants of Ulster,
we do express our admiration of the manner in which Dr. Cooke has

challenged and confounded Mr. O'Connell, and has thus demonstrated, that, however the question of Repeal may serve in *his* hands,
to excite an ignorant mob, it cannot stand the test of searching
argument".

A FULL AND AUTHENTIC REPORT OF THE
TWO GRAND
CONSERVATIVE DEMONSTRATIONS
Which took place in Belfast on the 21st and 22nd January, 1841.

IN consequence of the systematic and persevering attempts of O'Connell and his partizans to introduce the Repeal agitation into the North, as detailed in the preceding pages, a counter-demonstration was resolved upon on the part of the Conservatives, and the following Requisition was accordingly published in the Newspapers:—

"The undersigned request a Meeting of the Nobility, Clergy, Gentry, and other friends of the British Constitution and Connexion, in Antrim, Down, and the contiguous Northern Counties, to be held in Belfast, upon Thursday, the 21st January, 1841, at Eleven o'clock, A.M., for the purpose of expressing their opinion in favour of the principles of Lord Stanley's Registration Bill, and also in opposition to the attempt, now for the first time undisguisedly made in Ulster, to effect the Repeal of the Union."

This requisition was signed by Lords Downshire, Abercorn, Donegall, Hertford, Waterford, Ely, Londonderry, Lothian, Mandeville, Roden, Clanwilliam, Mountcashel, Enniskillen, Belmore, O'Neill, Castlestewart, Caledon, Clancarty, Ranfurley, Hillsborough, Loftus, Castlereagh, Corry, Dungannon, Ferrard, Newry and Mourne, Northland, J. Beresford, Claude Hamilton, S. Algernon Chichester, Adam Loftus; James, Dromore; De Ros, Blayney, Farnham, Dufferin and Claneboy, Sandys, Powerscourt, &c. &c. And, in fact, by the principal Nobility, Gentry, and Clergy of the Province of Ulster, while the meeting which ensued formed a striking contrast, both in numbers and respectability, to the ragged pauperism which two days beforehand had been gathered at the Royal Hotel. The dinner given on the following evening to J. Emerson Tennent, and G. O. Dunbar, Esqrs. Members of Parliament for the borough of Belfast, was proportionably brilliant. We subjoin ample reports of both demonstrations.

THE MEETING.

THIS meeting was held on Thursday, 21st January, agreeably to the requisition which appeared in the papers, and which was so numerously and respectably signed, by 1605 of the Nobility, Clergy and Gentry of the Northern counties in Ireland, consisting of 41 Peers and Noblemen, 14 Right Honourables and Honourables, 18 Baronets, 32 Members of Parliament, 11 High Sheriffs, 6 Lord Lieutenants of counties, 98 Deputy Lieutenants, 335 Magistrates, 257 Clergymen of the Established Church, 45 Presbyterian Ministers, 28 Methodist Ministers, and 28 Barristers. Such an array of the rank, wealth, talent, and respectability of the country, never before met in Belfast, to give expression to their sentiments, on any public measure. At the hour appointed for the meeting, the Circus was most densely crowded in every part. The front and side boxes presented a very imposing and splendid appearance, being principally occupied by ladies. In the front of the gallery, a platform was erected fro the speakers, and, even on this, a great many gentlemen were obliged to stand. Previous to the opening of the business, the assembled multitude gave demonstration of their feelings, by loud cries of "No Repeal", cheering, and the Kentish fire.—The following are as many of the names of the principal Noblemen, Clergy, and Gentry, who were present, as we could collect—the list will speak for itself:—

The Marquis of Downshire; Earl of Hillsborough, M.P.; Lord Loftus, Ely Lodge, Enniskillen; Lord Newry and Mourne; Lord Northland, M.P. D.L. J.P.; Lord Algernon Chichester; Lord Adam Loftus; the Hon. S. Hewitt, J.P.; the Right Hon. George R. Dawson; Hon. and Rev. S. Blackwood; the Hon. George Handcock; Sir George Hill, Bart. D.L. J.P.; Sir Robert Bateson, Bart., J. P. Castrue; Sir Hugh Stewart, Bart. Ballygawley House, county Tyrone; Sir H. Harvey Bruce, Bart.; Sir Robert Bateson, Bart. M.P. D.L. J.P.; Sir Arthur Brooke, Bart. M.P. J.P.; George Dunbar, M.P. D.L. J.P.; Thomas Greg, Ballymenoch, Hollywood, High Sheriff of Antrim;

Matthew Forde, Seaford, Clough, High Sheriff of Down; Simon Armstrong, Hollymount, Manorhamilton, High Sheriff of Fermanagh; John Lindsay, Loughry, Dungannon, High Sheriff of Tyrone; Lieut.-Col. M. Close, Drumbanagher, Newry, D.L. J.P.; Edmund M'Donnell, D.L. J.P., Glenarm castle; Rev. Walter B. Mant, Archdeacon of Down; Nathaniel Alexander, Portglenone House, D.L. J.P.; Rev. H. Cooke, D.D. LL.D; Rev. James Saurin, Archdeacon of Dromore; Rev. Robert Stewart, D.D. Broughshane; Con. R. Dobbs, Castle Dobbs, Carrickfergus, J.P. High Sheriff Elect for Antrim; Rev. John Chaine, Dean of Connor; John C. Moutray, Favor Royal, Aughnacloy, D.L. J.P.; John Rowan, Merville, Belfast, J.P.; Rev. James Stannus, Lisburn, Dean of Ross; Henry Richardson, Somerset, Coleraine, D.L. J.P.; Wm. Wilson, Esq. Belfast; R.B. Blakiston, Orangefield, J.P.; Jas. Courtenay, J.P. Glenburne, Portglenone; Marcus M'Causland, Fruit-hill, Newtownlimavady, D.L. J.P.; Rev. Daniel M'Afee, Belfast, Wesleyan Minister; John Harrison, Esq. Belfast; Matthew Anketell, Anketell Grove, County Monaghan, D.L. J.P.; Lieut.-Colonel Cairnes, K.H. J.P. Portstewart; Colonel Tisdall, Church-hill, Louth, J.P.; Wm. Cairns, Cultra, J.P.; Lieut.-Colonel Hawkshaw, Blaris Lodge, Lisburn, J.P.; George Joy, Galgorm Castle, J.P.; Rev. Dawson Dean Heather, Belfast; Major-General Coulson, Holywood; Charles Douglass, Grace-hall, D.L. J.P.; William B. Forde, Esq., Seaford; James Blackwood, D.L. J.P. Strangford; Sir George Hill, St. Columbs, Derry; John Mitchell, Esq. Monaghan; Rev. B.W. Forde, Seaforde; John Lindsay, Esq., Belfast; Lieut. Wm. Hall, R.N.; Wm. Herbert Hall, Esq. Belfast; Lieut.-Colonel Robert Lowry Dickson, J.P. Holybrook, county Fermanagh; Wm. Delacherois Crommelin, Esq. Carrowdore Castle; Rev. John R. Young, Rector of Tydonet; Rev. Charles Wood, Inch, Downpatrick;—Cross, Darton, county Armagh, J.P.; John Henry Loftie, Drumargall-house, county Armagh; J. Waring Maxwell, Finnebrogue, D.L. J.P.; Rev. R.A. Agar, Rathfriland; Rev. James O'Hara, Saintfield; Rev. Robert Hill, Aughalee Glebe; Rev. John Leech, Chaplain of St. Patrick's, Newry; Rev. Henry Martin, Larne; Rev. Charles Falloon, Shankhill Glebe; Rev. Robert Harvey, Belfast; Rev. Colin Ievers, Ballinderry; Rev. George M. Black, Strandmillis; J. Maxwell, M.D. Pointzpass; Henry Leslie, Esq. Leslie-hill; William Gamble, Esq. Magherafelt; Rev. J. Townley Macan,

View of the **CIRCUS** *as it appeared at the Great Protestant Meeting held in Belfast, 21st Jany, 1841.*

Greenmount; Rev. John Davis, Warrenpoint; David M'Connell, Esq. Belfast; Thomas Cather Maguire, Assistant Methodist Missionary; Richard Davison, Esq. Belfast; Thomas Stannus, Esq., Lisburn; Rev. James Shields, Presbyterian Minister, Newry; Thomas Crawford, D.L. J.P., Fortsingleton; S. Corry, Esq. J.P., Old Hall, Rosstrevor; James Robinson, J.P., Warrenpoint; Major Houghton, Springfield; Capt. Crawford, Lissen, Lisburn; A. Annesley, Esq., Ardilea, Clough; James J. Clarke, J.P., Maghera; A. Spottiswood, Millbrook, Magherafelt; Robert Thomson, J.P., Jennymount; Wm. D'Arcy, Necairn Castle, County Fermanagh; J.B. Beresford, Esq., Learmount; William E. Reilly, Esq., D.L. J.P., Hillsborough; George Callwell, Esq., Lismoyne; Captain Graves, J.P., Castledawson; William Caldbeck, Esq.; Hon. George Handcock, J.P., Randalstown; D.S. Kerr, Esq., Portavo; R. Kerr, Esq., Portavo; G. Macartney, D.L. J.P., Lissanoure Castle; J. M'Neile, Esq., D.L. J.P., Parkmount: B.C. Adair, esq., Loughanmore; Lewis Reford, Esq., Beechpark; Captain Garner, Garnerville; Chas. O'Hara, Esq., J.P., O'Hara-brook; Lieut. J.G. Lapenotiere, Castledawson; William Irwin, Esq., J.P., Mountirwin; James Watson, Esq., D.L. J.P., Brookhill; Col. Tisdall, J.P., Charleville, County Louth; John Robert Irwin, Esq., Carnagh House, Armagh; Hamilton Frail Johnston, J.P., Hollypark, Killinchy; Arthur Hill Reid, J.P., Goshen Lodge, County Down; James D. Rose Cleland, D.L. J.P., Rathgale House, Bangor; Bartholomew M'Naghten, J.P., Ballybogey; Richard Blackiston, Esq., J.P.; G.F. Coolderry, D.L. J.P., Monaghan; Arthur Hill Montgomery, D.L. J.P., Tyrella; James Goddard, Esq., Euston Lodge; Henry Rowley, D.L., Lough M'Rory Lodge, Tyrone; Major Richardson, D.L. J.P., Poplar Vale, Monaghan; William Archdall, J.P., Riversdale, Enniskillen; T.R.B. Evatt, A.M. T.C.D. , J.P., Mountlouis, Monaghan; John Montgomery, D.L. J.P., Benvarden; R.J. Smyth, J.P., Lisburn; John Owens, Ballyvoy, Ballyclare, J.P.; John Lindsay, D.L., High Sheriff, Tyrone; James Owens, D.L. J.P. Holestone; the Dean of Tuam; Thomas Lucas, J.P., Ballybay, Rev. A. Henderson, Lisburn; Wm. G. Johnson, Esq., J.P., Fortfield; James Henry, Esq., Fairview, Castledawson; John Thomson, Esq., Lowwood; Rev. Wm. Annesley, J.P., Ardilea, Clough; Hugh Leckey, Esq., J.P., Bushmills; Charles W. Armstrong, J.P., Cherryvalley; Roger Hall, Narrow-water Castle; H. Richardson, D.L. J.P., Somerset;

Wm. Keown, J.P., Ardglass Castle, Down; A. Miller, Ballycastle, Treasurer, County Antrim; Robert Potter, Esq., J.P., Ardview; Arthur Forbes, J.P., Craigavad; John Russell, Esq., Newforge; S. Cleland, Esq., Stormont; Thomas G. Batt, Esq., Purdysburn; Anthony Lefroy, D.L., Longford; Richard F. Anderson, J.P., Welshtown; Charles Fox, D.L. J.P., Keady; John Corry, D.L. J.P., Moutray, Favour-Royal, Auchnacloy; Edw. Archdall, D.L. J.P., Riversdale, Enniskillen; Duncan C. Getty, J.P., Solicitor, Moira; Samuel Davidson, J.P.; William Verner, Esq., M.P., Verner's-bridge; Francis Crossley, Esq., Glenburne; J. Stewart Moore, D.L., J.P., Ballydivity;—Baile, Esq., D.L., J.P., Ringdufferin; Peter Quinn, J.P., Acton House; W. Burleigh, Esq., J.P., Carrickfergus; Robert Lindsay, J.P., Mauleverer, Maghera; W.S. Blackwood, Esq., J.P., Saintfield; Sir Arthur Chichester, D.L. J.P., &c., &c., &c.

On the motion of T. GREG, Esq., High Sheriff of the County of Antrim, seconded by M. ORDE, Esq., High Sheriff of the County of Down,

The Marquis of DOWNSHIRE was called to the chair, amid loud cheers, and several rounds of the Kentish fire. When the applause had subsided—

His LORDSHIP said, that, upon so great, so important an occasion, he felt confident there was not an individual in that numerous and respectable assembly, who would not join with him and the Committee in feeling that it would be most proper and becoming, on the part of the meeting, to commence, by unanimously adopting an address of congratulation to her Majesty and his Royal Highness Prince Albert, on the birth of the Princess Royal; a resolution, and an address founded thereon, would be therefore submitted to their notice. (Loud cheers.)

It was then moved by J.S. WATSON, Esq., of Brookhill; and seconded by NATHL. ALEXANDER, Esq., of Portglenone.

"That John Bates, Esq. act as Secretary to this meeting."[63]

The Right Hon. GEO. ROBT. DAWSON then came forward, to move the adoption of the address, amid loud and long-continued cheers—a duty which he said he undertook with

great pleasure. He did so not only for the purpose of proving
his own loyalty upon this occasion—although he believed it
was not doubted[64]—(cheers)—but for the purpose of re-
echoing in voices, which he hoped would be appreciated and
heard from one end of the empire to another, the sentiments
of the loyal Conservatives of the North of Ireland—sentiments
which he believed to be not only those of the North, but of
every other part of the empire, where Conservatism existed.
(Hear and cheers.) Under ordinary circumstances, there might
not have been any occasion for this address to her Majesty
and her royal husband, congratulating them upon the recent
auspicious event; but they (the Conservatives) having been
taunted with disloyalty to their Sovereign, should seize the
first opportunity of proving the contrary.[65] (Hear, hear and
loud cheers.) Traitors to the country had dared to taunt the
Conservatives of Ireland with want of attachment to the
Queen. How dare they do so?—(Hear and cheers.) He was,
therefore, proud of having been selected. There was not one
bosom, from the noble leader's of the House of Lords, and
the eminent leaders of the House of Commons, down to that
of the humble individual who addressed them, that did not
beat with loyalty to the Queen. (Cheers.) He conceived that
loyalty and Conservatism were convertible terms, and that no
Conservative could be any thing but loyal. (Tremendous
cheering.) Loyalty to the Queen and Constitution of the
country were the very essence of Conservatism—(cheering)—
and the very essence of sovereignty was loyalty to the nation,
and conservation of the institutions of the country. He could,
therefore, understand no Conservatism that was not loyal,
and no Sovereign that was not a Conservative. (Cheers.) At
present, her Majesty was surrounded by persons who did not
profess those principles, but her Majesty, like a true and loyal
sovereign to the nation, bowed to the will of her Parliament,
and suffered herself to be surrounded by those who were
enemies to the country. (Cheers.) But it was the constant drop
that wore the stone, not the foaming torrents that made the
cavity; and it would be the Canterburys and the Walsalls that

would wear down the majority in the House of Commons. (Hear, and great cheering.) The day was coming, and the elections which had recently taken place, proved that it was not very far distant,—(hear and cheers)—when every difficulty which now presented itself will have entirely vanished, and, when the Queen of this empire will occupy the proud position which, as a member of the house of Brunswick, there was no doubt she wished to occupy—namely, that of being surrounded by those who sought for power, not for the purpose of merely basking in the sunshine of royal favour, but for protecting the institutions of the country—of being surrounded by those whose loyalty was the same, under all circumstances. They could say, in the words of the poet—

> "Our loyalty is still the same,
>   Whether we lose or win the game;
>   True as the dial to the sun,
>   Although it be not shone upon."—(Cheers.)[66]

Far different was the loyalty of those who professed different principles. (Hear.) Theirs was a loyalty which merely sought the enjoyment of patronage, and which had dared to call George the Third "a bloodthirsty tyrant". Theirs was a loyalty by which many persons were now pensioners upon the country; and who, while they lived upon the public money, ventured to call George the Fourth "a sensual and senseless voluptuary"; and who, when one of the noblest and bravest of British princes that ever adorned the annals of their country, was lying on his death-bed, ventured to propose, in reference to that illustrious person, "success to hemlock".[67] The loyalty of Conservatives was not of that description. (Hear, hear.) It was not a loyalty which would degrade or calumniate the royal character, when the party was out of power, but a loyalty which would at all times, and under all circumstances, be prepared to offer hand and heart to the Queen of Great Britain, and with both to support and defend the crown, the church, and every thing else noble or valuable in the land. (Loud cheers.) In saying this much, he felt convinced that he was but echoing the sentiments of every lady and gentleman in that building, which he was happy to see crowded by so brilliant an assemblage. (Cheers.) He hoped he would now be excused for offering a very few observations in reference to the events which had occurred within the last few days in Belfast. He could not express one-twentieth part of the indignation he had felt when he found that ruffian, O'Connell—(enthusiastic cheers)—when he found that political impostor daring to come down to disturb the peace of their homes, and to drag the country gentlemen of Ulster from their quiet firesides and from the bosoms of their tenantry, for the purpose of meeting as they had that day met, to tell him (O'Connell) in the face of the world, that he had belied the North of Ireland—(tremendous cheering)—and that he had no claim whatever either on their sympathy or their regard. He had come down to Belfast upon a bucaniering crusade, accompanied by some of his satellites or tail, or whatever he called it—(laughter) and for what?—to increase his beggarly funds, by denouncing the Union that had existed for forty years between the two countries. (Cheers.) Such was his professed object. But, surely, he might have known that his expedition must have failed as signally as it had done; when, if he had only referred to the fact, as recorded upon the books of his own Repeal Association, he would see that the contributions of the Province of Ulster, in favour of his revolutionary project, had amounted to just £2 2s sterling. (Laughter.) Surely that might have been sufficient to prove to him, that he would not have found either sympathy or money for his rebellious purposes, in the northern provinces of Ireland.—(Cheers.) He had said, indeed, that in coming down here, he had been actuated by a national spirit. But what was the fact? Why, that he had been led to do so, by his personal hatred of Lord Stanley, against whom he vainly and foolishly hoped to raise the cry of condemnation. It was, therefore, no desire for the public, no public spirit that had induced him to come among them; it was the spirit, the pervading spirit of selfishness,—or in a word, money, which had led him to the North. (Loud cheers.) He was sure, that the love of money must have been early instilled into his mind by some of his relatives, who, as he often said himself in reference to others, must have observed to him, "get money Dan, honestly if you can, but at all events, get money". But how had he succeeded. (Hear, hear, hear, and cheers.) He stole into town, and he left it under an escort of police, leaving it difficult to determine whether his entrée or retreat was the more glorious. (Laughter and cheers.) Although there was no doubt that O'Connell, at the next public meeting which he attended, would tell them that the enthusiasm with which he had been received in Belfast could scarcely have been repressed, he would continue to call it the "Black North", and say, after a little while it was blacker than ever. (Cries of "he would".) But they had treated him properly.—He had come into the town like a thief and he had gone out of it like a convict, both preceded and followed by a body of police, which he had obtained from the magistrates of the town, upon the affidavit of Tom Steele, one of his satellites, whom he had put forward upon every occasion during his visit, as the representative of his own person, so that had a blow been given it would have fallen on the pate of poor Tom Steele, instead of the rebellious agitator himself. (Laughter and cheers.) Tom Steele had made an affidavit that O'Connell was in danger from an infuriated Orange mob; and he therefore prayed for the support of the military and police to protect him from violence. Now, if the people of Belfast had any spirit, they would resent such an unfounded charge. (Cheers.) The man who had not the courage during the time he was in the town, to shew himself in the streets; but had he done so, he would not have been molested. (Hear, hear.) He would, doubtless, have been hooted, hissed, and cheered, and he (Mr. Dawson) would readily have made one of the Orange mob, as they were called, who would have done so,—but his person would have been safe. Ireland would have praised the loyal men whom O'Connell slanderously called an Orange mob, that had hissed Mr. O'Connell out of the country.

(Hear, hear and loud cheers.) The speaker then alluded to the challenge of Dr. Cooke, to whom he said, he believed they were indebted for the present splendid manifestation of public feeling. He rejoiced in this opportunity of paying his humble tribute of respect, to one who had been denominated a ferocious divine, but whom he would call a distinguished and high-minded gentleman. He therefore called on the meeting, for one unanimous cheer of approbation for his character and his conduct. (Loud and long continued cheers for Doctor Cooke, followed by several rounds of the Kentish fire.)— O'Connell had shrunk from meeting Dr. Cooke, as he had failed to meet every antagonist who had the courage to challenge him.[68]—(Hear, and loud cheers.) His visit to Belfast, however, would not be without its useful effects. (Cries of hear, hear.) The reception he had met with, while it would give encouragement to the Protestants of Ireland, would teach the demagogues of the country, with O'Connell at their head, that they could not trifle with the feelings or principles of Protestantism. (Loud cheers.) The Protestants of Ireland might be in a minority in point of numbers, but if forced to take their position, it would be found that they constituted by far the greater portion of the property, the intelligence, and the nerve of the country. (Loud cheers.) Let O'Connell and his tail continue if they pleased to draw a contrast between Roman Catholics and Protestants—the Protestants did not seek it; let their enemies if they pleased continue to draw that contrast— but, in doing so, let them recollect the events that had taken place at Aughrim, at the Boyne, and at Enniskillen. Let them recollect those events, for he could tell them, that if ever they sought for their repetition in the North, they would find that every river in it would become a Boyne, and every village an Aughrim. (Loud and long protracted cheering, with the Kentish fire.) The Protestants of Ulster would have what has long been the watchword of Derry—"No Surrender." (Cheers.) They would maintain their position. When the struggle came, be it sooner or later, they would have no fear whatever of their ability, by being united, as they had always been, to maintain the Crown, the Church, and the State. (Loud cheers.) The right honourable gentleman concluded by moving

"That addresses of congratulation be presented to Her Majesty and His Royal Highness Prince Albert, on the birth of the Princess Royal".

[At this period of the proceedings the doors were ordered to be closed, in consequence of the great pressure.]

Lord ALGERNON CHICHESTER seconded the motion, which passed unanimously, amidst loud cheers.

Colonel VERNER then came forward, amidst enthusiastic cheering, and one cheer more for the Deputy Grand Master, to move the adoption of the address. The applause having subsided, the gallant colonel proceeded to express his approval of the objects of the meeting, and observed that there never was an occasion when the province of Ulster was more peremptorily called upon to express its opinion than the present, two meetings having recently been held by a body professing to represent the province, and calling itself the Ulster Association; which he must say he regarded as a great piece of presumption, as that association did not speak the sentiments of the people of Ulster. If any body of men were entitled to assume that name, it was those he saw around him, for they represented the rank, wealth, and respectability of every county in the province. (Hear, hear.) The gallant colonel, referring to Lord Stanley's bill, said that in expressing their approbation of the measure they should not forget their admiration of the man. (Hear, hear.) Yes, they were deeply indebted to Lord Stanley for having brought forward that measure, and for having the courage to proceed with it, amidst insults the grossest, and language the most disgraceful, language which he believed no man would have dared to utter outside the doors of the House of Commons. As for a Repeal of the Union, the specimen they had had within the last few days, of opposition to such a measure, said more against it than he possibly could. (Loud groans for the Repeal of the Union.) It was, however, a measure for serious consideration, when they reflected from whom it was that

Mr. O'Connell received sanction, if not support, in his turbulent agitation of it. (Cries of hear, hear and cheers.) If the Government of the country were sincere in their determination to suppress that agitation, nothing could be more easily done. The Repeal of the Union was a measure which had been proved by Mr. Spring Rice, in a speech of six hours' length—a speech which he believed had taken half as many years to prepare—(loud laughter)—would work injuriously for Ireland; it was a measure to which a noble lord had declared in parliament, he would prefer civil war; it was a measure which had been denounced by the present Lord Lieutenant, and yet the military and police forces of the State were allowed to accompany that mountebank through the country, who was alone the cause of the agitation. (Loud cheers.) He (Colonel Verner) recollected when it was deemed advisable to put down a society very different in its nature from the Repeal Association[69]—a society whose objects were perfectly legal, which had existed for upwards of forty-one years, which had received the thanks of the Government and of both Houses of Parliament, and the admiration and approbation of every loyal subject. It was deemed advisable that it should be put down, and in obedience to that opinion the society of itself ceased to exist. (Hear.) The person whose presence had lately disgraced the town of Belfast, said, upon that occasion, that the Government had gone the right way of putting down the party, for it had taken the bull by the horns in removing the society. Now, the bull, he (Colonel Verner) thought, meant himself. (Laughter.) Well, if the Government were really determined to put down the Repeal Association, he would say to them, take the bull by the horns, and whether it was the bull of Rome or the Irish bull, he ventured to say, they would meet with success. (Loud cheers.)

The HIGH SHERIFF OF FERMANAGH seconded the motion. He began by alluding to the Belfast meeting which had been held for Repeal in this town; and called upon them to look upon that picture and upon this. (Loud cheers.) He referred to the prosperity and orderly state of one part of Ireland, as compared with the rest; and said, that Government ought to be sensible of the important advantages of Conservatism. Protestants claimed the right of reading their Bible, and no one could do that, and not be a Conservative and a loyal man. He assured the meeting, that the gentry and yeomanry of the county which he had the honour to represent, sympathized as fully as he did, with the objects of that meeting. He had sincere pleasure in seconding the resolution. (loud cheers.)

The resolution was then put and agreed to unanimously; and the following addresses were read and adopted:—

"TO THE QUEEN'S MOST EXCELLENT MAJESTY.

"MAY IT PLEASE YOUR MAJESTY,—We, your Majesty's most dutiful and loyal subjects, the Noblemen, Clergy, and Gentry, of Antrim, Down, and the contiguous Northern counties, assembled by public requisition, beg leave to approach your Majesty, with our heartfelt congratulations, on the birth of the Princess Royal. Whilst we tender our humble thanks to Almighty God, whose Providence watched over your Majesty's precious life, and has returned you to perfect health, to the joy of all your loyal and devoted subjects; and to God, by whom Kings reign, and Princes decree justice, it shall ever be our earnest prayer, that your Majesty may long be preserved, to reign over these inseparably united kingdoms, and that your illustrious line may be perpetuated,—the defenders under God, of our faith and our freedom, to all generations."

"TO HIS ROYAL HIGHNESS PRINCE ALBERT
OF SAXE GOTHA AND COBURG.

"We, the Noblemen, and Clergy, and Gentry, of Antrim, Down, and contiguous Northern counties of Ireland, by public requisition assembled, beg leave to congratulate your Royal Highness on the birth, and continued health of the Princess Royal, and the happy recovery of her Majesty; and we pray to Almighty God that her Majesty's union with your Royal Highness may be long and blessed; and that your posterity may be perpetuated to rule over a united, prosperous, loyal and happy nation."

JOHN BATES, Esq., then read the requisition, calling the meeting, and stated, that it had been signed by 1,605 noblemen and gentlemen.

The Marquis of DOWNSHIRE then came forward, and was received with unbounded demonstrations of applause. He said, that he had already used the phrase, "constitutional", and he now repeated it, as that best calculated fully to indicate the feelings by which this great meeting he saw before him were actuated. (Cheers.) He thanked them for the proud station in which he was then placed, and he should always endeavour so to direct his conduct, as to continue to meet with similar testimonies of regard from his fellow-countrymen. (Cheers.) He had always felt, that the cheerful support of the laws was the duty of every loyal subject, and that consideration brought him to the first object of the meeting, namely, the Repeal of the Act of the Union.—It appeared to him, that so destructive a measure could not be proposed by any of her Majesty's subjects, with a view to the interest of the throne, or the people of this realm, and he therefore joined in the proceedings of that day, to implore that the union of the three kingdoms might be permanently established. (Loud cheers.) The powerful endeavours made by Lord Stanley, during the last Session in the House of Commons, ought to inspire every loyal subject with the utmost confidence, that the future exertions which he proposes to make, would be ultimately crowned with success. He was firmly of opinion, that, if any meeting of the public, or expression of opinion, could have weight with the Legislature, the assemblage which he saw before him would be attended with the most important results; and he, therefore, for one, came forward cheerfully in support of the Act of Union, and for the purpose of returning thanks to Lord Stanley, for the judgment and perseverance which he had displayed in proposing and supporting, with extraordinary ability and judgment, his new Registration Bill.—(Loud cheers.) Too much praise could not be given to that nobleman, who held so distinguished a station in the public mind already, that they could do but little to exalt him more. He trusted, however, that the proceedings of that day would tend more powerfully to support those exertions for which they were so grateful. (Loud cheers.) The other point to which the attention of the meeting would be especially directed, was the necessity for advocating and adopting every course of conduct and action, which tended to the support of her Majesty's crown and dignity; and it gladdened him inexpressibly, to perceive that the Protestants of the kingdom required no urging on that point, but recognizing the necessity which had arisen for their interference, had come forward with unanimity to sustain the laws of the realm. (Loud cheers.) He was sure the proceedings of that day would be distinguished by that calmness and devotedness of conduct, which would best advance the cause they had at heart in both countries; for he could assure them, that the eyes of the empire at large were then directed to the events which were taking place in the north of Ireland, and he felt a strong hope that the conduct adopted by them would prove creditable to the high-minded and intelligent population, for which that part of the kingdom had ever been distinguished. (Cheers.) Of the Magistrates, Gentry, and resident nobility, he could not speak too highly, and the greatest honour which could be conferred on him, was to be considered one of that distinguished body. (Cheers.) It had been said by a noble friend of his, that Lord Stanley's Bill should be thrown out, because it was a restrictive measure on the rights of the people, but he would tell that noble lord, that such could never be the case in that part of Ireland; for those who were there permitted without interference to exercise their just rights, had never been disgraced by those acts of perjury, which had called forth so much just animadversion in other parts of the country. (Hear, and cheers.) The object of Lord Stanley's Bill was to put an end, for ever, to those enormities, and he trusted that it would not long be delayed. In the mean time, he would throw out a suggestion to his Roman Catholic fellow subjects, that they would not permit any body of men, whatever their spiritual influence might be, to interfere with the duties which they had to discharge to themselves, their landlords, their country, and their families. (Cheers.) He had mentioned their landlords, as persons to whom they owed something, because, if he knew any thing of the character of Irish gentlemen, he would assert, that it was distinguished above all other characteristics, for an anxious wish to improve their tenantry and dependants. (Loud cheers.) He would, moreover, say to the Roman Catholic clergymen themselves, that it was their duty to exclude from the house of God all political feelings—(hear, hear, hear)—and that whoever the individual might be, who commanded or desired it, they should not suffer individuals to be denounced from their altars, nor objects unconnected with the worship of the Most High, to be canvassed and insisted upon within the walls devoted to His services. (Hear, hear.) If this advice were acted on throughout the kingdom, more especially in the South of Ireland, it would soon present an appearance exactly the reverse of what they were so often called on to deplore, in every portion of the country except in the Province of Ulster. (Cheers.)—He said this from an anxious desire to benefit the whole of the country and thus serve that portion of it to which he was, from position and feeling, most attached himself; for he was firmly convinced, that, while a line of demarcation existed between the North and South, neither the one nor the other could thrive to the full extent of their capabilities.—(Cheers.) The most noble Marquis concluded, by thanking the meeting for the honour conferred upon him, and expressed his readiness, upon every occasion, to join in any undertaking which might be adopted for the benefit of the country. [He resumed the chair amid loud cheers, and several rounds of the Kentish fire.]

Mr. BATES proceeded to read the letters of apology which had been received from the noblemen and gentlemen who were unable to attend the meeting. He said the correspondence was very voluminous; and, if time permitted, every letter which had been received by him would be read to the meeting. A hurried selection had, however, been necessarily made. Mr. Bates then read letters from

Lords Donegall, O'Neill, Waterford, Ely, Mountcashell, Enniskillen, Belmore, Castlestuart, Clancarty, Castlereagh, Dungannon, Ferrard, Corry, Claude Hamilton, Blayney, Farnham, Lord Bishop of Clogher, General Meade, Counsellor Napier, E. M. Connolly, M.P.; Hon. A.H. Cole, M.P.; Hon. H. Corry, M.P.; Hon. S. Hewitt, J.P.; E. S. Hayes, M.P.; Sir James R. Bunberry, J.P.; Sir Thos. Forster, Bart., J.P.; P. Kirk, M.P.; E. Lucas, M.P.; E.J. Shirley, M.P.; W. J. Armstrong, High Sheriff, County Armagh; R. G. Montgomery, High Sheriff, County Donegall; J. M'Clintock, jun., High sheriff, County Louth; H.L. Montgomery, High Sheriff, County Leitrim; Colonel Ward, J.P; Lieut. General Cuppage; Rev. Alexander Ross, Rector of Banagher; W. Humphreys, J.P.

The secretary also announced having received letters form Lord Powerscourt, M.P.; Lord John Beresford; Lord De Ros; Lord Sandys; the Hon. and Rev. Charles Douglass; the Hon. John L. Cole; the Hon. Edward Wingfield; the Hon. General O'Neill, M.P.; the Hon, John C. Maude; the Hon. Somerset R. Maxwell; the Hon. R. T. Maxwell; Sir J. A. Stewart, Bart.; Lieut. General Sir T. Molyneaux, Bart.; Sir R. Gore Booth, Bart.; Sir John Lighton, Bart; Sir W. Macartney, Bart.; Sir Hugh Stewart, Bart.; the Marquis of Abercorn; the Marquis of Hertford; the Marquis of Londonderry; the Earl of Roden; the Earl of Clanwilliam; the Earl of Wicklow; the Earl of Ranfurly, &c., &c., &c.

The CHAIRMAN then rose and said that he had received, that morning, a letter from Lord Charleville, in which that noble lord expressed a hope, that the present meeting would be productive of all the good to the prosperity and liberty of the country, which it was so well calculated to effect. (Loud cheers.)

The Earl of HILLSBOROUGH came forward to propose the next resolution, and was received with cheering and the Kentish fire. He proceeded to observe,—My Lord, Gentlemen, and brother Protestants, I feel myself highly honoured in being called on to propose the resolution which has been put into my hand, and on which, after the able and eloquent speeches which you have just now heard, I will only trouble you with one or two remarks. (Hear, hear.) In the first place,

then, allow me to condole with you on the failure—the utter
failure—of the Repeal meeting which was held, or to be held,
I do not know which; for I assure you, that I could not hear
one word of the addresses said to be delivered, and I believe
no one else was more fortunate. (Hear, hear, and loud cheers.)
I have, it is true, seen a report of speeches alleged to have
been spoken; but I suppose they were all sent ready prepared
to the press. I condole with you, gentlemen, on the failure of
the political charlatanism which was attempted to be practised
among you. I condole with you in that way in which you
would expect to find me condoling—and that is, not at all.
(Laughter.) I now turn from this farce to a subject of a more
pleasing nature—that referred to in the resolution I am about
to submit to you. I thank you, gentlemen, for this meeting—
I thank you that you have enabled our enemies to say, that
Ulster has been roused at last. (Loud cheers.) I thank you as
a Protestant, like yourselves, for the determination you have
evinced, to stand up for your rights, and in support of the
Constitution. I thank you, finally, for this manifestation of
your approval of Lord Stanley's bill. (Hear, hear.) I am happy
to see that so many gentlemen have come here, from great
distances, at this inclement season of the year, to express their
concurrence in the objects of this great meeting. (Cheers.) Let
us hope that the assembly will be as useful in its proceedings,
and as successful in its results, as that over which I had the
honour to preside in 1834. (Loud and tremendous cheers.)
That meeting was called together by me in virtue of the high
station I then occupied, as High Sheriff of the County Down,
and not as a certain Radical has falsely stated, at the bidding
of my father. I wish the present meeting may turn out as well
as that did; for it not only turned the Whigs out of office, but
proved, to the despairing Protestants, that their dejection was
not without remedy. (Hear.)—I hope it will show the Sovereign
the strength and the loyalty of the Protestants of Ulster—that
it will prove to her how unworthily she is advised by her
present Ministers. (Hear, hear.) If the truth, the whole truth,
and nothing but the truth, were told to her Majesty, it would

not be necessary for us to hold such a meeting, merely to protect ourselves. (Cheers.) His lordship then read the resolution.—This resolution pledges us to the support of Lord Stanley's bill—(hear, hear, and cheers)—and, I think, that, when it is considered that that bill has already been agreed to by majorities in Parliament, composed of all shades of opinion—Whigs, Radicals, and Tories—(hear, hear)—you will excuse me for not going into details at this time; to do which, indeed, in a satisfactory manner, would require the perspicuity and acumen of a lawyer. I will say this much for myself, that I will, this year, act in the same way, with regard to that bill, as I did last year. I then attended every night in the House of Commons, and voted in every division, and I will be as punctual in the ensuing session; and I am as convinced of the honesty of Lord Stanley as I am of the necessity and success of the measure. Allow me to conclude, gentlemen, by expressing concurrence with the spirit of the resolution I have just read to you. (Loud cheering and the Kentish fire.) The following is the resolution referred to:—

"That the present state of the law for the Registration of Electors is confessedly ineffectual for the discrimination and enrolment of a duly qualified constituency, as defined by the Reform Act of 1832, and holds out most dangerous temptations to the advancement and support of factitious claims to the franchise, by means of perjury and fraud".

GEORGE MACARTNEY, Esq., Lissanore, then came forward, and was received with several bursts of applause. He said, in responding to their call, to second the resolution which his noble friend had just read, were he to consult his own feelings, and the comfort and convenience of the assembly, he ought, perhaps, merely second it, without making any observations; but it appeared to him, from the shadow of the coming events, that, let a man's position in life be what it might, great or small, who was connected with the property and institutions of Ireland, it would be both weak and criminal, were he to shield himself from declaring his sentiments, in the face of such a meeting as the present, and in the face of his country. (Hear, hear, and loud cheers.) He would own that, previous to the meeting in Dublin, on Friday,—when he saw the requisition and its array of names, forced from every point of the compass, by the influence of the Government and the exertions of the demagogues and the Priests, and which was styled "The Great Aggregate Meeting", to make a diversion against the proposed measure of Lord Stanley, which, when he withdrew it last Session, promised to introduce it again in the ensuing Session—when he (Mr. Macartney) saw the names at that requisition his mind misgave him, that a counter-agitation might damage the character of the measure, as approved of by the English House of Commons; but, when three days since, he received a report of that meeting, his fears were changed into admiration and surprise to find it so complete and so abject a failure. He felt had they (the Conservatives) not met there that day, the failure of Friday was sufficient to give that force and effect to the measure which Lord Stanley had introduced. (Loud cries of hear, hear, hear.) The requisition of the aggregate meeting in Dublin consisted of forty Noblemen, sixteen or seventeen Baronets, fifteen or sixteen Honourables, *cum multis aliis*; but what was the result? Why, that a Noble, deserted by his order, was in the chair. Two Baronets, ten or fifteen of the tail, with Dan at their head, and the renowned Peter, of imperial notoriety, and the last, not least, *par nobile fratrum*, Sharman Crawford and David Ross,[70] Secretaries of the still-born Ulster Association. (Cheers and laughter.) But who went under their wing? Why, only four gentlemen from the shores of the North of Ireland, representing the intelligence, prosperity, and respectability of the North; and whom it was found necessary to move and second resolutions. (A laugh.) Such was the meeting of Friday last. From that meeting the Conservatives had gained the greatest support to their cause. (Cries of hear, hear.) No resolution had been passed in his mind at that glorious meeting— (cheers)—the germ of an opposition to Lord Stanley's bill. (Hear, hear.) The question of Repeal had been brought to their doors by the connivance of a weak and vacillating

government—(cheers)—who, if they had the interests of the
country at heart, would have told Mr. O'Connell, "agitate in
your own district, where you have a mob of your own principles and party; but do not attempt to set your foot in that
district where you know, in your heart, this moment, the
question of Repeal is not entertained. (Hear, hear.) You had
people of your own religion and politics there, but even they
will not support that question; and he (Mr. Macartney) would
say, that many of the Roman Catholics who had foolishly
urged Mr. O'Connell to visit Belfast, were as opposed to Repeal
as any one then present. (Loud cheering.) Mr. O'Connell had
come twenty-four hours sooner than was originally intended,
and by doing so, he (Mr. Macartney) would say, that he had
libelled the people of the North—(hear, hear, hear)—for,
although they might have received him on his way with
disapprobation, he (Mr. Macartney) had that opinion of the
people, that he was sure they would let him pass in scorn.
(Cheers.) He had entered the town, as was truly said, like a
"thief in the night", with a carriage full of blunderbusses, in
which sat Steele and Co.—(hear, and laughter)—and in certain
places where they stopped to change horses, they took occasion to load the blunderbusses. (Hear.) Now, was that a proper
way for the great O'Connell to make an impression upon the
cool and thinking people of the North? (Hear, hear and cheers.)
No; he little knew them, if that was the course which had
been originally suggested by him. (Hear, hear.)—But he came
not only like a thief in the night, but he went away like a
criminal in the day. Thanks to the exertions, the attentions,
and the steady good conduct of the authorities assembled in
Belfast, from all parts of the country, no casualty had occurred,
or a blot been inflicted upon their county. But there was a blot
sought to be stamped upon Ulster by those who accompanied
him, Mr. Steele and others, who had, at the hour of twelve
o'clock at night, called on the Magistrates for a Police force
to protect Mr. O'Connell, making affidavit that his life was
not safe, if he had not the troops to guard him, whilst there,
and also to preserve the peace of his embarkation. Such

conduct as that was a libel on the North. It was the first time such a libel of injustice was done the Northerns, and he (Mr. Macartney) thought it would be the last. (Cries of "It is", and groans.) As to the question of Repeal, he (Mr. Macartney) would ask, what had made the North of Ireland flourish? Was it not their connexion with England; and was it not their communication with all the world through the means of England? (Hear, hear.) Was it not from their intercourse with men of intelligence, rank, property and manufactures, that the North was prosperous—(cheers)—and any measure that was calculated to sever that connexion would, and should, be detrimental to their country. (Loud cheering.) This demonstration would have its effect upon the mind of England, and show the English Members what the sentiment of Ulster was. The Southern population, and those of other quarters, were pleased to suffer the control of the demagogues, and the Priests. The North would never consent to any such influence.—(Cheers.)

The resolution was then put and carried.

Viscount NEWRY and MOURNE proposed the next resolution, which he stated to accord completely with his own opinions, and to which, he hoped, the meeting would unanimously agree to. The resolution was in the following words:—

"That the principles of the bill introduced, during the last Session of Parliament, by Lord Stanley, appears to us to be so consistent with justice, and the bill itself to embody such equitable provisions, as, if passed into a law, will be sufficient to grapple with the existing evil, and put an end to the demoralising practices which have prevailed at the Registering Sessions in Ireland, for the last eight years."

MR. EMERSON TENNENT, M.P.[71] rose and said,—The resolution of the noble Earl who had preceded him (Lord Hillsborough), and the speech in which it had been introduced, abundantly testified the imperative necessity which existed for legislative interference; that necessity had, in fact, been admitted by all parties for the last five years; but no sincere or effectual attempt had been made to grapple with and strangle the abuse, till Lord Stanley had, last year, introduced his Bill. The support which that measure received, from men of all parties, both in the House of Commons and beyond it, was the best evidence at once of their consciousness of the existence of the evil, and their confidence in the efficacy of the remedy, and against such a prevailing impression, the only weapons with which the opponents could contend were, misconstruction and wilful distortion of its parts. To some of these misrepresentations he (Mr. E.T.) would address himself. A few days ago, when the arrangements to hold this meeting were finally made, he (Mr. E. Tennent) took an opportunity of acquainting Lord Stanley with the intense feeling throughout Ulster in which it originated; and the attempts which had been made in the Ulster Association, under the shadow of an opposition to his Registration Bill, to obtain an expression of opinion, which would thus have been trumpeted as the genuine sentiments of the Province, in favour of reducing the franchise almost to the zero of Chartism. He enclosed to his lordship a copy of the report of the Association on the Registration laws generally, and his own bill in particular; and he concluded his letter by suggesting, that, as this vast and influential assembly had spontaneously met, in order to tender his lordship their support in effecting the enactment of that bill, he might, perhaps, be desirous of apprising them of his intentions, as regarded its introduction, as well as how far his own sentiments had been influenced by the discussions on the measure in the House of Commons, or the strictures of the Ulster Association and others throughout the country. To that letter, he (Mr. E. Tennent) had received an answer from Lord Stanley, the substance of which he would presently lay before them. And first, as to the time and manner of the introduction of the bill, Lord Stanley authorised him to say, that he stood ready for the first moment that his friends thought it desirable to move. (Cheers.) On the other point, as to any alterations which reflection, or the suggestions of others, might have led his lordship to contemplate in bringing the measure a second time before the House, his reply is as characteristic of the calm and mature deliberation with which the duty was originally undertaken, as of the temperate and conciliating spirit in which it will be followed up. "As to modifications", he says, "you know, no one better, that the task of introducing it was not of my seeking,—that having undertaken it, I most carefully considered its provisions, and, with the concurrence of our friends, put it into a shape in which we thought it both a just and an effective measure. I see no reason to alter the view which we then took, from any thing that has since passed in Parliament or elsewhere; but, I am not only ready, I shall be thankful to receive, and consider with respect, the suggestions of those who have more practical experience than myself, and too happy to adopt them, if, on the one hand, I am satisfied of their justice, and if, on the other, they will not throw additional obstacles in the way of passing the bill. No doubt, there are some of its provisions more important than others,— and I do not think that I can more conveniently, though I may more shortly, answer your questions, than by going through the manifesto which embodies the views of the Ulster Association, so far as they relate to registration." Now, with regard to the numbers of the Ulster Association, he (Mr. E. Tennent) was disposed to speak of them with every deference and respect, as well from their high rank and standing in society, as because there were among them individuals to whom he was attached by private friendship, not less than admiration of their talents, and appreciation of their sincerity. But these very circumstances, of the station and eminence of the individuals, rendered it the more incumbent upon them to protest against their acts and opinions being mistaken for a representation of the genuine sentiments of this wealthy and powerful Province. Against such a conclusion, however, the assembly whom he had the honour to address was the most effectual corrective and protection. (Cheers.) And his (Mr. E. Tennent's) most ardent hope was, that when the progress of events shall have accomplished that consummation, which he saw rapidly approaching—when all parties and denominations of Protestants would be driven to make common cause, in order to ensure their common defence—the Liberals of the Ulster

Association would discover nothing to contradict the assertion
which he (Mr. E. Tennent) now made in the face of the
assembled Conservatives of the province:—that their principles
were not aggressive, but simply and purely defensive—that
they seek to infringe no man's liberty—to contract no man's
rights; but, by God's assistance, and their own firm union, to
resist tyranny, from whatever quarter it may come—whether
from an individual or a multitude—and to preserve, with the
last pulse of their hearts, those rights of property and of person,
and, above all, those rights of judgment and of conscience,
which shone upon the world in the light of the Reformation,
and which must relapse into primaeval darkness, with the
occurrence of any catastrophe that would neutralize or overthrow it. (cheers.) The Liberal Protestants of Ireland misappre-
hended and wrong us, if they suppose that we have any
interest, or aspire to any, distinct and different from them;
they have the same objects in view, and the same privileges at
stake that we have—their welfare, their liberty, and their
happiness, are equally threatened with out own, by measures
now in agitation in Ireland; and we invite them—we entreat
them to weigh calmly, and aside from all jealousies of party,
the petty differences which separate us, and to make common
cause with those who are their brethren and natural allies, by
all the ties of country, of kindred, of friendship, and religion.
(Loud cheers.) Mr. O'Connell has told them, on Thursday
last, that they must either become Conservatives or Repealers:
his own violence will ultimately drive them to the one or the
other alternative—and with such a choice before them, he
(Mr. E. Tennent) had little doubt as to which they would
prefer to adopt. (Cheers.) He (Mr. E. Tennent) learned from
those tumultuous cheers, that they adopted these sentiments
as their own—(renewed cheers)—and, in that spirit of friendly
argument, he would now propose to meet the leading
objections which had been made in the report of the Ulster
Association to the provisions of Lord Stanley's Bill. "I hail
with satisfaction", says Lord Stanley in his letter, "the admission
in the report of the Ulster Association, that, *in order successfully*

to oppose any future attempt to carry a bill similar to that of last session,
it is necessary to be prepared to propose such amendments of the present
law, as are imperatively required to remedy its many objectionable
provisions and glaring defects.—And I rejoice to find also, that, in
many of the leading provisions of my bill, and some which
were the most decried, they are compelled to concur." And
his lordship then proceeded to notice the various points of
agreement and of difference, in the order in which they
presented themselves in the report. The first point at issue is
the establishment of an annual registration, as proposed by
Lord Stanley, or the continuance of the quarterly visits of the
assistant-barrister, as recommended by the report. There is no
individual who has had any experience of these three-monthly
attendances at the registration courts, that must not long for
their abolition, as a monstrous injustice to men on whose
habits of industry and occupation, it is a serious inroad in the
exercise of a constitutional vigilance over their political rights;
and an arrangement calculated to give an undue advantage,
either to those idlers to whom politics is a profession, and
lounging in the courts is a matter of ordinary business; or to
those wealthy candidates, who can afford to pay highly-salaried
agents for maintaining perpetual guard over their interests.
This prominent grievance Lord Stanley's Bill proposes to
remove, by the substitution of an annual for a quarterly registration; but to this the Ulster Association object, on the score
of the expense and delay which they apprehend would ensue,
if the whole body of the electors were to be congregated once
a-year at an annual sessions. Lord Stanley, however, contends
that the alteration is justified, not only by expediency, but on
the score of assimilation to the law of Scotland and of England;
and as a more than counterbalance to the inconveniency they
apprehended, he remarks, that "the Association take no notice
of the great additional facilities given to all parties, whether
claimants or objectors, by the provision of my bill, which
multiplies the places for holding registration courts, and
assigns a district to each—*a facility which could not be given by a*
quarterly registration". Another prominent objection taken by

Mr. O'Connell in the House of Commons, has been reiterated by the Ulster Association, with reference to the particulars of the voters description, as ordered to be set out in his notice of claim. Here Lord Stanley perfectly agrees with the Association, that the description given should be of such a nature "*as is necessary for the identification of the claimant, and such general description of the property as will prevent fraudulent registration*". "Perhaps", says his letter, "I should add, and they might admit, *as will enable the property to be identified;* and adopting this principle, the necessary forms are a matter of detail, and a fair subject for discussion." He (Mr. E. Tennent) would beg to direct the attention of the meeting, and of the country, to this and similar avowals of Lord Stanley, in reply to imputations of a desire to embarrass or intimidate the claimant. In the principle of the precautions he proposes, both he and his opponents are agreed, and he only asks for a calm and dispassionate discussion, to accommodate the machinery of the bill to the accomplishment of an object which is thus avowed to be common to both. This, and similar declarations are the best evidence of the animus with which Lord Stanley has undertaken the task in which he has been so egregiously misrepresented.— Another, and an important point of the bill, was the power which it proposes to confer of objecting to the registration of a claimant, or the continuance of a vote on the list, without any previous and minute notification of the several grounds to be taken, but under the penalty of costs upon whichever party failed in substantiating his allegations. Upon this point he could not do better than quote the words of his Lordship's letter, in reference to the difference of opinion between himself and the Ulster Association:—"The Association would admit any person to object, but limit the objections to those of which specific notice had been served upon the party, and on some public officer, as in Scotland. I restrict the right of objecting, as in England, to voters or claimants, or their agents, but require no notice except as against persons already on the registry, nor any specification of objections.—Indeed, if, *as they admit*, the claimant is in the first instance to prove his title, he must be prepared to prove it against any and every objection that can be raised. The Association are compelled to admit, that the system pursued in Scotland of requiring specific objections is open to abuse, as it contains no provision against an objector including in his notice every possible objection; and the remedy they propose is, to *compel* the registering barrister to saddle the objector with costs and evidence. Thus every objection stated must be gone into by the objector, (though the claimant may have been registered on the very first), under pain of being visited with costs, to be paid to the registered claimant; and a penalty is imposed on an objector, though it be distinctly admitted, that at the time of giving notice, he had every reason to believe his objection well founded. I propose to *authorise* the assistant-barrister to give costs, when he shall judge the application frivolous. Which is the most rational and the most practical course?" Another vital portion of Lord Stanley's measure is, the establishment of a periodical revision for the removal of the disqualified, and the names of the dead, from encumbering lists. Upon this point he (Mr. E.T.) would again read from Lord Stanley's communication his strictures upon the proposition of the Ulster association:—"We agree", says his Lordship, "that the Irish law should be adhered to, which requires the claimant to prove his title in the first instance, but the Association requires that 'he should then be protected from any further impugnment of his right to vote, except on account of some circumstances occurring, subsequent to his having been placed on the register, and not previously adjudicated upon'". I admit that a voter, once on the register, should be protected against vexatious re-investigations. My bill requires that the objector in such case should prove his objection (not show a *prima facie* case, but *prove* it), before the voter is ever called on for a defence—that he should prove it subject to costs for a frivo- lous objection; but we contend, that the extent of protection demanded by the Association will tend to keep on the register fraudulent voters, *provided they afterwards can prove to have been fraudulent when first put on*. Further, that in the difference which unfortunately prevails in the decisions of different barristers, a claimant successively rejected by a dozen different barristers, and having put objectors to the expense of substantiating their objections a dozen times consecutively, if he can at last succeed in persuading one barrister to revise the decisions of the other twelve, is immovably placed on the register. Again, a claimant having been placed on the register by the overruling an appeal of the objector on which he was first rejected is protected against objections, which *might* have been urged at his first claim, *and which would have been urged*, had they not been rendered unnecessary by his rejection on other grounds. I might multiply cases, but I think there will be sufficient to show, that protection to this extent passes the legitimate bounds, "and tends to the introduction for life of fraudulent votes". Another anomalous circumstance connected with the registration system in Ireland, was the imperfect nature of the appeal which was attached to them—the registering barrister having an absolute and irresponsible power in all cases of admission to the franchise, except in so far as they were cognizable by a committee of the House of Commons, and an appeal to a superior court being only allowable in the case of a rejected claimant. On this subject he (Mr. Emerson Tennent) would take the liberty to read an extract from the manifesto of the Association:—"Your committee", says their report, "consider it an object of the first importance, that an appeal to a committee of the House of Commons, on the right of a voter, should be rendered, so far as possible, unnecessary. They cannot, therefore, approve of the English system, because it gives no means of redress either to a claimant or to an objector, against an erroneous decision of a registering barrister, except by a reference to such a committee: nor of the Irish system, because it confines the right of appeal to the claimant. Your committee would therefore recommend, that the right of appeal, on all points of law, (the final decision on questions of *fact* having been already provided for in section IV.) should be conferred, both on the claimant and on the objector, and that a court of appeal should be constituted, before which

appellants might have such points decided." "I am happy", says
Lord Stanley, "to have the assent of the Ulster Association in
these main principles of my bill; 1st, That it would be of great
advantage to obviate the necessity of appeals in the House of
Commons; 2d, That for this purpose a court of appeal is
necessary; and 3d, That the right of appeal should be conferred, both on the claimant and on the objector. In fact,
these, together with the notice to be given by claimants, to
which the Association assent, the abolition of certificates, which
they also recommend, and the annual revision (and they
purpose a quarterly revision), constituted the essence of the
bill which was so acrimoniously opposed last session. I think
it doubtful how far questions of *law* and questions of *fact* can
be separated in the appeal, as proposed by the Association.
They do not suggest any new constitution of the court of
appeal. I found the judge of assize, already the authority
referred to, on the one-sided appeal, and I preserved the
same authority when the appeal was extended to the objector.
If any other tribunal can be established, as far removed from
temptation, and as free from the suspicion of partiality, I see
no reason for insisting that the appeal shall be to the judge of
assize. The substitution of the authority of a judge for that of a
jury, in cases of value, was suggested by the late Lord Clements,
sanctioned by the present Government, and adopted in the
House of Commons. The Association think that here again
the objector should be subject to *costs* by every case where his
objections are not sustained—the claimant in none in any
case whatever. I was of opinion that *both* parties should be
liable to costs, if there were no legitimate ground for bringing
the appeal or defending the vote. The course recommended
by the Association appears one-sided and unjust, and, if I
understand it rightly, gives costs against the objector whenever
unsuccessful, and relieves the claimant when he frivolously
puts the objector to expense, in substantiating an objection
already affirmed by the barrister". Another important question
connected with registration is, the period during which an
elector should actually occupy his premises previous to being

invested with any right, in order to avoid the evil of creating
batches of voters to carry any given election. The Association,
apparently forgetful of the object, propose that a man should
be registered immediately on coming into possession, and
should be enabled to vote in six months after registration. On
this Lord Stanley observes, "in England, freeholders and
copyholders, with some exceptions which extend to Ireland,
must have been in possession six months previous to the last
day of July, before the annual registration; and all other
claimants twelve months—that is, eight months at least before
registry. My bill proposed to give in Ireland the right of being
registered at the end of six months' possession, and of voting
at the expiration of the same periods which would entitle
English voters of the same class to *put in their claims*. What
ground can there be for a still greater difference in favour of
Ireland?" These were the principal points of the bill in which
Lord Stanley dissented from the amendments proposed by the
Association. He (Mr. E. T.) felt it to be unnecessary to trouble
the meeting with those points in Lord Stanley's bill of which
the Association fully approved. But there was still a third class
to which he would specially direct their attention—namely,
those alterations which the Association had suggested, and to
which his Lordship saw no good grounds upon the score of
principle to object. One of these, and one of the most important, is the right which exists in England of an elector to
register, if, for the necessary time beforehand, he has occupied,
not the same house, but another of equal value, and discharged
all the taxes due upon each, and also the right of partners to
vote out of their joint premises, provided their value, if divided,
would constitute a £10 qualification for each. To the proposal
of the Association, that this provision of the law should be
extended to Ireland, Lord Stanley says, "I am free to confess,
that, at this moment, I am not aware of the circumstances
which led to a difference in law, and that in such instances
generally the *prima facie* case is in favour of assimilation." For
his (Mr. E.T.'s) own part he could not but feel that there was
the utmost justice in asking the amendment of the law of

Ireland, when he saw and knew numerous gentlemen of
wealth and property in Belfast who were excluded from the
franchise on the score of their partnerships, whilst their own
porters were exercising all the rights of electors, being impeded
by no such legal restriction. Another point which he (Mr. E.T.)
had taken upon himself to recommend to the notice of Lord
Stanley, was the assimilation of the Irish law to that of England,
as regarded the taking of the poll and the duration of elections, reducing the period from five days to two in counties,
and to one in towns, an amendment on which there was, he
knew, some difference of opinion, but which, in his judgment,
would go far to secure the purity of election, and, in every
man's experience, would contribute much to the diminution
of turmoil and excitement, and the maintenance of peace and
good will. To this proposition Lord Stanley says, in reply,—
"Upon this subject I will only say, that if, as I understand, you
agree with the Association in discovering an assimilation to
the English law as to the multiplication of polling places, and
the duration of elections, I strongly recommend that that
question should be kept separate from registration, and be
made the subject of a distinct bill. If Irish members, without
distinction of party, are generally of opinion that the adoption
of the English law, in this respect, will tend to diminish
expense, and will, also, provide effectually for the peaceable
and impartial exercise of the elective franchise, I think I may
say, with confidence, that they will meet with no opposition
on the part of the representatives of England and Scotland."
There was one portion of this subject with which, in framing
his bill, he distinctly announced his intention to abstain
cautiously from intermeddling, namely, *the amount of the electoral
franchise*—a point on which such utter variance of opinion
exist, that to have disturbed its present settlement, in the least
degree, would have opened a door to discussions without end.
Even as it was, the entire gist and fury of the assault in the
House of Commons was ingeniously contrived to create an
impression that the bill, though its author distinctly disclaimed
all direct interference with the franchise, was so adroitly

designed as effectually to produce that result by an unseen machinery which its framers secretly aimed at, but shrunk from openly attempting. Again and again Lord Stanley spurned this disingenuous imputation, and professed what he professes now—that his object is not to destroy, but to *discover* the *bona fide* franchise. If his bill can be shown to him to be constructed so as in any degree to raise the franchise above the standard finally fixed by the Reform Act, he is most willing and ready to make any alterations that may render it accurately conformable to it, without adding one farthing to its annual amount. The opponents of the bill in the House of Commons calculated shrewdly when they sought to make the discussion in the Commons one upon *franchise* instead of one upon registration. Mr. O'Connell and his friends protested that there should be no registration bill without a clause to define (that is, to *reduce*) the franchise; none other would or ought to give satisfaction. This stratagem was wisely concocted, and not without a precedent. Five years, also, *no tithe bill* could or ought to be satisfactory without an "*appropriation clause*",—but so long as that clause was attempted, it was foreseen that no bill could be had whatsoever—no possible settlement could be arrived at; it was a seton that effectually prevented all healing of the wound. And such was precisely the design and desire of those whose interest it was to resist all amendments whatever in the registration system. Mr. O'Connell clearly perceived, that if Lord Stanley would only touch the franchise in any particular—extend it, diminish it, define it, or abolish it—alter it, in fact, in any shape, we should have had such a storm raised as would effectually prevent the boat from landing, and drive her back to sea again. (Cheers.) The Ulster Association, less wary and experienced than Lord Stanley, saw the seduction of the trap, but tumbled bodily into it. They had no doubts or misgivings upon the point. The settlement of a satisfactory franchise, it was true, had occupied the anxious thoughts of the legislature for years—it had protracted the final settlement of the Reform Bill itself, from 1830 till 1832—it might be sufficient to alter the whole constitutional complexion of the

empire, as the balance of judgment inclined on either side—
but for the Ulster Association, the subject had neither difficulties nor alarms. (Cheers.) With them, too, the settlement of
a franchise was to be the first and indispensable step to the
settlement of a bill, and the three tailors of Tooley-street[72]
never set to to cut out a coat or a constitution with more confidence and complacency, than Mr. Sharman Crawford and
Dr. Montgomery set about cutting up and trimming the
franchise of the Reform Act. (Laughter.) No one of the party
considered that the garment of 1832 exactly fitted the elector,
it was superfluously large—Dr. Montgomery was for cutting
it down to a modest and scanty covering. Mr. Sharman
Crawford preferred, in principle, no covering at all, but would
consent to a fig leaf—(cheers) —and so to it they went—
Dr. Montgomery took off the first slice, by reducing the
franchise from £10 to £8. Mr. Crawford would have something more—the electors were "industrious and intelligent",
and they were entitled to some further compliment. Well,
well, says Dr. Montgomery, a pound or two here or there is
nothing in dealing with such decent fellows; come, we'll throw
off £2 more, and make it £6 at once. (Cheers.) Very good,
replied Mr. Sharman Crawford, that is coming very near
what I want; but let us call things by their proper names;
people in Down or Antrim may understand you, when you
talk of a £6 franchise, but my new friends in Rochdale call
that "*household suffrage*"—give it that name, and I am content.
(Cheers.) Oh, no, replied Dr. Montgomery, the name with us
is a much more important matter than the substance, so, if
you please, we will take the franchise to-day, and christen
it at our next meeting—whereupon the assembly divided,
Mr. Crawford was vigorously outvoted by the eighty-five
gentlemen present, and so this very valuable Association
adjourned to meet again, whenever they can unanimously
agree on the terms of the franchise. (Cheers and laughter.)
And as, in their opinion, no registration bill can be had till the
results of that unanimity are embodied in it, Ireland must be
content to wait for this necessary reform, till all these great

and conflicting authorities shall have been calmly reconciled. (Cheers.) Now, *magna componere parvis*, just such a catastrophe as this, only not so good-humoured a one, would inevitably have followed had Lord Stanley instituted such a debate in the House of Commons, by attempting to interfere, directly or indirectly, with the question of the franchise, and the bill might have safely been postponed to the Greek calends to await any agreement upon its preliminaries, had such a step been unwisely attempted. The report of the Ulster Association is most copious and elaborate upon this topic, which occupies at least one-fourth of its entire contents but the following extract, from the notes of Lord Stanley, will show with how little show of justice a comparison has been instituted between the franchise of the three countries, with a view to establish the existence of any prejudicial discrepancy, as affecting the franchise in Ireland, as contrasted with that which exists in England and Scotland:—

"I have nothing to say to the remaining sections which support the vote by ballot, the shortening of the duration of Parliament (in the practical adoption of which principle, at the present moment, I apprehend they will meet with but little countenance on the part of her Majesty's Ministers), the qualification of representatives, or the proportion which ought to be established between the number of representatives form Ireland or from the rest of the empire; but, after all that has been said upon the subject of the comparative franchise in the three countries, I must say a few words on the 12th section— the franchise. The table furnished in this section as a comparative view of the franchise is a most useful document, and I gladly avail myself of it—1st. As proving that Ireland has not been unjustly dealt with: and, 2*d*, as furnishing, together with the comments, a strong argument in favour of our interpretation of the existing franchise.

"The table of the Association shews that, in two instances as compared with England, and one as compared with Scotland, the Irish freehold franchise is more restricted; while, as relates to the leasehold franchise, not only does Ireland possess to an equal extent, every franchise enjoyed by either country, with the exception of the

£50 tenancy at will (which is repudiated by the Association), but, *in almost every instance*, a less term of years, and a lower amount of value, will qualify in Ireland, than either in England or Scotland.

"First, as to the restrictions. In England a freehold of inheritance in any case, and a freehold not of inheritance, provided the party occupy to the amount of 40*s* entitles to vote; whereas, in Scotland and Ireland, the amount is £10, and in Ireland, for a freehold below £20, occupation is superadded as a condition. For the amount, it is needless to avert to the grounds which led to the abolition of the 40*s* franchise. At the period of the Reform Bill, the legislature found the 40*s* franchise existing in England, and did not abolish, though it restricted it, and where the restrictions applied, it fixed the minimum at £10. In Scotland it found no such franchise, and did not introduce it, but fixed the minimum at £10. In Ireland it had recently been abolished—the legislature did not restore it; but found the minimum fixed at £10, and left it so. Indeed the Reform Bill did not, in any way, deal with the freehold franchise of the counties of Ireland—it conferred no new one—it altered no old one, but it added the lease-hold to the previously existing freeholds, and in so doing conferred the right more extensively on Ireland than either England or Scotland. On the same ground the law requiring occupation remained unaltered; and it may be well for the 'Liberal' Association who select this point of comparison with Scotland as a grievance, to bear in mind, that so far from extending popular rights, the very want of this restriction in Scotland was found practically to give so much power to large land-owners to grant "fictitious" freeholds, that the Select Committee on Scotch Fictitious Votes, presided over by Mr. Horsman, recommended that in Scotland *occupation* should be required of the smaller freeholders, and that two successive Lord Advocates, with the sanction of the present government, have gone so far as to advise that *residence* should be enforced as a condition.

"And now let us turn to the leaseholds, and, adopting the plan of the Association, place side by side the franchises possessed respectively by the three countries, leaving a blank in each case where no corresponding franchise exists."

LANDED FRANCHISES IN COUNTIES

	England £	Scotland £	Ireland £
Original lessee or assignee of a term of 60 years (57 in Scotland)	10	10	10
Original lessee or assignee of a term of 20 years	50	50	20
Ditto, ditto, 9 years		50	20
Ditto, ditto 14 years			20

FRANCHISES REQUIRING OCCUPATION.

	England	Scotland	Ireland
Sub-lessee or assignee of sub-lease of a term of 60 years (57 in Scotland)	10	10	10
Original lessee or assignee of a term of 20 years,			10
Sub-lessee or assignee of sub-lease of a term originally of 20 years,	50	50	10
Ditto, ditto, 19 years,	50	10	
Ditto, ditto, 14 years		20	
Tenant at will, liable to a rent of	50	50	

"Examine this table, the table of our opponents, and then say whether if inequality of the franchise be ground of complaint, Ireland be the portion of the empire entitled to make it.

"But the table is valuable in another point of view, because, for the purposes of comparison, it sets side by side the £10, £20, and £50 franchises enjoyed by England, Scotland, and Ireland respectively, as being co-extensive with each other; and either the Association act most disingeniously in instituting a comparison between similar amounts with different meanings, or else the several franchises, though in each country conveyed in different terms, are in reality (as we contend they are) the same in substance in each. I close with them on the most creditable assumption, and it will be a great point gained in the controversy if we concur in this view, because in that case the interpretation given to the law in one country ought to influence the interpretation of the corresponding words in the other. It is right, however, that we should see what the words really are, which, with reference to the Scotch Act, the Committee of the Association incorrectly quote. You are well aware that the Irish county freeholder votes under the terms not of the Irish reform Act, which does not confer the franchise upon him, but of the 10th Geo. IV. c.8, 3, 2, and that the oath which he is required by the reform act to take is that "I am a freeholder, &c. and that I have a freehold therein" of the clear yearly value of ten pounds over and above, &c. The English act borrows its phraseology from the preceding Irish act, and provides that the freehold shall be of the clear yearly value of ten pounds", words identical with the qualifying words of the Irish freeholders, and with the words of his oath. Can it be contended their construction is different?

"The Scotch words relating to owners (and to owners only, not tenants) are, that "the subject on which he claims *shall be of the yearly value of* £10, and shall actually yield, or be capable of yielding, that value to the claiment, after deducting feu duty, ground, annual, &c."—The words in italics have been ommitted by the Association in quoting the franchise, which they do with approbation.

"The leasehold qualification in England is conferred on the lessee, &c. of any term originally for a period of not less than—years "of the clear yearly value of—pounds"; in Ireland, on a lessee, "having a beneficial interest therein of the clear yearly value of not less than—pounds". In Scotland, "where the clear yearly value of such tenant's interest, after paying the rent and any other consideration due by him, for his said interest, is not less than—pounds". And it is worth remarking, that in Scotland the leasehold qualification applies to a franchise which in Ireland would be called a freehold, viz. a lease for the life of the tenant. I know not how the difference of expression arose between the English and the Scottish acts; I do know that the words of the English and Irish bills, as introduced, were identical: and the reason of the change which was made publicly, and for which the grounds were publicly assigned, are known to all. I am confident the franchises were intended to be the same in principle; I believe they are the same in effect; and I do not believe that any English or Scotch lawyer has placed on the English or Scotch franchise the interpretation which is sought to be attached to the words of the Irish act.

"But I have neither time nor inclination to argue this question at length, still less to consider the propositions made by the association for the alteration of the franchise. I will just direct your attention to a proposal (p.19), while they repudiate the £50 tenant at will, as unduly dependant on his landlord, to place on the register all persons rated for a twelve-month upon a holding *valued* not higher than £10, whatever be his rent, without any reference to his beneficial interest in the tenement; and to another passage in the same page, where, is speaking of a franchise depending on the excess of *annual rated value* above his rent, such excess is correctly enough called the tenant's 'beneficial interest'. One other argument, however, I must borrow from the Association in favour of our construction, too remarkable to be omitted. They quote with approbation p. 12, and 18, a Scotch franchise given to a tenant having paid a sum of £300 for his interest, whatever his rent may be. A very little reflection shews the ground for this. The tenant who has paid £300 for his lease, subject to a rent, has given 30 years purchase of a *profit rent* of £10; whatever his rent may be, he could dispose of his farm for £10 per annum more than he pays. His lease is to him, in the words of the English Act, "of the clear yearly value of £10". In those of the Scotch, "his interest, after paying his rent, is not less than £10". "In those of the Irish he has a beneficial interest therein of not less than £10"; and lastly, in the words of that part of the Irish oath now abrogate, "a solvent tenant could fairly and without collusion, afford to pay him £10 over and above the rent to which he is subject". The argument is new to me, but I own it strikes me as both sound and forcible.

"I am ashamed of the length to which my letter has run. It has been written in haste, but as you well know I am tolerably familiar with the subject, and as I am not aware of having stated any thing erroneously or unfairly, you are perfectly at liberty to make what use of it you think fit. I have nothing to conceal or disguise. I rejoice at having an opportunity of bringing into a narrow compass the points at respect to the registration bill, on which the Ulster Association and I are at variance: and of obtaining an admission from them of those in which we concur; and I heartily wish, though I hardly dare expect it, that the result may be a more temperate discussion in Parliament of the points at issue, and the passing of a measure which shall give due protection to the bona fide voter, and adequate means of purging the register of the fraudulent claimants.

Believe me, my dear Sir, very sincerely yours,

"STANLEY."

J. Emerson Tennent, Esq.

With this ingenious and manly declaration of the objects and opinions of its author, he (Mr. E.T.) would confidently leave with the meeting the adoption of a resolution approving of Lord Stanley's bill. Before he sat down he would have been desirous to be permitted to say a few words on the other subject of their meeting, *the Repeal of the Union*; but it was too great a one to be dismissed in the few sentences which was all he could with propriety claim from the time of the meeting, and he preferred leaving it all together to those who were to come after him, and confining himself strictly to the resolution in his hand. The hon. gentleman then resumed his seat amidst loud cheers.

Colonel CLOSE, of Drumbanagher Castle, proposed the next resolution, and expressed his conviction, that from the concentration of opinion in favour of Lord Stanley's Bill, in the last Session, there was every possibility that it would pass during the present. The resolution was as follows:—

"That the fact of this Bill containing provisions identical with those introduced on numerous previous occasions, by the various Law Officers of the Crown in Ireland, together with the favourable reception which it met with by men of all parties in the House of Commons, affords the best possible grounds for confidence in its being carried during the present Session of Parliament."

GEORGE DUNBAR, Esq., M.P.,[73] in seconding the resolution, said—My lords and gentlemen, I thank you from my heart

for your flattering reception. (Hear.) I have every confidence
that this bill of Lord Stanley's will pass at no distant period.
It is scarcely possible to suppose it will not, when you
consider, as stated in the resolution, that bills containing
provisions, identical with those in Lord Stanley's have been
introduced by various law officers of the crown; and, that this
bill, as the resolution goes on to state, met with a favourable
reception from men of all parties. (Hear.) As I went very fully
into the proofs of the first of these propositions, on a recent
occasion, at a meeting held in May last, in this town, at which
your lordship was present, I do not think I would be justified
in occupying your time, and the time of this meeting, by
again going into them at length; besides, my lord, I observe
that the opponents of the bill do not persist in denying the
fact—I shall enumerate the bills as briefly as I can. The first
bill was brought in by the present master of the rolls for
Ireland and Judge Perrin, in August, 1835—passed the
Commons, but was lost in the Lords, in consequence of the
very late period of the session, at which it was sent up.
(Hear, hear.) The next was in 1836, by Lord Morpeth and
Mr. O'Loghlen; another in 1838, by Mr. Maule, the then
member for the town of Carlow, a Liberal, and supporter of
the government; and in 1839, Mr. O'Brien, the member for
Limerick, brought in his bill. Now, my lord, those bills, one
and all were, in principle, the same as Lord Stanley's, and
brought in by the very party now so strongly opposed to it;
and the very man who now applies such gross epithets to
Lord Stanley, not only supported the bill of 1835, but he was
the very first man that proposed to alter the registration law
in this country. On the 29th of April, 1835, he gave notice of
a motion to consolidate and amend the law of elections and
of registry in Ireland, so as to assimilate it to that of England.
But, my lord, there is a much stronger reason to justify me in
supposing, that this bill of Lord Stanley's must soon pass, than
the mere fact of her Majesty's ministers having introduced
similar measures. I say, my lord, the state of crime, of bribery
and perjury, acknowledged to exist, and to arise from the pre-

sent state of the registration law, and to which this bill is calculated to put an end, justifies me in concluding, that the bill must pass. And what are the objections to the bill? That it will have the effect of reducing the number of electors in Ireland; and, therefore, some of the Radicals propose to amend the law in this way, by bringing in an act that will enable those men who now obtain the franchise by perjury to have it legally—that is, legalise what has been obtained by perjury and fraud. Was such a proposition as this ever heard of? There is another reason given, and one more absurd than the one just mentioned, and the only, by the by, that was stated by any of the speakers (for I carefully examined the speeches as given in the *Monitor*, which I hold in my hand.) At the *great little meeting*, held in Dublin—(hear, hear)—at which there appears to have been great noise, but little wool, and where, too, a friend of mine, Dr. Montgomery, was very badly treated, because he ventured to speak the truth; but I can assure the Doctor the account has been settled, and com-pound interest paid on it to Mr. O'Connell, at the Repeal meeting here—where the very reporters that were close beside could scarcely hear him, and at last he was obliged to give it up in despair. But, my lord, to return to the reason given at that meeting by two gentlemen who spoke: it was this—"why attempt to do away with bribery and perjury in Ireland, when it exists in England and Scotland?" One speaker says—"The counties in Scotland were swarming with fictitious voter, but why was not that immorality removed? (Hear, hear.) Because it was at the Tory side." (Groans.) Again, he says—"I read that the counties of Scotland swarmed with fictitious voters to such an extent, that corruption now existed there to as great an extent as it did before the passing of the Reform Bill.' Well, my lord, the speaker again says, this is not put down because it is on the Tory side; but he does not venture to deny the existence of perjury and fraud in Ireland. But one gentleman does—one, I believe, not in the habit of stopping at trifles, as you will hear—"Lord Stanley has been taunted here to-day, and justly taunted, for not turning his attention to the bribery which is carried on in England; and bribery so manifest and so disgraceful, as that which was practised in Ludlow and Cambridge, never was witnessed. In Ireland we have no bribery, with the exception of one small borough in the South; and I will name it, as I consider it a disgrace to the country. With the exception of the borough of Kinsale, bribery is not heard of in the land". (Cheers.) Oh! my lord, is it any wonder there should be bribery, perjury, murder in the land, when a man in such a situation would be found to utter such untruths, and find men to cheer him? There is but one answer to be given to this statement respecting crime in England; that, if such is the case, why not bring in their bills, and then they shall see that they shall have good for evil, they shall have our hearty support, though they deny us theirs. (Cheers.) Another reason, my lord, why Lord Stanley's bill is likely to pass, and it is the last I shall offer—the Conservatives are an united body, while our opponents are the very reverse—(hear, hear, her and cheers)—or, as Dr. Montgomery at that meeting has eloquently expressed it:—"Our enemies (he says) are linked together like a chain cable which binds the mighty vessel, whilst we are like the rope of sand." Why are we like the chain cable?—it is because of our firm, simple, unbending, unyielding principle to bend or connect them; and I tell them, my lord, they never can, and need never expect, to hold together. (Hear.) I do hope before our Roman Catholic brethren will again surrender their judgment to designing demagogues, and endanger the peace of this great and prosperous town by again renewing the Repeal question, they will consider that object never can be obtained except by bloodshed; and, if obtained, must lead to the dismemberment of this great empire; but if they will per-sist, I do trust the Liberal Protestants will unite with us in heart and hand in defence of the throne and implore her Majesty to put this question at rest for ever. Nothing shall induce us to say a severe or harsh word against the Roman Catholics, but I do beg they will recall that they are under many obli-gations to their Protestant brethren in this place—look at our charitable institutions—are the doors not thrown open to them? I shall just mention one, our poor-house—one third of the inmates are Roman Catholics, while the Roman Catholics do not subscribe one-ninth part of the funds by which that institution is supported. I shall now, my lord, conclude in the words of Lord Charlemont, at the meeting in Dublin—he would say to these men about to assemble in Belfast, persevere in supporting the *atrocious* measure of Lord Stanley, and you will serve essentially the cause of Ireland." (The hon. gentleman then sat down amid loud cheers.)

MARCUS M'CAUSLAND, Esq., Fruithill, with some brief remarks, proposed the following resolution:—

"That we distinctly and unequivocally disavow and repudiate the imputation, which has been unsparingly directed against the supporters of Lord Stanley's Bill, of a design, indirectly and covertly, to abridge the elective franchise, as confirmed by the Reform Act of 1832; but that, on the contrary, we desire the enactment of that measure, solely as a means of declaring and carrying out the intention of the existing law."

MR. RICHARD DAVISON said, he rose to second the resolution just read, and he said it with unaffected sincerity, that he regretted that this duty had not devolved on one of more influence; because there were hundreds of those around him, whose rank and station would give double effect, in a meeting like the present, to the sentiments he was about to express. But the committee were pleased to signify a wish, that he should undertake it, and as he felt that that wish was not the language of compliment but of sincerity, and as he had long entertained the opinion, that individual feeling should, in almost all cases, yield to public duty, he consented. (Cheers.) He knew of no principle, the cultivation of which should be more strenuously enforced, on occasions like the present, than that of *individual* activity. It is a combination of atoms which forms the mass—(loud cries of "hear, hear")— and as well might you expect commerce to flourish or manufactures to exist, where all was apathy or indolence around, as that a great political measure could be accomplished without strenuous individual exertion. (Loud cheers.) The twin sister of *individual activity* is *union*. (Hear.) Union is strength; and what family—what community—what nation as such, can prosper without it. As well, therefore, may we hope, that Ireland can independently exist, or that her national prosperity can continue, if severed from Great Britain, as that we Conservatives can secure and maintain our now opening position, if we become divided—or that the seeds of strife, religious or political, be sown among us. We have not only a common enemy to contend with, but we have to remove some existing prejudices from the minds of many excellent and amiable men, now but slightly separated from us. (Cheers.) Let us not, therefore, he implored them, cast stumbling blocks in their way. Treat them not as enemies, but as friends; win them over by gentleness and forbearance, which, in cases like the present, conquer more than the sword of a Wellington. (Hear, and great cheering.) The design and objects of Lord Stanley's bill have been most ably and satisfactorily explained by his esteemed friend, Mr. Emerson Tennent; but the portion of it to which he meant to confine the attention of the meeting was that embodied in the resolution—the alleged design, indirectly and covertly made, to abridge the ELECTIVE FRANCHISE, as conferred by the Reform Act of 1832. And here, in the outset, he begged to repeat a fact already stated and observed upon, by Mr. Tennent, with the view more fully of impressing it on their minds, *that Lord Stanley's bill, in no one clause or section of it, interferes with the elective franchise as established by the Reform Act.* It does not create any new—nor does it abolish any existing one. The Reform Act established, according to the nature of the property and the occupation or non-occupation of it, a certain franchise, varying in value from £10 to £50 per annum. In counties, the words are, persons having a *beneficial interest* of the *clear yearly value* of so much *over and above all rent and taxes.* In boroughs, the franchise arises form the mere occupation of a house, warehouse, or shop, *bona fide* of the clear yearly value of £10. So that from these words it is clear that the value was not intended as a fictitious or colourable one, but a substantial and *bona fide* interest. One would whip a schoolboy if he put any other interpretation upon it. (Loud cheering.) On this point all parties are now agreed. The working of the Reform Act, like many other pieces of Whig machinery, was found unsatisfactory—he had almost said impracticable—and lawyers were at issue as to the true interpretation of many of its clauses. This afforded fine scope for ingenious minds, and it proved also a fertile one for deep and designing ones.—(Hear, hear.) The first assault made upon the franchise was through the instrumentality of some of the Radical and Roman Catholic Assistant-Barristers, the nominees of the present Government, by the admission at the registry sessions of persons who swore up to the franchise in a qualified way, thus, that their house or land was worth £10 a-year *to them*, and thus the occupiers of oyster-shops, sheds, and hovels, became entitled to the elective franchise. (Cheering.) No town in Ireland can attest this fact more strongly than Belfast, but it stands recorded from various parts of the kingdom in the evidence taken before the Fictitious Votes Committee. Now, a £10 franchise, one would have thought, meant a £10 franchise; but, according to the law laid down by some of Mr. O'Connell's registering barristers, it meant no such thing—for if a house was worth only £5 or £6 a-year, and that you produced witnesses to prove that a good and solvent tenant could not afford to give more for it; yet, if the claimant swore that it was worth £10 a-year *to him*, that is, by a combination of the profits of his trade, no matter what the actual value of his house might be, he was admitted; and this, in times past, has, over and over again, occurred in his (Mr. D's) own presence, against the true interpretation of law, in opposition to argument, and in defiance of common sense. (Hear, hear, and tremendous applause.) Thus they would perceive that the law was perverted, that the *bona fide* test of the franchise, as established by the Reform Act, was trodden under foot, and that fictitious votes, through the instrumentality

of perjury, became crowded upon the lists. He did not desire
to give offence by the statement of any opinion, as to which
party most availed themselves of either this or any other of the
demoralising courses alluded to by his friend, Mr. Tennent;
but this he did know, that the Conservatives had long felt and
laboriously struggled for the abolition of one and all of them,
whilst the Government, Mr. O'Connell, and their Radical
opponents—these boasted friends of liberty—by their conduct, during the whole of the last session, and apparently up
to this hour, seem resolved to encourage and perpetuate the
evil. (Hear, hear.) The patriots of the present day are a spurious
race; they can talk largely of liberty, but they neither know
nor feel its ennobling influence. (Hear, hear.) Place, power
and popularity are the gods they worship, and they prefer the
tainted atmosphere of a corrupt borough system of their own
manufacture to the pure and balmy air of the mountain top.
(Hear, and loud cheers.) Patriots, now-a-days, are traders in
politics, and it is as much part of the business of a man of the
people, when he wants to accomplish a political end, to clothe
it in the garment of popular rights, as it is of a hypocrite,
when he has personal ends to accomplish, to deck himself in
the habiliments of sanctimonious humility. (Hear, hear.) But
whilst our opponents agree with us, that Lord Stanley's bill does
not directly touch the franchise, they assume, from certain
machinery he has employed, that his design is indirectly and
covertly to do so. (Hear.)—We fling back upon them the
unworthy imputation, because it rests on an ill-directed sur-
mise. But as they have assigned reasons for such their opinion,
he felt bound, in fair dealing, to grapple with their arguments.
First, then, they allege that Lord Stanley, by establishing *rating*
as the TEST of value, aims at the reduction of the franchise.
(Hear.) Now it struck his (Mr. D.'s) humble judgment, that a
more erroneous or ill-founded argument never was used by
rational men—(hear)—and he trusted he should be able satisfactorily to prove, that a fairer or more impartial test could not
well have been selected, nor one so wisely calculated to strike
at the root of the awful perjuries which the present system has

engendered. (Hear.) Rates are an uniform system of taxation
imposed on property according to the estimated annual value.
That value is ascertained by competent, sworn, and impartial
valuators, who have no personal end to obtain, political or
otherwise. If the rate be too *high*, the party aggrieved has
always the benefit of an appeal—if too *low*, other ratepayers
have the same remedy in order to reduce their own taxation;
or, by the institution of a just comparison, the attention of the
authorities is directed to the omission, and thus errors are
corrected. And if a man pay his county, municipal, poor, and
other rates, according to an estimated value, placed by indifferent parties upon his property, why not also take the same
ascertained value as the criterion for estimating his political
franchise? The Ulster Association report says:—"It is a constitutional principle that taxation and representation should go
hand in hand". He quoted this as corroborative of his view.
Can any man, in the spirit of fairness, say, that this principle
is unjust, or that it is not calculated to work impartially
towards all, without distinction of sect or party? In Belfast we
have our *municipal tax*, our County, or *Grand Jury tax*, our *poor
rate*, and we shall shortly have our *water tax*, and, under each
of these, a separate and distinct valuation. (Hear, hear.) Now,
surely from such criterions there can be no difficulty in arriving
at a fair estimate of value for our political franchise, and there
is no corporate or borough town in the kingdom, which has
not two or more of these assessments. By adopting these, then,
as the criterion of value, you not only accomplish the end
impartially, but at one blow sweep away both the temptation
and power of committing perjury from the claimant. (Loud
cheers.) Secondly—But then they say, admitting all this in principle, in practice rating is an uncertain test of actual value—
1st, because the valuators always estimate under the real
amount; and 2d, that they make certain deductions for repairs,
insurance, local taxes, &c., &c., all of which diminish the
gross value, as appears on the face of the rate book, by 25 or
30 per cent., and that, by this means, they say, if you take a
£10 rating, it would have reference to a £12 or £14 house

instead of a £10 one. Now, all this is *quite true*, and has been admitted over and over again by Lord Stanley, and his reply is—I don't want, in that case, to take a £10 rate which would represent a £12 house, but I will take an £8 rate, or any other which will truly represent the £10 house. Or I will adopt any one defined principle on an unvarying system, which can be raised or diminished on such a scale as will represent a *bona fide* £10 house. (Hear, hear.) Let this be settle thus— take first the actual full value of a tenement; deduct from that,—1st, a fixed percentage, as a general security against our valuation, but let both be fixed the *full value*, and the *exact and invariable proportion* by which it is to be reduced;—2nd, a fixed proportional sum for repairs; 3d, a fixed proportion for insurance, and let the balance represent if it will, *bona fide*, the £10 house. Now if this principle is to be admitted, and he defied reason to contradict it, what remains then is to be discussed and enquired into and fixed is, what exact amount of rate will represent £10 of actual value. This, if fixed on any unvarying and ascertained scale, Lord Stanley will adopt, and thus preserve the franchise and the Reform Act, and sweep away for ever the amalgamation which has followed in its train. (Hear.) Thirdly—Trial by Jury, in all cases of disputed value, is a course recommended in the report published by the Ulster Association. Any one conversant with the practice of the registration court, as at present constituted, will see the impracticability of this course. (Hear, hear.) In the first place, the empanelling of a jury, and the trial of all these cases by them, would, of itself, consume several days. Such a practice has no precedent elsewhere, and you might just as well take also the remaining civil bill cases out of the barrister's hand, and try them all by jury—the thing is impracticable. It would make the court machinery too ponderous for the necessary active discharge of its duties. Besides, who would constitute your jury? Why, your borough electors, parties having a direct interest in the question at issue. (Hear.) The Committee of the Ulster Association, feeling this, actually suggest a hint, under the words, "*due provision should be made for the impartial empannelling of the jury*", either to place some coercive enactment on the Sheriff in this respect, or to take the matter wholly out of his hands, and place it, I presume, in the hands of "The Ulster Association". He (Mr. D.) could not, for the life of him, understand the opposition which this bill had encountered on this single point of taking rating as a test of value, without attributing motives, which, as they gravely reflect on the character of a party, he should abstain from imputing. He might call them factious without offence, for he thought, to all rational minds, he had demonstrated them to be so. But that no misunderstanding may exist on the point, he called upon their opponents, as fair men, to suggest some other equally safe and certain test of value—(hear, hear)—embracing the objects he had enumerated, and they held the pledged honour of a British nobleman made in the senate, that he is ready to adopt it. If this be refused, what signifies then, their boasted patriotism? He called upon their opponents, as moral men, to join them in interposing against the commission of the foul and deadly crime of perjury, by resting, on the key-stone of this bill, an arch which will enable claimants to pass over the polluted streams of infamy, which but too many have waded through, to the attainment of those political rights which we neither desire to abrogate or annul. Mr. Davison then related an anecdote he had heard, relative to a plan laid to intercept Mr. O'Connell in his progress to Belfast. An innkeeper in a town on the route, not a hundred miles from Belfast, was applied to to have post horses in readiness. He peremptorily refused to supply them, but, on being remonstrated with, complied. Still reluctant that even his *hacks* should be disgraced in taking part in such a mission, he consulted a friend as to how far he would be justified in giving Dan a course or two round the Market-house, almost opposite his door, and sending him out of town by the road he had entered. (Cheers and laughter.) Had this innocent plan succeeded, he (Mr. D.) would have deeply regretted it, because it would have prevented the demonstration which Mr. O'Connell's visit had given of his unwelcome errand. His visit was an absolute failure; as must always prove the visits of an agitating demagogue in peaceable, Protestant Ulster. So long as they thus presented such an array of constitutional resistance to the common enemy, they had nothing to fear. It would intimidate him—it would reflect honour upon them. (Loud and long continued cheering.)

Sir Robert Bateson, Bart., proposed the next resolution, and was received with loud cheers and Kentish fire—He was sensible of the honour done him, but was not vain enough to attribute the applause to anything in himself, but to his being one of the members for the Protestant county of Derry—a title he would not barter for anything the ministry had it in their power to bestow. (Cheers.) He felt proud of standing side by side with that great and good man Doctor Cooke, who also s a Derry man. (Tremendous cheers, and cries of "Derry", and "No surrender".) The men of Derry stood forward that day in a proud position. As a member for Derry, he would read them what he was sure would meet their assent. He held in his hand a resolution, which was a vote of thanks to Lord Stanley, for introducing his bill; it was but a just tribute, that the thanks of Ulster men be given to his noble friend for advocating their cause. (Cheers.)—No man of integrity could object to the bill; it was calculated to put down the system of perjury which was carried on at present. Lord Stanley never was met by fair argument, but was assailed by low, vile, abuse and scurrility, which was a disgrace to the lips uttering it—he was termed a "hypocrite", a "miscreant lord", and "scorpion Stanley"; but he may laugh such ribaldry to scorn, emanating, as it does, from the lips of the disturber of our peace—I won't pollute my lips by mentioning his name—(Cries of "you're right")—who had the audacity to call Dr. Cooke and Dr. Stewart "brutal monsters". (Cries of "Oh! oh!" And why? Because they came forward to protest against perjury and fraud, and thus your ministers are assailed by ribaldry, for supporting measures which do credit to themselves and their country; but we despise the low abuse of that imperial disturber of the peace, whose name, I say it again, I won't pollute my lips by mentioning.—(Cheers.) He (Sir R.B.) was surprised in reading the account of the Dublin meeting, where there was a long list of high-sounding names, that it would have been tolerated to call Lord Stanley a "miscreant". (Cries of "it was base".) This meeting is a defensive meeting; had we been let alone, there would have been no meeting; the Association might have gone on, though it dwindled down to 85 present; but when "the disturber" came to agitate this peaceful town, then it was time for the "lion of the north" to rouse itself. Had he come quietly among us, we might have treated him with silent contempt. Troops of horse and artillery have been brought among us, to the great inconvenience of our gallant defenders, brought from a distance to protect the disturber of our peace, at this inclement season. What an idle—what a ridiculous farce—each town in Down is filled with troops, and who's to pay the expense? Why, we are! (cries of "it's too bad"); and if you ask the soldiers what brought them here, they would tell you they did not know. Regarding the resolution in his hand, which was a vote of thanks to Lord Stanley, he would only say he was so fortunate as to know that gentleman—he was amiable in every respect, and even his tenants, on his Tipperary estate, call him the best of Irish landlords—he resides among them when Parliamentary duties permit, and is beloved by them all. (Loud cheers.) He (Sir R.B.), in conclusion, would only say, what he was sure all would re-echo—

"On Stanley! On!"

(Long-continued cheering.) He then read the resolution, as follows:

"that the thanks of the meeting are gratefully offered to Lord Stanley for the laborious zeal, the discretion, and sound judgment, which characterised his proceedings with regard to the bill, during the last session of Parliament; and that we desire earnestly to impress upon his lordship, the urgent expediency of his taking the earliest possible opportunity for its re-introduction."

Lord ADAM LOFTUS in seconding the resolution which had just been proposed by Sir Robert Bateson, said, that he fully concurred in the object of the present meeting. The meeting was one of no little importance and interest, not only to the country, but to the empire at large. Such a demonstration as the present must have a considerable influence on the acts of the approaching session of Parliament. (Hear, hear.) the present was a crisis that must lead to some important changes in the government of the country. (Loud and long-continued cheering.) Could it be supposed, that, while the foreign and domestic relations of the empire were rendered so precarious in their issue, by the conduct of the present ministry—that, while the government had received, by the repeated minorities in which they were placed, manifest proofs of the want of public confidence and public support, could it be imagined, he repeated, that a government, proceeding in such a manner, and so opposed by the public opinion of the country, could possibly remain much longer in power? The present meeting was calculated to hasten an answer to the question. He was glad to have an opportunity of stating his sentiments thus publicly on such a subject, and, at the same time, of expressing his unqualified confidence in the benefits likely to result from Lord Stanley's proposed measure.—Lord Stanley's bill was of such a tendency as to put down the attempts of the Catholics and their priests, to destroy the franchise of the country, by turning it to their own purposes. The present demonstration was calculated to effect much good in the attainment of such an object. Its consequences would produce a new and bright era in the history of the empire, by regenerating the representation of the country, and raising the Protestant interest of the people, on a sound and immoveable basis. (Great cheering.) The noble lord then referred to the present agitation for a Repeal of the Union, and observed, that the subject should occupy the attention of the approaching session. (Hear, hear and loud cheers.) He said that a measure ought to be introduced into parliament, condemnatory of the present proceedings of the agitator; he would not condescend to call him by his name.—He hoped that Parliament, in its deliberations, would pronounce such agitation as treasonable and rebellious. (cheers.) The sedition and rebellion implied in the proceedings of the Repealers, called on Parliament to pronounce their opinion on such treasonable purposes, and at once put an end to their agitation. (Hear, hear and cheers.) His lordship then argued that the Imperial Parliament had testified their fostering care towards Irish interests, by affording them the same protection as was extended to England and Scotland. (Cheers.) He further stated, that the Imperial Parliament had granted to the Roman Catholics of Ireland, that emancipation which was denied them by the Irish Parliament. The noble lord concluded his observations, by calling on the government to adopt some measure, proclaiming the repeal agitation as identified with treason, and calculated to promote the dismemberment of the empire; and sat down amid loud cheers.

J. W. MAXWELL, Esq., J.P., of Finnebrogue, moved the next resolution, for the adoption of a petition in favour of the bill.

"That a petition to Parliament be adopted, and signed by this meeting, in support of Lord Stanley's bill, and forwarded for presentation as soon as the forms of the House of Commons admits of its reception."

JOHN BATES, Esq., of Belfast, in seconding the resolution, said they had every encouragement in sending the petition; all Ulster is with us (cheering)—and every one present shall be furnished with copies of the address, before the meeting separates, in order that it may be circulated to the greatest possible extent. Lord Stanley's bill, instead of meeting with fair argument, was met by the greatest misrepresentation; so gross, in fact, as to mislead many. He here alluded to the miserable falling off in the Ulster Association, which had dwindled down to eighty-five, and even these eighty-five disagreed in opinion, and were, at last, represented by five, who, it might be said, were now the Ulster association. Not only opposition to Lord

Stanley's bill had decreased, but the supporters of it had greatly increased. The requisition for the present meeting was signed by 1605 persons—and of what class were these? There were 41 Peers and Noblemen, 14 Rt. Hon. and Honourables, 18 Baronets, 32 Members of Parliament, 11 High Sheriffs, 6 Lord Lieutenants of counties, 98 Deputy Lieutenants, 355 Magistrates, 257 Clergymen of the Established Church, 45 Presbyterian Ministers, 28 of that influential body, the Methodists, and 28 Barristers. (Cries of "How many Priests?") These requisitionists consist of men of all parties, and several Whigs, I am happy to say, have signed the requisition. If the measure were so destructive, would the Ulster association have decreased, and the numbers in favour of the bill be now 1605? And I appeal confidently to the state of feeling as a proof of what I say. But, unfortunately, it has been opposed by government, and, to advance its ends, government resorted to the meeting in Dublin. Now, I beg of you to contrast their meeting and ours—(cries of "Comparisons are odious") and there could be no better test of the influence and wealth of each. And first, select the Sheriffs. They (the Repealers) had three. The North had eleven Sheriffs in support of Stanley's bill. (Cheers.) They had for them but 290 Justices of the Peace, and the North alone has 355 out of 3,000, the whole number in Ireland. Another test is afforded. Out of the entire Established Church, 24 Clergymen signed for them. In Ulster alone 257 Clergymen signed our requisition. (Cheers.) The dissenters agreed with us; they had but two Presbyterian clergymen, and even they did not belong to the General Assembly. (Cheers.) We have 45 Presbyterian clergymen. They had not a single Methodist—(immense cheers)—we have 26—(great cheers)—and of Priests they had only 76. We rejoice that they courted the discussion, and they have been signally overthrown. I, too, as well as Mr. Dunbar, read the speeches made at the Dublin meeting, and I think any man reading them must become a convert to the bill. Mr. Bates here read a part of Henry Grattan's speech, as a specimen of absurdity and non-sense, and begged the pardon of the meeting for mentioning

his unfortunate name. (Groans for Grattan.)[74] He concluded
an excellent speech, by expressing his trust, that the same
spirit that assembled them, would send forward names to the
address, the resolution for the adoption of which he now
seconded. (Loud cheers.)

The following is a copy of the petition alluded to:—

To the Honourable the Commons of the United Kingdom of
Great Britain and Ireland in Parliament assembled.

The Petition of the undersigned Nobility, Clergy, Gentry,
Merchants, and Yeomanry of Down, Antrim, and the contiguous
northern counties, in the kingdom of Ireland, adopted at a public
meeting, convened for the especial consideration of the subject –

HUMBLY SHEWETH—That Petitioners feel deeply convinced that
the present state of the law for the registration of Electors in Ireland,
is confessedly ineffectual for the discrimination and enrolment of a
duly qualified constituency, as defined and intended in the Reform
Act of 1832, while it holds out the most dangerous temptations to the
advancement and support of fictitious claims to the franchise, by
means of perjury and fraud.

That Petitioners, having seen a Bill introduced into your
Honourable House, during last Session of Parliament, by Lord
Stanley, Lord Granville Somerset, and Mr. James Emerson Tennent,
which appeared to them so founded on principles of constitutional
justice, and to embody such equitable provisions as, if passed into a
law, Petitioners believe would be found sufficient for discriminating
between fictitious and well-founded claims, and for securing a *bona
fide* constituency, and putting an end to the demoralising practices
which have prevailed at the Registering Sessions during the last
eight years in Ireland.

That Petitioners distinctly disavow any desire of abridging the
elective franchise, as conferred by the Reform Bill of 1832; but, on
the contrary merely desire such amendments as would frustrate the
frauds, and put an end to the perjuries by which it is eluded or
counteracted, and efficiently carry out its intentions and provisions.

Petitioners, therefore, trust that your Honourable House will be
pleased to sanction the introduction of a similar Bill to that introduced

as aforesaid by Lord Stanley during the last Session of Parliament, and pass the same into a law. And Petitioners as in duty bound, will ever pray.

REV. DR. STEWART of Broughshane,[75] then rose and said— My Lord, my excellent friend Mr. Davison has stated that we are, in the opinion and by the confession of our opponents, like a chain cable, while they are but a rope of sand. In this there is certainly much to please and delight us, yet to me there is a very considerable inconvenience. Our opponents having as many opinions as there are members, have a vast variety of matter for discussion. It has been stated that the eighty-five members of the Constitutional Association have eighty-five different opinions upon the subject of the franchise; but in our unanimity there is comparative poverty. We are so fully agreed on the subject that has brought us together, that it is exceedingly difficult to find scarcity of observations, or to avoid a tedious repetition of the statements which have been already made. (Hear and cheers.) I shall begin, my Lord, by begging leave to defend myself against some imputations which, from past experience, I know will be brought against me. I know it will be urged against me, in common with my clerical brethren here, that we are out of our proper place in such meetings as the present. That we have forsaken the Gospel for the study of politics, and in place of preaching and promoting peace, we are labouring to stir up animosity and strife. Now, my lord, I will not plead the example of the party to defend myself against it; though, this I could most easily and success- fully do. It has been most correctly stated already, that we are only on the defensive, and that our opponents are the aggres- sors. It was upon a former occasion, their meeting against Lord Stanley's bill, that gave origin to ours in support of it, and had it not been for the inauspicious visit of the Arch Agitator, we should not have been assembled here this day. I will not, however, my Lord, satisfy myself with the "*argumentum ad hominem*", or because I can show that there is a large beam in my accuser's eye, rest contented under the imputation that

there is a mote in my own. I submit, my Lord, to this most
respectable and influential meeting, and to the public at large,
that there are two departments in politics. In the one, no
minister of the Gospel ought ever to be found, and in the
other, it may be his bounded duty, on many occasions, to take
even a prominent part. There is, in the first place, the
department of the demagogue, where, from the altar or the
pulpit, the street or the platform, the passions, feelings, and
prejudices of the ignorant and excitable multitude are mad-
dened and inflamed—where, with the art and tact with which
education, eloquence, and the habit of public speaking usually
invest the orator, the speaker magnifies and dwells upon
abstract or imaginary rights, and exaggerates supposed or
constructive grievances,—interposing exhortation to peace
and forbearance, as Vulcan sprinkles water on his furnace,
that the flame may not blaze forth and waste itself uselessly,
but be internally condensed;—where the portion of the
community placed lowest in the arrangement of Divine
Providence is artfully taught to consider itself exclusively the
people;—where rule and government are alleged to belong to
the populace, whom God, by the position in which he placed
them, shows that he intended to be ruled and governed—just,
my Lord, as though it would improve the art of navigation to
transfer the helm or rudder from the stern to the stem of the
vessel;—where, I say, by such artful and plausible misrepresentations as these the working classes are seduced from their
industry and inflated with a vain, delusive and unprofitable
ambition, no minister of the Gospel—because no good man
of any profession—ought ever to appear or take a part. But,
on the other hand, as a minister of the Gospel, in becoming
a clergyman does not enter into a cloister, or cease to be a
citizen, as he still remains a member of the civil community,
and has some, though it may be a small stake in the public
hedge, he has a right, nay it is his duty upon any emergency
affecting the peace, stability or welfare of the state, rationally
and calmly to deliberate and consult with intelligent and
rational men upon the plans and measures most proper to be

adopted. (Hear, hear.) This, my Lord, I maintain is upon all occasions the case, but where truth, religion, religious liberty, and the glory of God, are, as on the present occasion, the interests in peril or in question, the minister of the Gospel would be a Judas to betray, or a Peter to deny, his Lord and Master, were he to permit false delicacy to prevent him from taking a post. (Hear, hear, and cheers.) In the second place, I protest against the imputation, that, because I am hostile to the errors of Popery and take every opportunity to expose and refute them, I am an enemy to my Roman Catholic fellow subjects. Against this imputation, I, in common with your Lordship, endeavoured at a former meeting to defend or guard myself, and I have somewhere since seen upon that defence, the observation, that the distinction between Roman Catholics and Popery was hypocritical, absurd, and insulting to Roman Catholics, while the question was triumphantly asked, how can we separate between a man's errors and himself, so as to hate the one and love the other? (Hear, hear.) How is it possible to hate Popery and yet love Papists? (Cheers.) I positively do not recollect who was the philosopher and logician who made these observations. I do not know who was the Philanthropist and apostle of peace and truth, who thus exerted himself to expose to the infuriated personal hostility of Romanists, every person who exposed the errors of the Romish system—[here several persons called out, it was Dr. Montgomery]—well if it was Dr. Montgomery, I am sorry for it—(hear, hear)—he is a man whose intelligence and talents I have ever admired, and I fearlessly assert that the author of the above observations is to be pitied either in his understanding or honesty. (Hear, hear.) "We cannot" says he, "separate between a man's errors and himself, so as to hate and correct the one and yet love the other!" Why can we not make this separation? Can we not love and wish to save the soul of a thief or of even a murderer, while we detest both the theft and murder? (Hear, and cheers.) Is it not possible to hate idolatry, even with a perfect hatred, and yet love and pity the poor dupes who are under its influence? Did not our blessed Lord, while they were enemies and sinners so love mankind, as to die for their sakes; and will it therefore be alleged, that because he loved them, he must have loved their enmity and their sins? (Hear.) Will the author of the above observations follow up his principles in the case of our Lord, or can he do so without blasphemy? (Great cheering.) If he believed the observations when he made them, I do most sincerely pity his ignorance; and, if he made them *ad captandum*, to serve a pur-pose to [ex]pose the enemies of Popish error to the personal hostility of Roman Catholics, and fortify the minds of the dupes of error against the ingress of the simplicity of Divine truth, I pity his want of good taste and good feeling.—(Great cheering.) It is because we love Roman Catholics—because we esteem their generosity, patience, cheerfulness, and numerous amiable features of character—because we see that they have a zeal of God, but not according to knowledge—because they are building the house of eternal hope, with wood, hay, and stubble—that we labour for their enlightenment and conver-sion. And it is because we believe that while under the influence of error and delusion their ascendancy would be ruinous to Protestants, and injurious to themselves, that we oppose their advancement to power. In the next place, I protest against the imputation that I am here this day as an enemy to civil or religious liberty. I am here this day as the opponent of Popish ascendancy which is, unquestionably, the ultimate object of the Arch-Agitator in his Repeal and other movements, and Popery and liberty are the most perfect incompatibles in nature—they are the antipodes of each other.—(Hear, hear, and cheers.) Popery commenced its career in usurpation, and tyranny over God's heritage and household, and it rapidly advanced its unhallowed claims to domination over the persons and properties of men. Popery will not permit slaves and subjects to think, speak, or act, except as it pleases to dictate. Witness the Inquisition and its inhuman acts. You might, therefore, as well expect to unite together fire and water, light and darkness, as Popery and liberty. (Cheering.) Projected usurpation and intended tyranny have ever employed the catch-word liberty to decoy their dupes and accomplish their purposes; and accordingly the grand leader in the Popish ascendancy scheme now too successfully dupes the soft and easy Protestant Liberals with fairy and fascinating promises and prospects of liberty. But as we find, in the whole history of antiquity, that the demagogue who most flattered the populace, and made the most zealous display of zeal for public liberty, was the intending and approaching tyrant—so in the present case, let but the *soi-disant* Liberator and his staff, the Romish priests, have an opportunity to accomplish their object—let them get quit of Protestant bonds and Protestant obstacles, and if they do not say to their dupes, as Rehoboam did to the nation of Israel, "Your yoke was heavy, but we will add to your yoke". Protestant ascendancy chastised you with whips, but we will chastise you with scorpions. They will bely their parentage, and demonstrate, in the face of her own pretensions, that Popery is neither infallible nor unchangeable. (Cheers.) For these statements, the truth of which no sane man, unblinded by prejudice, can for a moment question, I shall, no doubt, be favoured by the Dictator, with the classical epithets of "beast" and "brute". These are names with which, as my respected friend, Sir R. Bateson, has told you, he on a former occasion honoured me, and I am exceedingly obliged to Sir Robert for defending me when I had no opportunity of defending myself. (Hear and cheers.) As these names are words from the vocabulary of Dan's usual society, I will not say of some of his late entertainers in this town, I should have considered them of no more consequence than had I heard them repeated in passing through Billingsgate, were it not that in passing through the lips of Dan they have derived an adventitious importance. (Cheers.) As a general rule, the reverse of what this man publicly states is always the truth. (Hear.) To illustrate this fully I should be obliged to trouble you with the whole history of Dan's public life, take however, the following late samples, in the same breath, nearly in the same sentence, he publicly and unblushingly declared that he read a certain letter three times and that he only read the first three lines till he threw it into the fire. (Hear, hear and loud cheers.) He publicly promised to come boldly into Belfast on a Monday, and he cowardly and privately slunk into it on the Saturday evening before. (Loud cheers.) When, therefore, as one of his opponents, he calls me brute and beast, it follows that he is speaking of and describing his own friends, and that I am *toto caelo* removed from such creatures. (Loud cheers.) The history of Popery, in its extinction of Protestantism in Spain and Italy, its fiend-like persecution of it in France, down, wherever it has opportunity, even to the present day. (cheers.) Its cruelty towards it in Great Britain and Ireland, until its claws were cut and its fangs pulled out. (Loud cheers.) The tyranny exercised by Dan, and his staff, the Romish priests over Raphael, of London,[76] Purcell of Dublin,[77] and Sharman, my jewel of Down, and every man who has ever dared to breathe dissent from their dictation, demonstrate that Satan would be just as tolerant of holy-water in Pandemonium,[78] as Popery in the ascendant would be of liberty. (Hear, hear.) For the sake of liberty, then, for the sake of Roman Catholics themselves, I stand here this day to contribute my humble mite to prevent Popish ascendancy in this country. (Hear, hear and loud cheers.) 4th. I shall further protest against the imputation that I am here to-day as the enemy of the equitable extension of the elective franchise. (Hear, hear.) It is Dan's constant or reiterated complaint, that the numbers of electors and members of parliament for Ireland is not equal, in proportion to the population to the number in Great Britain; but he never even glances at the cause. The mass of the population in the two islands is of a very different character and description. In Great Britain the people are taught to think and rest upon personal responsibility; In Ireland they dare not think, except as directed by an Italian Church, and they rest upon the ghostly responsibility of the priest. (Cheers.) In Great Britain the population are trained up in piety, industry, and economy; In Ireland they are trained up in superstition, idleness, and extravagance. Let, then, Dan, and their reverences, his staff, relax their spiritual tyranny, abolish their numerous holy, or rather idle, days; let them tech the people to think, to be industrious and economical; let them civilise and bring the population to a moral level with the population of Great Britain, and then the demand of equality will be more like justice for Ireland. (Cheers.) Besides, are not the provisions of my Lord Stanley's Bill intended and calculated to apply to all classes in the community—to Protestants and Papists, Conservatives and Liberals? Why, then, should its provisions be considered so grievous to one party? Are not Dan's party Ireland? And does not justice to Ireland, in his mouth, mean favour to his party? If then, they be a party so powerful and important, why are they not able to cope with their weaker and more insignificant opponents, upon equal terms? Let not Daniel say that his party, though numerous, are poor and ignorant, for this is the error of himself and his staff. Ulster while Popish, was the most turbulent, sanguinary, and wretched province in Ireland; and now, except where a number of Dan's "fine pisantry" are located together, it scarcely yields to Great Britain in civilization, prosperity, and comfort. (Hear, hear.) Let, then Dan become a real liberator. Let him overthrow priestly domination, and introduce civilization. Let him make the country safe for Scotch and English capital, and then he will no longer have cause to complain of his party's poverty. (Cheers.) I submit, my Lord, that, were I pleading against the extension of the elective franchise to poor Roman Catholics, which I am not, I would not be arguing against its equitable extension. (Hear.) There is a manifest difference between Roman Catholic and Protestant electors. When the State confers the franchise upon a Protestant, poor or rich, it creates an elector, but when it gives it to a Roman Catholic, it only confers another vote upon the priest. (Cheers.) The question of a £5 qualification in place of a £10 qualification would not be, in the case of Roman Catholics, shall a number of poor householders have votes, but shall the priest have a number of additional votes? (Loud cheers.) He can already command 200. Will you raise him to 300 or 400? The Romanist elector is a cypher, and the priest the significant figure. In himself he is nothing; but place him on the right side of his ghostly confessor, and he will swell his reverence's importance. (Renewed cheers.) Nor will the priest permit him to act otherwise. He who keeps his conscience must also keep his vote; and should he shew himself refractory, he would be excommunicated in time and eternity. (Hear, hear, and cheers.) Such my Lord, is the liberty which Romanists at present enjoy—the liberty of obeying their priests' commands. Such is the liberty to a share of which they invite Protestants, when they shall have obtained a Repeal of the Union, and a Popish Parliament in College Green. And it is, my Lord, because I have no taste for such liberty, that I appear here this day. (Great cheering.) When I last had the honour of addressing your Lordship, I stated, that according to the doctrines of Popery, oaths made against the interests of the church, and of which interest the church itself was the only judge, were not oaths but perjuries, and that, of course, it would be sinful not to violate, but to keep them. For this and a collateral statement, I was previously called to account by two priests. One of them peremptorily demanded my authorities for such a statement, foretelling, at the same time, that as I could not join them, I must be branded as a calumniator and a liar; I, however, gave him authorities for much more on the subject than I had asserted in the Music Hall; he replied and admitted the fact, by asserting, that the churches of England and Scotland held the same doctrines; I rejoined, and following him in his sophistical wanderings, exposed Auricular confession and extreme Unction in such terms, as, I believe, led him to think he had caught a Tartar. He therefore divided his reply to my rejoinder into three parts, two of which, with rigmarole statements, 100 miles from the subject, slowly appeared, but the third appears to have gone to keep company with Dan's moral courage. I have proved my position through the press, and I now throw down the gauntlet to all the priests in Ireland, to prove it on the platform. I will meet them one to one, two to two, or three to three, as they please. (Loud cheers.) I now, my Lord, conclude by moving the resolution.

"That the Petition now read be adopted, and that the presentation of it be entrusted to Lord Stanley."

THOMAS BATT, Esq., Belfast, seconded the resolution, which passed unanimously.

Doctor COOKE then came forward, and was received with deafening cheers, and several rounds of Kentish fire. He said, my lords and gentlemen, I have now in my hands one of the most important records, and, of course, one of the most veracious statements that has ever been exhibited to a Belfast audience. (Hear, hear.) The record to which I allude is taken from undoubted authority—that from which none of us can be supposed to dissent. It is from no less an authority than the *Belfast Vindicator*.[79] (Laughter and groans.) This record is worthy of preservation, and my anxiety for its safe keeping was such, that, in coming to the meeting, and in dread of its irreparable loss, I actually carried it thus—placing it next my heart. (Hear, hear.) It is deeply to be regretted that so invaluable a production should remain confined to oil and lamp-black. But if the Repealers be the grateful men I take them to be, they will speedily have it printed in letters of gold, framed in the most exquisite manner, and handed down in their wills to their posterity, as one of the most valuable and truthful descriptions of the greatest event that ever occurred in Ulster. (Laughter, and great cheering, that continued for several minutes.) Lend me your ears. (Laughter.) We may presume that half-a-dozen of gentlemen, with coats as black as my own, had lent their joint-stock assistance in preparing this document. And if I may be allowed to make as free with my own name as our great visitant has done; and if, after his illustrious example, I may ascend to that sublime department of oratory called a pun, I should say that those congregated black coats clubbed all their wits in *concocting* this invaluable dish. And, in my mind's eye, I can see the fire rolling beneath, and as the several ingredients descended into the cauldron. (Loud cheering!) I can see them dance, and hear them sing around it, like the weird sisters on the moor—"Double, double, toil and trouble; fire burn and cauldron bubble". (Cheers.) And as each tosses in his "foot of newt", or "toe of frog". I can fancy a curl from Daniel's official wig descending into the foaming vessel to make the broth complete.[80] (Laughter and cheers.) But hear the document—it is worthy of attention:—"O'Connell in Ulster—Words are too weak to express our joy, our exultation, our triumph, in the success of O'Connell's visit to the North". (Ironical cheers.) Why do you not believe them? I tell you, they are worthy of all credit. Words were actually "too weak", and therefore it was they had recourse to sighs and tears, the only language of such a joy as theirs, the brief history of which lies in one brief sentence—He *lied* himself into the town, and his friends *swore* him out of it. (Vehement cheers.) Be silent, I entreat you, for not a word should be lost.—I shall do my best to read it well, and so well, that, at the next election of professor of elocution in the College, I expect—though in that quarter my interest be rather weak[81]— that I shall carry the election against every competitor, and be unanimously installed in that important office. (Loud laughter and cheers.) And certainly the document deserves the best of reading, for beyond all doubt, it is either the most sublime or the most ridiculous of all writing; and the most true, or the most false, of all history. (Cheers.) "Never since Ulster was Ulster", proceeds the *Vindicator*, "Never since Ulster was Ulster"—and I believe that's a long while—(laughter) "did she witness any demonstration approaching in importance the least of the three that has honoured his arrival amongst us". (Laughter.) Don't laugh; it is every word true, and I'll prove it. Yes, these demonstrations prove, to their hearts' content, the vanity and folly of the men that called him hither. (Hear.) They prove the vanity and folly of the man that obeyed their call; and they have demonstrated to the three kingdoms, that, whatever his influence might be in the South, his name is an utter abomination to the freemen of the North. (Loud cheers.)— "The Reform dinner", proceeds the *Vindicator*, "when the number, the respectability—(laughter)—the enthusiasm and all the accompanying circumstances are considered—forms

an era, even in the life of O'Connell". (Laughter.) Why will
you not believe it? Again I undertake to demonstrate its
absolute accuracy. There is no doubt, in this extract, a pretty
considerable spice of what I have elsewhere attributed to
Mr. O'Connell, "a genteel talent for invention"—a choice
expression which, after much research in the best authorities,
I have employed, as it casts out an offensive and very vulgar
word, and converts a source of blame into an occasion of praise.
(Laughter.) The *Vindicator* declares, "that the three glorious
days" of Belfast "forms an era even in the life of O'Connell".
(Hear.) I know your blinded incredulity may lead you to say—
not that this out-herods Herod, but that out-daniels Dan.
(Great laughter and cheers.) The thing is true, nevertheless;
and as the Mahomedan era was dated from the Hegira, or
flight of Mahomet from Mecca, so shall the Danielan era be
henceforth dated from the flight from Belfast, and future
chroniclers shall write it thus—*Anno Hegirae Belfastiensis I.*
(Cheers.) I shall, however, just treat you to "the least taste in
the world" more of these "elegant extracts", from this paragon
model of truth and accuracy.—The article proceeds to say
"The Repeal meeting was every way worthy to stand beside
it", that is, I presume, "beside the dinner".—Now did not he
who penned that passage find his goose quill swell within his
fingers, till it were transmuted as into the baton of Wellington—
(laughter)—and ready to point the way to as terrible a charge
upon Ulster, as when the hero pointed to the columns of
France with "Up guards, and at them". (Great laughter and
cheers.) I beseech you do not laugh—the eloquence of the
Vindicator is really no laughing-stock, as the next extract will
show: "In Belfast"—mark you, in Belfast—"no place could be
found, not even the immense Pavilion *erected* for the dinner, and
which, after the removal of the tables, was capable of accom-
modating 6,000 persons—which could contain a fifth of the
assembled Repealers. They were *forced* to adjourn from the
largest building in the capital of Ulster to the open air". This
immense Pavilion. (Laughter.) Immense Pavilion. (Great laughter and groans.) And *erected* for the occasion too. (Renewed

laughter.) Why, I fear, after Daniel's examples, their memories are all fled together. Do they think we forget when and for what that Pavilion—(laughter)—that shed was erected? Do they think we forget what sort of animals were formerly exhibited there? Was it, or was it not, erected some years ago, for the exhibition, either of a menagerie, or a succession of low comedies, pantomimes, and farces? (Continued cheering.) Did the Repealers not find it like an old pair of cast-off boots, which by vamping, toeing, heel-tapping, and sparrow-bills, may be coaxed to wear a fortnight longer? (Hear, hear and laughter.)— Was not the street encumbered with uprights and props to ensure for a few hours its miserable and rickety existence. (Cheers and laughter). Yes, they exhibited King Daniel where the kings of shreds and patches were wont to fret their little hour, but where he and his entertainers fretted a great one. (Long-continued cheering.) I believe folks, still less majestical, have also figured in the same place; and, perchance, those dignified characters, "Punch and Judy", have been exhibited in the same locality to not less dignified spectators.* (Hear, and laughter.) I do trust the *Vindicator* will send the props to the *Museum*, and that the singular service they have done in holding up the "immense Pavilion", will be recorded in their archives, in *perpetuam rei memoriam*. (Cheers and laughter.) But that most faithful chronicler of the times, the *veracious Vindicator*, tells us, that the "Pavilion"—(laughter)—could contain 6,000, and that for want of room the Repealers were forced to adjourn to the open air. No, whether it might not contain 6,000, as herrings lie in a barrel, I will not say; but that it would not contain 3,000 standing, I will undertake geometrically to demonstrate, and that, at the time of adjournment, there was

---

* This history of the Pavilion is correct, so far as it goes, but a *defect* has to be acknowledged. The origin and design of the Pavilion was as described: but another old shed, erected for purposes of similar histrionic dignity, and that had long stood the weather in *Smithfield market-place*, was brought to eke and patch its brother shed, in Chichester-street. The Pavilion, therefore, was *"erected for the occasion"*, when the one old shed was *taken down*, and stuck to the side of the other old shed that stood.

vacant room for 500 persons, I will undertake by eye-witnesses to prove. (Hear, hear.) Why then did the Repealers adjourn? I'll let you into that secret. Besides their "genteel talent for invention" the Repealers have a nice capacity for the ingenious art of money-catching. (Laughter.) Ay, Daniel's the boy for that. (Roars of laughter.) Accordingly, when they *invited* "Protestants, Presbyterians, and Dissenters", to the Repeal meeting, they first *invited* them to pay for every man, woman, and child, six-pence or a shilling. (One voice, 2*s*. 6*d*., another 1*s*.) Well, be that as it may, the value of the sight vibrated from a shilling to half-a-crown. (Hear.) Now, the sage managers of the Pavilion farce well knew the Protestants had the money—(hear, hear, and cheers)—and though sound enemies to heresy, to a little heretical cash they had no insuperable objection. (Hear, hear, and cheers.) But when they had got the Protestants into the trap, they determined to test their numbers by introducing a green flag, affectedly the emblem of Ireland, but perennially the symbol and stimulant of rebellion. (Loud cheers.) And when they cried "hats off" to the idol, while a part of the audience readily obeyed the summons, another, and a large part, paid the idol no respect. (Cheers.) The Irish descendants of the blue-bonneted Scots stood covered, to a man—(cheers and laughter)—and when the priests and potentates of the old, original, new Pavilion (cheers and laughter)—found, by this test, they were in danger of being out-numbered, then was the green flag smuggled away to Kern's Hotel, and followed by the adjournment. (Hear.) And it is well, my lord and gentle-men, that strangers to Ireland should know the real meaning of the green flag, by the interpretation of Mr. O'Connell himself. He has not forgot either the time or place, when, in the midst of *his own shouts*, it was explained in the memorable stanza—

> "We tread the land that bore us,
> The green flag waving o'er us;
> The friend we've tried
> Is by our side,
> *And the foe we hate before us*."—(Cheers.)

Yes, there's the true meaning of the emblem of Repeal, by which they tested the minds of the Pavilion audience. (Hear, hear, hear.) And when they found they had "caught such Tartars", they adjourned them to the open air, having first honestly cheated them out of their money. (Laughter.) And this was a wise manoeuvre, for had they remained in Rickety Hall, the Repeal, beyond all question, would have met an overwhelming negative. (Cheers.) It was under this well-founded dread, and not for any want of room, that the adjournment was a forced march; and, no doubt, in the open air, Mr. O'Connell thought, that with proper management he might still achieve a victory over the North. (Cheers.) Yes, and let the press tell it—when, what he calls "the honest Northern shout" made the welkin ring, a shout which, with such exquisite taste, he vows he loves so dearly—and who his word will doubt?—(laughter and cheers)—yes, when that honest, well-loved shout arose, Mr. O'Connell's words to the myrmidons around him were, "I pause, my good fellows, till you shout them down". And a shout they did raise, both loud and long. But when they had expended the last puff of their most sweet breath, still nigh at hand arose a louder shout, imposing upon Mr. O'Connell the Protestant penance of silence. (Cheers.) Again his followers tried their lungs, and strained their throats, until, as is suspected, it will require the entire amount of the pavilion cheatery money to purchase gargles. (Cheers and loud laughter.) But all in vain was the effort. For still as the voice of Repeal became silent, the voice of the North arose, and

> Again, again, again,
> And the battle did not slack,
> Till a feebler cry, Repeal,
> To our cheering sent us back.

(Cheers and laughter.) It was under these circumstances Mr. O'Connell was forced to speak in pantomime and dumb show—a speech that has been printed, and may have been uttered, but which certainly never was heard—(cheers)—and

which it had been wise in Mr. O'Connell had he never
attempted in Ulster. But he has received a lesson he will never
forget. He has looked into the faces of the men he threatened
to drive into the sea with "kail stocks". In vain has he tried
either to bully them or to blarney them; the one attempt they
do not much dread, the other they most heartily despise.
(Cheers.) And here, my Lord, I feel compelled to notice the
only part of the story that furnishes any cause of regret, unless
the coming of Mr. O'Connell, the real cause of every evil that
follows in his train. Unhappily, during his sojourn in Belfast,
a few windows were broken—the breakers, very properly—so
far as in such a case the word properly can be applied—the
breakers, I say, very properly dividing their favours between
Protestants and Roman Catholics.* (Hear.) That any man's

---

* The *Ulster Times*, in referring to the window-breaking by the O'Connell
mob, observes:— "We are led to these reflections, by having had shewn
to us the *identical brick-bat* with which the *Vindicator's* said *gentle protégées*,
actually struck a Protestant female, by projecting it through a window on
the second story. But we suppose being a Protestant, her windows and her
life are matters of minor importance in the moral code of Peter Dens.
Weighed in a patent machine the missile is exactly 1 lb. 15 oz.; and is carefully preserved by a gentleman who promises to shew it, if needful, in Exeter
Hall; and we judge it no bad *set off* against both the "*sling*" and the "*stone*"
flung through the windows of the Music Hall—and which, Mr. Chas.
O'Connell affirms, actually drew the blood of one of the "lovely and the
good"—and which blood Mr. D. O'Connell did not *see* but merely heard
of. If the thing were so, we deplore and condemn the actor and the act.
But, though little given to speculate in curiosities, we do hereby offer one
pound sterling, for the discovery of the surgeon who dressed the wound;
with one shilling a drop, for all the blood shed by the "slung stone"; and
a good half-sovereign, for the adhesive strap and bandage by which the
head was dressed; and we do promise to preserve them in a bottle as carefully as the relic of St. Januarius—and, upon every anniversary of Daniel's
"*Repeal Triumph*", to cause the desecrated blood to flow afresh as veritably
as ever did the blood of "old brazen face" at the pious objurgations of the
Neapolitan Lazzoroni.

The brick-bat is still preserved, with the following inscription:—"A
Dan-ish antique, (not found in an Irish bog), but picked up in a drawing-
room in Cromac-street, Belfast—into which it had been projected, (not from
the moon) but from the arm of one of the 'finest pisantry in the world'".

window should have been broken is cause of regret; but that
the window of any Roman Catholic should have been broken
is cause of regret still deeper. (Hear, hear.) And I feel bound
to give expression to this sentiment in this great Protestant
meeting, because I know it will meet a response in every true
Protestant heart. (Loud cries of hear, hear, and great cheering.)
And every gentleman here, and every man who possesses the
least portion of influence over the more moveable portion of
the community, I would beg leave to remind of that great
religious and political truth, that it is in the life of peace, and
that alone, that Providence will enable us either to defend
ourselves or to conquer our assailants. (Cheers.) I also beseech
all to remember, that our religion is not merely a religion of
peace, but of long suffering. Therefore, let Mr. O'Connell heap
on us all the ribaldry and abuse he can muster—let him vilify
and traduce my friend, Dr. Stewart—let him call me by as
many names as his tongue can utter, or his worshippers re-
echo—it is our part to bear all this and more with patience,
to wash it out by forgiveness and repay it, not with injury, but
with kindness. (Cheers.) Mr. O'Connell is doing all in his
power to stir up and exasperate the Roman Catholics against
their Protestant fellow-subjects. With one breath he inculcates
ingratitude to their landlords—with another he enkindles their
hatred to the Protestant clergy—with a third he denounces the
bloody Orangemen (meaning thereby all Protestants)—while
he hugs the gentle and extirpating Ribbonman (hear, hear,
hear)—aye, to his heart of hearts. (Continued cheers.) But no
matter for all this—Protestants may not be provoked to any
retaliation. They must live by the Bible that they love. (Hear,
hear.) And while they mingle their loyal determination with
peaceful conduct, the Providence that guarded and guided their
fathers will take care of their safety and ensure their success.
(Hear, hear). But as this unhappy breaking of a few (and I
rejoice to say they are but a few) panes of glass, though so
equally apportioned between Protestant and Roman Catholic,
has already, with Mr. O'Connell's usual dexterity, been
distorted to calumniate us as a body, and to vilify and expose

an individual to vengeance, it becomes necessary to put the public, and especially the English public, into possession of the real origin of this occurrence, which, however trifling in itself, we lament most deeply, not only as wrong in itself, but as a never failing source of calumny to our great traducer. (Hear, hear.) Now, the origin of the whole affair was this:— When the boys—and most of them were literally so—found themselves turned out of the "immense pavilion", which they say was expressly erected for the Reform dinner and the Repeal meeting—(loud laughter)—and transferred to the open street, where certainly they had as good a right to hear *gratis* as Mr. O'Connell had to speak, they thought—for many of them were descended of the canny Scot, who knows both how to make, and how to lay out his money—they thought themselves unjustly choused out of their sixpences, shillings, and half-crowns, and therefore crowded to the *Vindicator* office, where the tickets had been bought and sold, demanding back their money. At the *Vindicator* office, as I have learned, they were referred to the Linen-hall, and at the Linen-hall they were handed to the *Vindicator* again. Under these circumstances the cold-blooded Northerns became hot, being provoked at the trickery practised on them—literally that of obtaining money under false pretences. And then, and there, was the first pane of glass demolished. (Hear, hear.) Now, I grant that to any one, but especially to boys, this conduct was provoking— because insulting; and exasperating, because dishonourable and dishonest. (Hear, hear, hear, and cheers.) Still they should not have allowed their passions to triumph over their better judgment. What they should have done was this—they should have brought the breakers before my learned and highly respected friend, the *Assistant Barrister*. (A laugh.) Every man, every boy that was cheated should have issued a process against the ticket-sellers, and a Belfast lawyer would have shown up their fraudulent proceedings to a Belfast jury, whose verdict, under the direction of our learned, and truly urbane, and sweet tempered Barrister—(laughter)—would have taught them to avoid embarking again in so hazardous an experiment

as that of obtaining money on false pretences—and so unprofitable a trade as that of being decreed for the sum abstracted
and the expense of prosecution. But, while we have laws,
and juries, and Barristers—such "*second* Daniels come to
judgment"—let no man take the law into his own hand.
Above all things, let no one, whether young or old, offend
Roman Catholics or injure their property. (Hear.) Though
their whole house were glass, remember they are your fellow-
creatures, and that we owe them nothing but love; and that,
however we may oppose, nay abhor, some of their doctrines,
we are still bound to love them, as Christ Jesus loved us, poor
sinners though we be, and misguided though we have been,
by manifold errors, and polluted in heart and action by many
sins. (Loud cries of hear, hear.) Having given this advice,
which your cheering of its sentiments has so heartily enforced,
my next duty is to turn your attention to the proceedings of
our great friend and illustrious visitant. (Laughter.) And, where
all is so admirable, I scarce know where to begin—but I must
begin somewhere, and to select the following at random. The
admirable reporter of the *Vindicator*, whom I cannot fail to compliment on the acuteness of his hearing—(a laugh)—has noted
as follows: "The Hon. Gentleman said, I come here to-day to
address you, and I brought with me some extracts from the
ancient history of the North." Now, I am glad to find he has
studied history—indeed Daniel is a great historian—an excellent historian—a perfect *improvisatore* in history, *making* it without
either reading or study, as easily as he recollects the unwritten
paragraphs of the *Ulster Times*. (A laugh.) But, in the present
case, he tells us he is drawing from our own modern dates, and
favouring us with a resolution passed at the great Dungannon
convention, affirming that the claim of any but the King, Lords,
and Commons, to govern Ireland, was unconstitutional, illegal,
and unjust. But what is the real meaning of the resolutions at
Dungannon, contrasted with the avowed perversion of the
expositor of Darrynane?—(Cheers.) Why, the volunteers at
Dungannon were men who loved their country, but were
Protestants to their heart's core. (Hear, hear, and cheers.)

They were, consequently, men who feared God and honoured the King—(hear, hear)—and who loved the constitutional and united supremacy of King, Lords and Commons. But by whom is this piece of ancient modern history adduced to be perverted? By that servant of all work, who was despatched as a missionary through England and Scotland in open hostility to the House of Lords.—(Cheers.) And did he not undertake that unholy and unconstitutional crusade with all the zeal of one of the followers of Peter the Hermit? And did he not declaim against the House of Lords with all the tender mercies of a *delenda est Carthago?* And is this the man who dares, and in a Belfast street to boot, to quote and pervert a resolution of the loyal men of Dungannon? Men, with some of whose political views I cannot claim identity, but men, of whose honour, honesty, truth—yes, Daniel, truth—and loyalty, no man ever doubted. (Cheers.) Men, who, had the House of Lords been threatened, not merely by an itinerant charlatan tickling the masses of the populace into attention by his harangues, that, while their attention was so fixed, he might more easily pick their pockets. (Laughter.) Men, who, had the House of Lords been threatened by the whole influence of the Crown, betrayed by an enslaved and besotted Ministry, would have rallied around them in all the panoply of principle, and, if need have been, would have warded off the "heavy blow" from their best protectors at the point of the bayonet, and with the thunders of their cannon. (Loud cheers.) Yes, these are the men whose resolutions Mr. O'Connell dares to quote, and labours to pervert; but, however his authorities may impose in the South, we are too far North to take them on his shewing. (Hear, hear.) I shall give you just one specimen of Mr. O'Connell's vaunted crusade against the House of Lords. He had marched through England to the tune of the Radical and Chartist pipes, and invaded Scotland as great as another Edward hurrying to Bannockburn. (cheers.) But just as he found in Ulster, so he found in Scotland—"a new climate". But not the climate of the frost, or the mountain mist, but the climate where he still shivers and hugs his mantle tighter—(a laugh)—the climate of the men that listen and think, and judge before they shout. (Cheers.) Yes, truth it is, that even a Scotch Radical is a thinker, whose mental vision, though for a time impeded and perverted, seldom goes far astray, and generally soon returns to its healthy functions. (Hear, hear.) Accordingly, he marched through Scotland with silence for his almost constant, though unwelcome companion. At Glasgow, nothing but Conservative forbearance protected him from a bath in the pure streams of the sweetly flowing *Molindinar*! Arrived at Paisley, he had learned some wisdom from experience, and I have it from an eye-witness, when he stood up to address the steady and the silent crowd, he looked the very image of Client Dishonesty consulting Counsellor Duplicity—both thoroughly convinced of the badness of their cause, yet searching for any shift, or plea, or evidence by which it might be sustained. (Loud cheers.) Well, at last, like a cowardly horse, the lash of necessity com- pelled him to take the fence. (Laughter.) "Men of Paisley", he exclaimed, "what are we to do in our present circumstances? (*Deep-Scotch attention.*) I'll tell you what we must do—we must annihilate the House of Lords. (*An expected cheer, but no cheer came—continued Scotch attention listening for what would come next.*) For what are the House of Lords? A number of old women— yes, of old women up in London; and, if old women in London, with petticoats on them, are permitted to govern the nation, why may we not as well appoint the lovely young ladies of Paisley (and I suppose he pronounced them "the lovely and the good")—(a laugh)—to govern the nation in Scotland?" At this effusion of wit, a staid and elderly Paisley weaver—one of the tasteful cultivators of carnations, quietly observed to his neigh- bour, "Am suspeckin, may be, that's a lee". (Some laughter.) In this tasteful and persuasive Corn-Exchange style, he continued for a time to rave and rail against the House of Lords, but the full tornado of his eloquence could scarcely produce a ruffle on the surface of the Scottish mind, and he was privileged to return to Darrynane to his own "much loved and respected Lords",[*]

---

[*]   Mr. O'Connell's title for the Romish Bishops.

and *re infecta* it, to permit the "old women" in London to
retain their "old petticoats" till he can quietly filch them to
make him a new gown.[82] (Loud cheers and laughter.)—Yes,
thank God, they still muster around the throne, interposing
an impassible barrier between King, and Commons, and
people; preventing the precipitancy of the one from hurrying
onward to the throne of their unfashioned and often abortive
attempts at legislation, and shielding the other from that
"fierce democracy", that would rob the rich and rifle the
industrious, to endow the pauper, who will but beg, the lazy
that will not work, or the factious and seditious demagogue
who lives by maliciously retarding the progressive improve-
ments of his country. (Vehement cheering.) Yes—well may we
adopt the liturgy of Lord Brougham, and say, from the
bottom of our hearts, "thank God we have a House of Lords".
Well, now, I must furnish you one or two others of those precious extracts. "It is said", says O'Connell, "that we are
looking for ascendancy, but this I utterly deny". Not much the
more credible for that, my friend Daniel. (A laugh.) "Recollect
that this is not a sectarian or party contest—our struggle is
for the Protestant as well as the (Roman) Catholic. The
Orangeman, the Protestant, the Presbyterian, the Dissenter—
Irishmen of every class will be all equally benefited." (Aye, so
said Brutus when he had murdered his dearest friend "for *the
good of Rome*".) (Hear.) "And all are therefore alike bound to
assist in promoting it."—Now, for a wonder, there is truth in
this; and in that word "we" lies the hidden mystery, that appears
to speak truth, while it conceals the mystery of iniquity. (Hear,
and cheers.) True, Mr. O'Connell, you may well say of the
collective Repealers, "*we* are not seeking ascendency". No—
you, and *you* alone, are sent seeking it—(cheers)—and when
under the more pompous name of King Daniel the I!!! or the
less imposing, but no less powerful one, of "*Lord Protector*" of
the commonwealth of Old Ireland—(cheers and laughter)—
or, merely under the bewitching title of "Liberator", and the
death's head and cross bones of the resistless "Dictator".
(Loud cheers.) It is all the same to Daniel. Power, like the

roses' perfume so sweet under any name,—power is still power, whatever title your humility is pleased to assume.— (Cheers.) You must remember how, even the mitred head and croziered hand of Doyle must veil their high dignity in your presence. Yours is the sole O'C. ascendancy, and ever since the days of "Honest Jack Lawless" and downwards, your every act is an additional proof that you are just the man who can bear "no brother near the throne".—You say you are not for (Roman) Catholic ascendancy. Well, I will believe you— yes, I will believe you—and I tell you when—whenever you produce the number of the *Ulster Times* in which you "recollected" to have read my "authorised contradiction of the report that I intended to challenge you to discuss Repeal." (Hear, and cheers.) Now, do not delay to do this—for not only is your veracity at stake, but the moment you produce the document you so clearly "recollected" to have read, and on the credit of which you so courteously pronounced me, and the gulls shouted me, a double convicted LIAR, that moment I am bound to be your convert, and you may perhaps find me as active and as useful a partisan and helper as either Mr. Tom Steele or Mr. Dillon Browne. But though I thus agree to believe you, whenever your "recollection" will believe for me— a laugh—yet, must I entreat you—pray, Mr. O'Connell, stand a little aside, till I see who is that black-coated, rosy (not pale) faced gentleman that is peering so wistfully over your shoulder? Ah! Is that you, the mild and gentle John of Tuam, Lord paramount of Maronia, and patron of the Isle of Achill?[83] (Loud cheers and laughter.) And who, "my beloved and most respected Lord", pray who is that beside you? Ah! It is that gentle, amiable, and apostolic man, Father Hughes—(hear, hear, and cheers)—whose "ascendency" is the "ascendency" of the "pitchfork", whose level is that of the "Ban dog" and whose descendency is that of the "boghole".[84] (Laughter and loud cheers.) You, my Lord John, and you Father Hughes, you never once dreamed of "ascendancy"; no, never "once", for it was the lullaby of your cradle before reason dawned; it was the lisp of your childhood before the day it was developed; it was the object of your manhood, it has been the idol of your age; and with a perspicuity as clear as if I read your hearts, I can discover, from your acts and your words, that you eat, drink, and sleep, and wake, but on one thought—the hour when the priest shall be transmuted into the lord of the parish. (Hear, and cheers.) And, whatever it may please you, Mr. O'Connell, to whisper in sweet words to the ears of the North, right well I know that when your Southern conclave meet, "ascendancy", and ascendancy alone, is the magnet that conglomerates the filings of the mass—the fire, and the anvil, and the hammer by which it is welded, till, forged into a sword for the hand of rebellion, it goes forth to overturn the passive Government, and the credulous fellow subjects who foolishly looked on till it was formed and sharpened for their destruction. (Loud cheering.) Yes, Mr. O'Connell, say what you will, we interpret your meaning, not by words, but by deeds. We still remember "the ugly figure" as you called it, of the "death's head and cross bones", and on an authority that we know to be infallible, we have concluded that "out of the abundance of your heart your mouth spoke". (Hear, hear and loud cheers.) And when, with honied words, you would persuade us to follow you to Repeal, we know it is the vision of ascendancy that is flitting before your mind's eye, and that were we to follow you, it would be only to witness the last scene, where Popish ascendancy, like the phantom dagger of Macbeth, is beckoning you to the chamber where our liberty reposes. (Tremendous cheers.) But in the hands of Mr. O'Connell, miracles will never cease. In another part of the report of this *unheard* of Repeal speech, he tells the ignorant and unreading Northerns a thing that they never knew before—he tells them that since the Reformation, the Romanists of Ireland were three times in power, and yet never once attempted to persecute their Protestant brethren. As they say in some parts of England, "that's a whopper". (Laughter.) I would Mr. O'Connell, that I had been your con-sulting counsel when you briefed that figment. I should have strongly advised you to adopt a wise, though I admit it is a vulgar principle "let sleeping dogs lie". (Cheers.) I cannot, however, deny it to be a specimen of your "very genteel talent for invention". Standing here as a Conservative, a Protestant, a Christian, I would you had permitted me to allow the by-gone events of other days to moulder in the tomes of our history. I would you had allowed the dust and the cobwebs of time to accumulate around them. I wish you had permitted his lenient surgery to bind up the wounds both of ancient and of recent days. I wish you had permitted oblivion to draw her veil over occurrences that were better forgotten than recalled—or that we had been allowed to unite for the economical, moral, and spiritual regeneration of our common country, I would you had not compelled us, by raising up the records of the past, to sow the seeds of differences for the present; I would you had not compelled me to call history to my aid, nor to demonstrate to my fellow Protestants the tender mercies of your "ascendancy" in other years, both in order to warn and arouse them to resist your restoration. (Loud cheers.) And, as you know you are not entitled to credit for any quotation from ancient history, till you have verified your "recollection" from the more modern chronicle of the *Ulster Times*—(hear, hear)—permit me then to say, I have taken some pains to examine your "recollections" of ancient history; and though I admit I am far from your equal in history—nay, though I admit, as your followers assert, that I am utterly your inferior in all your greatest qualities, and that, to have met me in argument, would have lowered beyond restoration the dignity of your character—still as your humble fellow-student in history, I proceed to examine your three epochs of "Popish ascendancy"—epochs that will augment into four as I proceed—and to furnish you with a few records of that mild, and tolerant, and fostering spirit with which it invited, housed, fed, and cherished its truant, but beloved Protestantism. And now, Mr. O'Connell, lay aside for a moment "your genteel talent of invention". To your book, Daniel, to your book, boy; and now for as good a lesson as ever you received, since the day when you first touched battledore. (Loud cheers, laughter,

and cries of hear, hear.)—Now, I presume, Mr. O'Connell's
first period is that of Queen Mary; and, with respect to that
most kind-hearted and gracious gentlewoman—it is said she
did not persecute any one. Shades of Cranmer and of Ridley,
and all ye fire-tried martyrs and noble army of confessors,
who kindled up in England the unextinguishable fire—ye who
not only taught her Church to know the truth, but her gallant
sons and her tender daughters to die for it—(hear, hear.)—
bear witness to this generation of the deeds of the past, and
say whether your Papist Queen was a gentle mother or
a bloody persecutor. (Hear.) And yet while the fires of
Smithfield still burn in the pages of history, Mr. O'Connell
tells us Mary was no persecutor. (Hear, hear.) But perhaps
he means to insinuate that her favours were reserved for
Ireland—that island of saints—that oasis of mercy in the
desert of war and persecution—where Popery like a bene-
ficent foster-mother, hugged to her bosom England's orphan;
where she furnished the outcast with a home, and the
disinherited with an estate. If this be the figment he means to
palm upon us for history, we tell him, the man who persuaded
him to the attempt must be either an *ignoramus* or a *knave*. And
utrum horum mavis accipe—is good Latin even in Kerry, and Mr.
O'Connell well understands it without my translation. (Cheers
and laughter.) I know not, and I guess not, to what veracious
chronicler he may have reference for his assertion, but I pin
him down to his own assertion, and for the forgery he has
attempted will "nail the rap to the counter".[85] (Vehement
cheering and laughter.) First, then, does Mr. O'Connell know
that a merciful Providence, to counterwork the bigotry and
cruelty of Mary, had led to the appointment of a Lord Deputy,
who was a concealed Protestant? (Hear.) Does he not know
that the proof of this lies in the fact, that when Elizabeth
came to the throne, and employed all her energies to foster
Protestantism, so far from dismissing Mary's Lord Deputy, she
continued him in office, out of gratitude for the protection he
had extended to the Protestants; because being no longer a
concealed, but an avowed, Protestant, she could fully confide

in him for the care of her Protestant subjects? (Hear, hear, cheers, and loud laughter.) But, as Mr. O'Connell is a lawyer, I shall restrain him from his historic gambols, by the fetter of legal authority. (Hear, hear.) I have accounted already for any favour the Protestants enjoyed; and now I shall discover to him the tender mercies which Mary intended them to enjoy. And here, it well becomes Irish Protestants to look back with gratitude to that overruling Providence which called her to her last account just when all her plans of persecution in Ireland were about to be carried into terrible execution. The denial of this, Mr. O'Connell, lies happily beyond the limits of your "genteel talents for invention". It lies in the authentic record of Mary's instructions to the Lord Deputy, touching the tender mercies she proposed for her Irish Protestant subjects. The first article contained the following words:— "That they should, by *all good means possible*",—(no doubt, Mr. O'Connell, the means the Queen and her counsellors had found "so very good" in Smithfield)—(hear, hear)— "advance the honour of God and the Catholic Church; that they should set forth the honour and dignity of the Pope's holiness". His holiness, Mr. O'Connell, his holiness!—the holiness of an heretical Liberius!—of a "fasting", self-denying Hildebrand!—of a modest Joan!—a gentle Julius! and an upright Sixtus the Fifth.[86] (Cheers.) Yes, the Pope's "holiness" the Irish Government were visibly to set forth, together with "the honour and dignity of the See Apostolic of Rome". But how, Mr. O'Connell? By deeds of forbearance and mercy to her poor Protestant exiles who, as you say, were invited over to be cherished in Ireland? No. But the Lord Deputy and Council were ordered "to be ready, from time to time, with their aid and *secular force*, at the request",—mark it well, Mr. O'Connell,— at the "request of *all spiritual ministers and ordinaries* to"—do what, Mr. O'Connell?—to provide houses rent free in Dublin?—to feed Protestants with food convenient?—to clothe them in nakedness, and cherish them in sickness?—to visit them in prison? No, not one of all these mercies to shew—but to "PUNISH AND REPRESS ALL HERETICS and Lollards, and their

damnable sects, opinions, and errors". (Great cheering.) Ah!
Mr. O'Connell, read that, and if you ever blushed when
detected in a misdeed, spare "one blush more" when exposed
in the most palpable historic forgery that ever was attempted
to deceive the ignorant, or to gull the credulous. (Loud
cheers.) I have no doubt you may plead the authority of
Taylor—an historian exactly after your own heart—(hear,
and a laugh)—an historian that will be held for an authority,
when you discover the number of the *Ulster Times* containing
my *authenticated contradiction* of a report concerning you, which,
like Taylor, you "recollect" to have read;—(cries of hear,
hear)—and when the *Vindicator* shall prove that the crazy old
shed that, for some years, has degraded one of our streets,
was an "immense Pavilion", expressly "*erected* for the dinner".
(Loud cheers and laughter.) But I have more heretic comfort
still in store for you. The better to carry those instructions into
effect, an act, in the following year, reviving three statutes for
the punishment of heresy—of which the preamble—a true *ex
pede Herculem*—runs as follows:—"For the escuying and avoiding
of errors and *heresies*, which, of late, have risen, growen, and
mouche increased within this realme; for that the ordinaries
have *wanted authority* to proceed against those that were infected
therewith; be it therefore ordeyned and enacted by the authority of this present parliament, that the statute made", &c.
Now, Mr. O'Connell, please chew these two legal mouthfuls.
(A laugh.) Yes, chew them well, and I will venture to affirm,
that never was there an animal that had munched, by mistake,
a mouthful of rue, that chewed a more "bitter cud of disappointment" than will Daniel chew when he has swallowed the
two bitter historic pills that I have now administered. (Hear,
and loud cheers.) But, passing from crabbed law, I shall now
select for Mr. O'Connell's historic study, a leaf out of my
Lord Plunket's "old almanac" history. And this shall bring us
to period the second of Popish power in Ireland, subsequent
to the Reformation—the never-to-be-forgotten year 1641.
(Hear.) In that year the Romanists again assumed political
power—acting, as they then asscrtcd, and as it is now certain

they did, under the commission and order of the unfortunate King Charles the First.* Who has not heard of Sir Phelim O'Neill. (Hear, and a laugh.) Aye, of Phelimy Roe, and his slaughter? (Hear, hear.) Who has not heard of his march upon Belfast, and how he was compelled to call a halt, by the gallant men of Lisburn. (Hear, hear.)—And surely this great meeting will permit me to indulge an honest joy, when I mention the historic fact, that the first effective resistance to his invasion, was headed by the gallant Lawson, of Derry, who was a Presbyterian—(loud cheers)—a Presbyterian, not actuated by the miserable prejudices of a repulsive sectarianism, but bound to his Protestant brethren of the establishment, by the attractive and uniting impulses of common principles, and of common danger. (Loud cheers.) The Romanists, as I have said, had their royal authority and political power—and gently and tenderly did Sir Phelim and they employ it! But Mr. O'Connell, in his hurry in consulting

---

* The Royal Commission from Charles I., for the movements of 1641, has been strenuously denied. The evidence of its reality seems, however, beyond controversy. The evidence may be summed up as follows:—(1.) The Royal Commission was published by Sir Phelim O'Neill himself, in his proclamation from Newry, 1641. (2.) It was reprinted in the *"Mysterie of Iniquity"*, 1643. (3.) In *"Viccar's Parliamentary Chronicle"*, 1646. (4.) In "Milton's Works", 1698. And those who desire to see the genuineness of the Commission fully canvassed, may consult Brodie, vol. III p.190–9; and Godwin, vol. I. p. 225–30. (5.) Even Reilly, a staunch Romanist, admits that Lords Auburn and Ormond were instructed by Charles to seize the Castle, the Lords Justices, &c., and that Sir Phelim merely endeavoured to have the first hand in the work. In this statement, it is not intended to implicate King Charles in the guilt of the massacre, but merely in the folly of commencing a *movement*, he afterwards could not control. Just as there may now be some weak-minded Repealers who, by the plausible speeches and professions of the agitators, are deceived into the opinion that they mean to benefit their country, and maintain the integrity of the empire, and who would in vain, hereafter, express their regrets, when the Repeal they had foolishly encouraged had finally ripened into Rebellion and dismemberment. No doubt, by the power of England, that Rebellion, like its "Precursor", would be finally suppressed. But, is the suppression of the monster any consolation for its mischief? None. Prevention is still better than cure.

authorities, must have skipped over this page of Irish history; or perhaps, some one had cut out the page, and, so Daniel could say, like an unprepared schoolboy, "that's not in my book"—(a laugh)—or, perhaps,—for there is no end to possibilities where Daniel is concerned—perhaps some printer's familiar, had pasted the leaves together; or, certainly, as he cannot distinguish between *John* and *Henry*, his eyesight is failing—(a laugh)—and to that cause we must attribute his short coming. And undoubtedly, his memory is gone—and no living man has need of a better—(a laugh)—for he cannot "recollect" what number of the *Ulster Times*, is to prove me doubly "*a liar in my own person*", although the files were courteously offered to be laid on his table, and we might opine he had leisure enough during *four long nights*, and *three short days*, in the *lock-up house*, Donegall-place, to have made the important discovery. (Loud cheers and laughter.) I tell you, Mr. O'Connell, in more seriousness than the subject seems to warrant, that, in this your northern tour, like Madam Piozzi's old man, "you've had more than your three sufficient warnings": first, your memory's gone; secondly, your eyesight; thirdly, your judgment; fourthly, your popularity; fifthly, your bullying; for though the House of Commons were roused when you called them ruffians, and quailed beneath an apology, that doubted the insult; still, your skulking from a personal encounter, through your genteel "talent of invention", will not only encourage others to assail you, but will furnish them a weapon from which even "triple brass", will not be sufficient to defend you. (Loud cheers.) With these warnings, Mr. O'Connell, it is full time you should prepare for your change. As to your natural life, I pray, it may be long and happy. I pray that you may have grace to see all your errors; and, in good time, exchange this scene of turbulence, for one of rest and peace. But, in the mean time, I call you to another change—put off that painted mountebank coat, in which you gull your poor countrymen to buy and swallow your nostrums. (Hear, hear.) Put off that false profession of mercenary patriotism in which you traffic alike for shouts and for halfpence—above all, put off that visor of hypocrisy beneath which, while you profess religion, you practice untruth.—(hear, hear)—and put away that lip-loyalty by which you would flatter a Queen, while you would rend her empire—(loud cheers)—and stand forth, what you are, a venal disturber of your country, a traitor to your Queen, and a liar to your God. (Vehement cheering.) Yes, Mr. O'Connell, I call you by your proper name; and I take the brand of unquestioned history to enstamp it deep on your forehead. (Hear, hear.) You say the Romanists in Ireland, during the three periods of their political power, never once persecuted, but on the contrary, invited to their shores, and fostered and protected the Protestants. Now, lest you should hold parley with me about 1641, I shall return to 1553, the era of your beloved Mary, in whose auspicious reign, Taylor's 53 apocryphal houses were opened by the Romanists in Dublin, for the reception of the British Protestants. In June of that memorable year, Mary ascended the throne, and, in the following month of September, either commenced or was completed the persecution of Bale, bishop of Ossory, one of the brightest ornaments for learning, piety, and zeal, that ever adorned the Established Church of Ireland. Five of his servants were murdered in one night, and he was forced to fly for protection of his life to Kilkenny. Here he remained for some time, in the faithful utterance of his testimony, but being in daily danger of his life, he obeyed his Lord's injunction; and "being persecuted in one city, he fled to another"; and, after many difficulties and dangers, succeeded in reaching the continent. And never, Mr. O'Connell, did the Established Church, or any other Church in Ireland, possess a nobler son, a brighter ornament, than Bale; and, as once I did travel a pilgrimage of some miles, that I might stand by the tomb of Bedel of Kilmore, as many, yea more, would I travel to stand by the tomb of Bale of Ossory—the man justly characterised as *facile princeps* amongst the mightiest of the Reformers, and ranked above Luther, Platina, and Vergerius, in his faithful exposure of the heresies and usurpations of Rome.[87] (Hear, hear and cheering.) There, Mr. O'Connell, is an example for

you of the manner in which the Romanists treated an Irish
Protestant Bishop, in the reign of the mild and tolerant
Queen Mary—(hear, hear)—and if you wish to know on what
authority it is founded, I refer you to "Reid's History of the
Presbyterian Church in Ireland", vol. I., pages 40 and 41. We
now revert, Mr. O'Connell, more particularly to the second
period of Popish ascendancy in Ireland, 1641. (Hear, hear.)
Yes, you do well to cry, "Hear", and let Ulster hear; and let
Ireland, in all her provinces, hear; and let England's Court
and Parliament hear; while, contradicted by the testimony of
unquestioned history, Mr. O'Connell stands elevated on the
pillory of public condemnation—"the bad, bad eminence"
from which he will never descend, unless he break off his sins
by repentance, and fly to the mercy of an offended God.
(Cries of "Hear, hear".) And here, Mr. O'Connell, allow me
a word of apology for the heavy sentence and portentous
denunciation I have just uttered against you. You have often
delighted to call yourself "the best abused man in the kingdom", but you have always forgot to tell you were yourself the
most abusive man in the universe. (Hear, hear.) I state not this
oversight of yours to vindicate myself for any severity of
language I may have applied, or intended to apply to you.
No, I remind you of it, that I may grapple with that feeling
of sentimentality, that will not distinguish between abusing the
man and denouncing his sins. (Hear, hear.) As a sinner I
speak, knowing the grace of God in his Son—and I speak of
your sins but as I desire to speak of my own. I abuse you not
as a man, but I do denounce you as a sinner—not as a man,
however, truly confessing, ashamed of, or forsaking his sin—
but as a man whose very "trade" is sin—sin, the first that
beclouded Paradise—sin, the meanest practiced on earth—
sin, the last condemned in the lake that burneth—where is
every thing that "loveth or maketh a lie"! (Hear, hear.) I lead
you back, accordingly, not in anger but in pity, to your speech
in Dublin, where you twice denounced me as a liar. Have you
apologised for the injury—have you repented of the sin? I
know you have not done the first, and, till that take place, you

cannot have attained the other. (Hear, hear.) I have led you
to the reign of Queen Mary, and exhibited you, by irre-
fragible documents, as a wilful perverter of the history of that
reign, and now I offer, through you to the public, some means
of further testing your truth, when you assert that toleration,
nay kindness, was extended to Protestants during every post-
reformation period of Popish ascendancy in Ireland. And
here, my Lord, I shall read to the meeting a few brief extracts
from Dr. Reid's History, as specimens of the mercy, toleration,
and kindness, enjoyed by the Irish Protestants, during that
disastrous period of their history—a period which, I solemnly
believe, Mr. O'Connell is either intentionally or practically
labouring to re-produce—(hear, hear)—and from which may
God in his infinite mercy protect this distracted land! (Hear,
hear.) The extracts which I now read in brief, I have noted on
the margin of the books before me, and shall afterwards
furnish to the newspapers in full detail. Now, this being the
second post-reformation period of Popish ascendancy in
Ireland, it must be the second period, during which, Mr.
O'Connell says, Protestants were not persecuted. Lest it
should, however, be called ill manners, I will not accuse
Mr. O'Connell of telling an historical lie; but I must say with
the good-natured Scotsman—"He's a great economist of
truth!" (Cheers and laughter.)

"Ireland was now in a state of universal tranquility.—At no
former period had the country enjoyed so much real prosperity,
and so long internal peace. All dissatisfaction or anxiety with
respect to defective titles, had been removed by the confirmation of the graces, and by other conciliatory acts of the
sovereign and the English Parliament. The Roman Catholic
party enjoyed ample toleration. Their nobility were unrestricted
in their privileges, and shared in the titles and dignities
conferred on the peers of Ireland by James and Charles. Their
gentry were members of parliament, judges, magistrates, and
sheriffs. Their lawyers occupied the same station at the bar as
Protestants, and practised as freely in the courts of law. Their
clergy were unmolested in the performance of their religious

rites, and their other ecclesiastical functions. In obtaining the redress of national grievances, both Protestants and Romanists cordially co-operated. The constitutional administration of the Lords justices were universally popular; and a new era of national improvement and civilization appeared to be opening on this long distracted country.

"But these anticipations were awfully disappointed.—'The hopes conceived from a peace of forty years, from the gradual improvement of the nation, from the activity of its parliament, from the favourable disposition of the king, from the temper of the English parliament, were in an instant confounded; and the calamities of former times revived in all their bitterness.'

"In Ulster, the rebellion broke out at the appointed time; and, owing to the defenceless state of the Protestants, and their consternation at so sudden and simultaneous an attack, it met, for a time, with no effective resistance."

"On the 23rd of October, 1641, and within a few days after, the Irish rebels made slaughter of all men, women, and children, which they could lay hands on, within the county of Antrim, that were Protestants, burning their houses and corn."

"Sir Con Magennis took possession of Dromore, and treated with wanton and unprovoked cruelty the few Protestants who had ventured to remain. Having burned the town, he fell back to Newry, where he effected a junction with Sir Phelim O'Neill, who, finding himself placed, without controul, at the head of a much more formidable force than he had ever anticipated, immediately abandoned what may be called the royal, and prosecuted the original, scheme of the insurrection; and henceforth openly aimed at the extirpation of the entire Protestant population, whether of English or Scottish descent. He, therefore, encouraged his infuriated followers to give free vent to the direful passions of hatred and revenge, which the Romish priesthood had for years been fostering in the breasts of their people, against their protestant neighbours. The insurrection was speedily converted into a religious war, carried on with a vindictive fury and a savage ferocity, which have been seldom exceeded. Though the enterprise was now formally disowned by Charles, and though Sir Phelim, by his brutal excesses, had disgusted some of the more ardent of his original associates, yet urged on by Ever M'Mahon, Roman Catholic Bishop of Down, he plunged into the deepest atrocities.

"The shocking tale of the cruelties perpetrated by the undisciplined and bloodthirsty levies of O'Neill, during several months, has been often told; by none more effectually than by the female historian of England (Mrs. Macauley).[88] 'An universal massacre ensued; nor age, nor sex, nor infancy, were spared; all conditions were involved in the general ruin. In vain did the unhappy victim appeal to the sacred ties of humanity; companions, friends, relatives, not only denied protection, but dealt with their own hands, the fatal blow. In vain did the pious son plead for his devoted parent; himself was doomed to suffer a more premature mortality. In vain did the tender mother attempt to soften the obdurate heart of the assassin in behalf of her helpless children; she was reserved to see them cruelly butchered, and then to undergo a like fate. The weeping wife lamenting over the mangled carcase of her husband, experienced a death no less horrid than that which she deplored. This scene of blood received yet a deeper stain, from the wanton exercise of more execrable cruelty that had ever yet occurred to the warm and fertile imagination of Easter barbarian. Women, whose feeble mind received yet a stronger impression of religious phrenzy, were more ferocious than the men; and children, excited by the example and exhortation of their parents, stained their innocent age with the blackest deeds of human butchery.'

"The persons of the English were not the only victims to the general rage: their commodious houses and magnificent buildings were either consumed with fire, or laid level with the ground. Their cattle, though now part of the possession of their murderers, because they had belonged to abhorred heretics, were either killed outright, or, covered with wounds, were turned loose into the woods and deserts, there to abide a lingering, painful end. This amazing, unexpected scene of horror, was yet heightened by the *bitter revilings, imprecations, threats and insults* which everywhere resounded in the ears of the astonished English. Their sighs, groans, shrieks, cries, and bitter lamentations, were answered with—"Spare neither man, woman, nor child; *the English are meat for dogs*; there shall not be one drop of English blood left within the kingdom'. Nor did there want the most barbarous insults and exultation on beholding those expressions of agonizing pain which a variety of torments extorted.

"Nor was the rage of the rebels confined to the unoffending Protestant clergy. Every thing which could be considered in any way identified with Protestantism was wantonly destroyed. The BIBLE, in a particular manner, was an object on which the Romanists vented the detestation of the truth. 'They have torn it in pieces', says the commissioners in their remonstrance presented, by the agent of the Irish clergy, to the English Commons, scarcely four months after the breaking out of the rebellion, 'they have kicked it up and down, treading it under foot, with leaping thereon, they causing a bag-pipe to play the while: laying also the leaves in the kennel, leaping and trampling thereon; saying 'a plague on it, this book hath bred all the quarrel', hoping within three weeks, all the Bibles in Ireland should be so used or worse, and that none should be left in the kingdom: and while two Bibles were burning, saying that it was hell-fire that was burning, and wishing that they had all the Bibles in Christendom, that they might use them so."

The devastations committed during this second period of "tender mercies" it is now impossible, accurately, to ascertain, but the following are some of the various calculations which the writers nearest the melancholy period have left upon record:—

"The following is a brief summary of the calculations of the more eminent Protestant writers. May (p. 81) estimates the number slain at 200,000 in the first month. Temple makes it 150,000 in the first two months, or 300,000 in two years. Rapin (ix.343) gives 150,000 in about four months. Lord Clarendon (i.290) says that about 40,000 were murdered at the first outbreak before any danger was apprehended, and he is followed by Hume. Sir William Petty, a very expert and accurate calculator, computes that 37,000 perished within the first year."

I come now to what I suppose Mr. O'Connell's third period—that of the ill-fated James II. I doubt not I am addressing the descendants of some who were driven under the walls of Derry. I know I hold the card of one honoured individual whose ancestor acted a conspicuous part in its defence.* And I wot of another who had no name to be either honoured or recorded; but, at the first outbreak of the rebellion, all his family was murdered but one little child; driven from a distant part of the county Down, with thousands of starving Protestants, he carried his child in his arms to Derry, and was happily one of those admitted into the city for its defence. But when he mounted guard at night he had no nurse for his little one, so carried it with him to the wall, and placing it between the embrasures, where the cannon frowned defiance on James and slavery,—(cheers)—Providence protected him in the midst of famine and death; and when, in after years, he was questioned how he fared at night for shelter, "well enough", was the reply, "I had the shelter of my father's gun". (Cheers.) Yes, God protected that motherless and homeless boy, and he who now addresses you is that boy's humble descendant. (Enthusiastic cheers.) Repulsed from the walls of Derry, James hastened to meet his mock Parliament in Dublin; and then proceeded, not in military, but in Mr. O'Connell's true and legal style, the third specimen of Popish ascendancy tolerating and fostering Protestants. But how? Why, by the most barefaced act of wholesale robbery ever put on record; and what renders the robbery still more execrable, under the royal hypocritical mask of liberty of conscience, and respect for property. (Hear, hear, hear.) By one dash of the royal pen, the Acts of Settlement and Explanation

---

* Lieutenant-Colonel Cairnes—the allusion to whom, as occupying a place on the platform near the speaker, produced an instantaneous burst of applause.

were repealed,—(hear, and a laugh)—and all Protestants who
held their estates under these acts, whether as original
grantees, purchases, or by mortgage, were deprived of them
in the true style of O'Connell slapdash. (Hear, hear.) Yes,
O'Connell is the boy for a slapdash. (A laugh.) He promised
to breakfast in Newry, and attend a procession 50,000 strong,
and to give an hour and a half, to deploy and march, "the
green flag waving o'er them". But he passed through at a
slapdash,—(loud laughter.)—and silence smiled at sleeping
echo in Trainor's lonely hayloft.* (Loud Laughter.) By
slapdash he was spirited through Hillsborough, and looked
sadly askance at the valley where the army of William reposed,
on their glorious march to the Boyne. (great cheering.)
Through Lisburn, another slapdash, with colours flying. (A
laugh.) It is true; but they were the colours of his rosy face, for
a danger that existed but in his own heart. (Hear, hear.) And
by final slapdash he "invaded" his hotel, and speedily
bivouacked in his bed-room. (Laughter and cheers.) And there
he lay *perdue*, like a hare in her form, without one ray of
comfort, even from the ghostly consolations of Donegall-
street. (Cheers.) Now I should not have troubled you with this
"tedious brief history"—(a laugh)—of Mr. O'Connell's talent
for slapdash, were it not that every article of his Repeal project is borrowed from the slapdash Parliament of King James.
(Hear, and cheers.) In that parliament, Protestant property
was, - what shall I call it? Annihilated? No, no, that cannot
be. Mr. O'Connell, that learned and profound historian, has
discovered that, during every period of Popish ascendancy in
Ireland, Protestants were always fostered! Bravo, Daniel—
(cheers)—when *you* say it, it must have been so; aye, and it
was so, with a witness; for—witness the king's hand—the
Protestants were so cherished, that they were delivered from
the intolerable trouble of managing their estates,—(cheers and
laughter)—and the labour of both recovering and spending
their rents, most generously undertaken by the ascendancy.

---

* The place of *the great O'Connell Banquet* where there was no dinner to eat.

(Hear, hear, laughter and cheers.) And this, doubtless, is, what Daniel calls fostering the Protestants. Had James prevailed, we should not to-day have been surrounded by the Hills, the Chichesters, the Needhams, the Loftuses, and the Watsons; they would have been foster-nursed, *a la Daniel*, with a vengeance—(cheers)—and the next time he sits to H. B. for his picture, I trust he will consent to be represented in the character of an Irish nurse, with Protestantism as baby, which he is rocking with his one hand, whilst stealing its pinafore and frock with the other.[89] (Roars of laughter and cheers.) Mr. O'Connell has given us three periods of Popish ascendancy, and if he can say—hum—with the benevolent Uncle Toby,[90] I'll treat him to a fourth—the very days we live in. (A voice, "You forget Scullabogue".) Oh! I thank you; I had indeed thought of that period, but it would have escaped me but for this refresher. Yes, yes; there was a time when the people of Ulster were nearly lured between the Scylla and Charybdis of disaffection and rebellion, and the genius of Popery was the syren that sung them amidst the breakers, the whirlpools, and the rocks. (Hear, hear, and cheers.) But the time will never come when the Presbyterians of Ulster will be found at the tail of O'Connell. (Cheers.) He tells of 33 houses, charitably provided in Dublin by Romanists, for the persecuted Protestants of Bristol. I would his antiquarian search would tell where they were situated. He knows what house was provided for them at Scullabogue! (Hear, hear.) The burning roof above, and the bristling pikes without—(hear, hear)—where the helpless infant, whose cries might have moved some pity, was cast back into the flames it had escaped, a victim to the Moloch of a fiendish and perennial intolerance. (Hear, hear.). And does he know the house prepared for them at Wexford? The heavens their only covering, the bridge their kneeling-place, the demi-savage and his pike their only judge and executioner. (Hear.) Why, why, Mr. O'Connell, do you force us, in self-defence against your falsifications of history, to revert to those evil days? Already we have forgiven: why will you not permit us to forget? I tell you, Mr. O'Connell, the

unhappy men and women who fell victims at Scullabogue
barn and Wexford Bridge have been the political saviours of
their country. (Loud cheering.) Though they perished, they
live. They live in our remembrance—their deaths opened the
political eyes of the many thousands of Ulster; and the names
of Wexford and Scullabogue form an answer to all your
arguments for Repeal. We have heard some days ago from
Dublin, that the Presbyterians are great Reformers. With this
I agree, for they wish to reform Mr. O'Connell; but, that they
are Reformers in any other sense, I prove by the 85 witnesses
that lately assembled in Belfast, and who, in the genuine spirit
of a precursor society of reform,

> "Resolved, that all resolves are vain –
> Resolved, we ne'er resolve again. (Laughter.)

No, no. The time will never come when the mass of
Presbyterians, now united in the General Assembly, will
become sharers in any department of the present conspiracy
against the Queen, the country, and the constitution. (Cheers.)

I come now to the fifth period of Popish ascendancy—for
two more have grown out of Daniel's three—(a laugh)—and
the fifth period is, the reign of King Daniel himself—(Cheers,
and a laugh)—lately crowned in the "immense Pavilion" by
the title of the "*Peaceful Conqueror*".* Now, of King Daniel's own
method of cherishing Protestants, I can say no more than that
he takes great pleasure in starving them—(hear, hear)—but
that, I may presume, is merely to initiate them in his own art
of "fasting".† (Cheers and a laugh.) But of the manner in
which his loving subjects cherish them, I can speak more
distinctly. They, when they can, just kill them for kindness.

---

* His bust was, for a time, presented to the spectators with this inscription.
  And the motto contained not the first disappointed prophecy of Daniel
  and his Belfast friends.
† See his proclamation of his fasting achievements, in his Dublin speech, in
  which he declined Dr. Cooke's challenge. Yes; Daniel *says* he *fasts*—and he
  has great need of it.

(Hear, hear.) I recollect once, in an argument on establishments of religion, I was taunted with the assertion, that no established church ever produced a martyr. I immediately retorted upon my antagonist by a list of many recently produced by the Established Church in Ireland; and, when I now repeat to Mr. O'Connell the names of a Foote, a Ferguson, a Huston, or a Whitty, does not this array of the murdered ministers of Protestantism render him utterly ashamed of the assertion, that ascendant Popery has always been mild and tolerant? Yes, Mr. O'Connell; and it ought to render you more than ashamed—for, no matter by whose hands these victims fell, upon your soul rests the aboriginal guilt, for you planned and fostered the agitation from which these murders sprung—(hear)—and if ever there comes a time when your darkened eyes shall be enlightened, and your hard heart softened, the phantoms of the sheeted dead, whom your agitations consigned to early and bloody tombs, will flit before you, whether in waking or in sleeping hours, and become the means, in mercy, of leading you to repentance, or the means, in judgment, of plunging you in despair. (Hear, hear.) Or think you, Mr. O'Connell, that Protestants can ever forget, that to you they are indebted for the cherishing project of extinguishing some hundreds of their churches in Ireland? I lent my feeble aid to extinguish that most wicked proposal; and look back, with grateful satisfaction to the day when our combined efforts in Exeter Hall expunged the disgraceful record from the journals of the House of Commons. (Cheers.) I rejoice in recollecting the scathing ridicule—ridicule, never a test of truth, but an inextinguishable consumer of imposture and hypocrisy—Providence enabled me to cast on the guilty project and the enslaved projector. My proposal was, to institute a Society for the extinction of Lighthouses, and an estimate of the boundless gratitude of merchants and sailors, and of widows and orphans. Never was I apparently so unable to speak: but God strengthened me mightily: and I was one of those who were privileged to give a death-blow to your cherishing kindness, and to deliver the country from the guilt of extinguishing the light in the dark places where it was most needed. (Hear, hear, and cheers.) But I had almost forgot how, in referring to the cruel purpose of Queen Mary against the Protestants, you call *Ussher* "superficial", because he gave credit to the commission of Dr. Cole, to "lash the Heretics of Ireland".* I can pardon you, Mr. O'Connell, when you call Ussher *superficial*—and, I think, you will pardon me, when I pronounce you *profound*. (Cheers.) Ussher superficial!— Mr. O'Connell being the judge. Ussher *superficial!* The man whose historic memory embraced all time—the man whose research no record could escape—the man who had digged in the very darkest mine of learning, and returned to upper air, not merely like him that returns with precious ores, but like him that ascends with the gems that lend ornature to beauty, or splendour to crowns! Above all, the man whose mildness won every heart to cling to him, and to love him—the man whose eye of faith, and wing of devotion, looked and soared— yea, lived in Heaven—he *superficial*! I can only answer, Daniel, Daniel, you are certainly profound; "and in your lowest depth a lower still". (Cheers and laughter.)

Another of Mr. O'Connell's Repeal propositions must be understood to declare, that his efforts are not "*sectarian*", and

---

* In October, 1558, Dr. Cole was despatched by Queen Mary with a commission to Lord Deputy Fitzwalter, authorizing him to proceed in the detection and punishment of Protestants. When at Chester he shewed her commission to the Mayor, at the Blue Posts Inn, kept by Elizabeth Edmonds. She, having Protestant relatives in Dublin, watched her opportunity, took the box out of the Doctor's cloak pocket, and substituted, for the Commission, a parcel of a similar size. Arrived at Dublin, Dr. Cole waited on the Council, and produced his box. When lo! Instead of a commission, out came a pack of cards, with the emblematic *knave of clubs* uppermost. Dr. Cole was astounded; but the Lord Deputy facetiously observed—"Let us, then, have a new commission; and, in the mean time, we will shuffle the cards." Dr. Cole returned, and obtained his commission; but, before it could be executed, the wretched Queen was called to her account. Leland seems to throw doubt upon this account; but there appears no ground to question its accuracy, beyond the word of that "*profound*" historian, O'Connell, and he is believed to have a "hereditary" antipathy to "THE KNAVE OF CLUBS".

that a man without "*toleration*" cannot be a Christian. Now, this last assertion is a point upon which I shake hands with Mr. O'Connell. (Cheers and laughter.) But, if so, Mr. O'Connell, what will become of the Pope? (Hear, hear.) Gregory XVI (I am scarcely sure of the name, but I pledge myself to the fact),* in his famous Encyclical Letter, denounces liberty of conscience "*a most pestilential error*", and liberty of the press, as "*never to be sufficiently execrated*".[91] Now, is not your Pope infallible?—or so you affirm; and had he power according to his will, where were human liberty, if conscience were fettered, and the press annihilated? (Loud cries of "Hear, hear.) Ah! Perchance under that happy *regime* the veracious *Vindicator* that built the "immense Pavilion"—that beautiful "house that Jack built"—(cheers)—might find it necessary to look more narrowly to his words, else a missive from Rome might furnish a new "distribution" to his types, and a new employment for his blackball. (Cheers and laughter.) Daniel, if you be a judge, the Pope's no Christian—(cheers)—and I will pay you an annual rent, the longest day I live, if you will go to Rome and tell him so. (Cheers.) And I really think you should go, and I'll tell you why. Rome is a good place for the study of painting; and, as you have lately turned portrait-painter, and have exhibited great precocity of genius for the art, I think a little Roman finish would render you a Parliamentary Vandyke. (Cheers and laughter.) I have myself lately had the honour of your pencil, and with the true dignity of a Milesian gentleman you have drawn me as "a pale-faced, bland-looking, cunning-eyed cleric—with a countenance in which there is very little worth borrowing". Well, believe me, Daniel, I'm glad of that last touch of your pencil, for it's little you would leave me that was at all worthy your "appropriation". (Roars of laughter.) You paint me "pale-faced"; I am glad you didn't draw me "white-livered". (Cheers.) No,

---

* Dr. Cooke was right, both in name and fact. The Belfast Priests—at least, their press—have denied the existence of such a letter. They may just as well deny their own; and perhaps they will: and if they do, who can prove it?

that I suspect is too much your own colour—(cheers and laughter)—a tinge in which you have greatly improved since your late jaunt to Belfast. (Loud cheers.) Daniel, I have such a pale face as God was pleased to give me—but thanks be to Him, it has never yet had cause to blush for my saying behind any man's back, what I dared not utter to his face. (tremendous cheering.) But to relieve this *tedium*, I shall tell you a story of Mr. O'Connell's mild and tolerant Queen Mary. (Hear, hear.) It was in her inauspicious reign that Calais was taken by France—and when she was dying, she said to her attendants, "If you open me when I am dead, you will find 'Calais' written on my heart". Now, while I heartily wish Daniel O'Connell long life and good health, yet Daniel at last will die; and, when entombed in the appropriate retreat of "Bully's-acre",* Michael Cullen,† if yet you tread the purlieus of Channel-row, you owe me an ancient kindness—and, when "clothed are the skies in black, and the winds howl horrible round the mansions of the dead", grub up the body of the defunct Daniel, and bear it for my sake, gently, to the Richmond theatre of Anatomy; and let some curious hand, with sharpened scalpel and hooked tenaculum, carefully dissect Daniel's larger eye—and indelible upon the retina, you will, perhaps, discover the image of a "pale-faced" man—(loud cheers)—whose picture follows the charlatan, like the shadowy visions of the hypochondriac, pointing with steady finger to an unopen file of the *Ulster Times*, and repeating in the ear of a convulsive conscience—"where, Daniel, where?" (Loud cheers.) My lord, I owe to your lordship, and to this vast and splendid assembly, a most profound apology, not merely for the length of this address, but for the pervading *egotism* with which it has been so largely occupied. (No, no—

---

* The burial-place of Dublin beggars, and formerly the chief resort of the unhappy race of "body-snatchers".

† A once well known attendant of that valuable School of Anatomy and Surgery; and, perhaps, the only member of his profession who ever raised a body, and with the aid of the mob, in open day light. This fact, however, he actually achieved.

go on.) And yet, I may not conclude, without a few words
more relative to myself, and explanatory of the too prominent
position, I felt it my duty to take. (No, you are in the right
position.) My lords, I am thankful for the kindness that judges
so, but I am no less sensible, that this kindness is partiality.
Now, my lord, I will say, that in common with many, I have
long been an attentive student of Mr. Daniel O'Connell. He
is a mighty man. But long before he entered Parliament, as
the wooden horse entered the walls of Troy, Mr. O'Connell
had laid open to me the secret powers upon which he
depended. The one I learned when in the streets of Ennis, he
knelt to a Popish Bishop[92]—the other, when he registered a
vow against two English Baronets—which, if he don't
remember, I have not forgot. The first I did not dread, for
Babylon is doomed to fall—the second I did not fear, simply
because God had shown it me; and I therefore have waited
till opportunity and duty should meet in leading me to the
encounter, in which, I verily believe, not I, but God and truth
would utterly cast him down—(cheers)—I believed in the
fact—I, in some degree, mistook the means. Mr. O'Connell
has been unscathed by me—but he has fallen an intellectual
and political suicide by the blow of his own hand. (Loud
cheering, and cries of "Hear.") The moment, my lord, his
portentous visit was threatened against Belfast; my duty on
the occasion, became matter of solemn prayer to Him who
can employ the "weak to confound the mighty". And thought
he world was pleased to conjecture, my secret purpose rested
in my own breast breathed to none but God; and it was not
till I saw my duty in what I judged the leadings of Providence,
terminating with the expressed opinions of men of God—that
I finally determined to meet the giant, who has so often and
so loudly defied the armies of the living God. (Cheers.) I did
believe, my lord, whatever others may say, I did believe that,
in 1841, I saw the fearful shadow of 1641. (Hear, hear, hear.)
I saw the circumstances merely so far changed, that, in 1641,
physical force marched in the van of rebellion and massacre;
but, in 1841, intellect and eloquence, enlisting argument,

prejudice, and passion, advanced in the front, to mark and to cover the array of physical force that fearfully gathered behind. (Hear, hear, hear.) I judged the spirit of the terrible movement to lie in pretended appeals to reason, interests, and facts. And I said, in my heart, shall we see the "sword coming", and will no man give warning, and "grapple with it, ere it come too nigh?" (Hear, hear, hear.) I did believe, my lord, and I do still believe, that this mighty conspiracy may, under Providence, be met and averted—therefore did I, all unworthily, take one step in advance to meet it. My fellow-Protestants will pardon my presumption, for if I know my own heart, it proceeded not from vanity, but from love. (Hear, hear and loud cheering.) I did not miscalculate when I counted on Mr. O'Connell's abuse—nay, as God is my judge, I did know I was "taking my life in my hand"; but I did also calculate, that my life was in the hands of Him that gave it, and that, if one hair of my head was molested, or one drop of my blood spilled—were my children left fatherless, and my wife a widow—yet would the event be overruled to unite still more closely all true Protestant hearts—and that the loss of one humble and worthless man might still be the salvation of our Churches and our country. (Loud and vehement cheering.) I may not, my lord, overlook the newspaper statement, that Mr. O'Connell has challenged me to twenty-six hours of a discussion upon civil and religious liberty.* I take him at his word. (Tremendous cheers.) The time, the place I leave to himself; but London and Exeter-hall I take to be the best— (loud cries of "Hear, hear, hear")—and I claim but one condition—the issue of half the tickets. (Cheers.) And never, by the blessing of God, since truth tore the cloak off hypocricy,

---

* It is a fact, since vouched to us by an eye and ear witness, that Mr. O'Connell's challenge ran in these words:—"As to Dr. Cooke,—I challenge him!—I challenge him!!—I challenge him!!!—(*Then a considerable stutter during which he applied his handkerchief to his mouth, and seemed deeply puzzled to find out what to say—when at last he brought out*)—to a discussion of civil and religious liberty, for twenty-six hour if he dare!!!" Dr. Cooke has dared. Has Mr. O'Connell redeemed his pledge? Will he? *Nous verrons*—but we shall see.

did man stand for such a stripping as awaits you, Daniel
O'Connell. (Vehement cheering.) This is no braggadocio, my
lord, it is the certainty of the aid of Heaven against the doomed
apostacy; it is the consciousness of the truth that lies enshrined
within our bibles and our Churches—(hear, hear, hear and
loud cheers)—it is the knowledge of the falsehoods and the
tyrannies that lie unchained in the tomes of the Vatican, from
which we are preserved in our Protestant liberties, only as we
are preserved in the presence of the foreigner of the jungle, as
he paces before us, and measures us, behind the iron of his
cage, and is tame and inoffensive—because he is imprisoned.
(Vehement cheering.) Oh! for these vaunted twenty-six hours,
in which his deluded followers here are beginning to boast—
that Heaven might, in mercy, permit me to exhibit O'Connell
to the country, on "a fair stage, and no favour"—where he
must speak not to his favourite mob, but to an audience of
educated men; where assertion must be supported by proof,
and facts must be substituted for fancy. There should I exhibit
him sitting this moment in the councils of the land, as the
transformed hero of Milton sat at the ear of the sleeping Eve.
So sits he whispering his dreams of Repeal into the ear of the
people, and infusing the poison of his Popery into the vitals of
the constitution. But as the spear of *Ithuriel* compelled the foul
and ugly toad to start into his native satanic form,[93] so shall
the history of the past, and the condition f the present compel
O'Connell to appear in form, what he is in heart—the genius
of knavery, the apostle of rebellion. (Hear, hear, hear and
overwhelming cheers.)

There is another gentleman who has figured here, and
whom I should have left "alone in his glory"; but that, like
other cast-off habiliments, "being of no other use to the
owner", Mr. O'Connell has been pleased to make him a
present to Belfast. This gentleman rejoices in the name of Mr.
Dillon Brown. (Cheers and laughter.) I know Daniel can well
part with him—let him, however, first take the opinion of
some folks about the lobby. (A knowing laugh from the M.P.'s)
Mr. O'Connell comprehends me. Yes, and let Mr. O'Connell

send him to one of David Stow's admirable training-schools, in Glasgow, where they teach something more than letter and manners, where—Mr. O'Connell understands me—they go one step higher, and then we shall consider of accepting or rejecting his present. (Loud cheers.)[94]

There is another aspirant for reforming fame, whom it were the grossest injustice to pass over unnoticed. Mr. Henry Grattan, who cut so great a figure in the "great" demonstration lately enacted in Dublin. (Hear, hear, hear.) For one act, on that solemn occasion, one shadow he was pleased to furnish of the march of "coming events", I honour him far above all competitors for "liberal" fame. Yes, he seized with emblematic hand, the list of requisitionists to this vast meeting—and as tenderly and as tolerantly as if he had been a born child of Queen Mary, did he trample and stamp on it amidst the cheers of the "great" meeting. (Loud cheers.) "The wish was father, Harry, to that thought"; and when, with iron heel, you trampled on the names of our noblemen, clergy, and gentry, 'twas not upon the *names*, but on their *necks*, you longed to tread. (Hear, hear.)—And who are you, Henry Grattan!—that thus would tread upon the noblest names in all the land? Thou feeble son of a mighty sire!—Thou unworthy bearer of an illustrious name! Think you the men of Ulster worms, that thus you trample them? (Cheers.) If so, we will turn! (Continued cheers.) Not in aggression, but in self-defence; and instead of our bowing to Dagon, Dagon shall bow to us, as sure as he fell prostrate and broken on the threshold of his own temple.— (Vehement cheers.) Yes, who are you, Henry Grattan, that thus insultingly dares trample us? (Cheers.) Are you not the Hotspur of Coldblow-lane?* (Hear, hear, and loud laughter.) Are you not the enfranchiser of cabbage-stalks? (Cheers.) Are you not the magical converter of gooseberry-bushes into green-

---

* A famous—rather, infamous—scene of the manufacture of fictitious votes that quite equalled, or, rather, surpassed any thing in *Ovid's Metamorphoses*. Ovid turned men into bushes and birds; but Coldblow-lane turned bushes and cabbages into freemen and voters.

grocers? (Loud cheers, and laughter.) I do see your image as
you stand behind O'Connell, with a begging placard bearing
the following inscription, which I furnish you from a new
edition of a well-known poem, at once a memorial of your
Coldblow achievements of old, and the modern act of
emblematic kindness which your heel—your heart—inflicted
upon our names. (Cheers.)

> "Pity, *kind gentlemen*, friends of *humanity!*
> COLD BLOWS my courage, but heat's coming on.
> See how I trample in "*liberal charity*"—
> A shout and a penny—and I will begone."[95]

(Cheers and great laughter.) And, following Henry Grattan,
I must also begone. (No, no—go on.) I feel I cannot—I feel I
need not.—Before me, all unopened, lie those piles of documents, with which I had hoped to overwhelm our Repeal
antagonist. (Cheers.) They will keep, however, for Exeter
Hall. And whosoever desires to see the Repeal question set at
rest, needs only to read my friend Mr. Tennent's Anti-Repeal
speech, lately republished in the columns of the *Ulster Times.*
But I dare not move my resolutions without saying one word
about it. I ask, then, the great Repealer, "Pray, Mr. O'Connell,
did you ever see Belfast?" (A laugh.) You say you did not—
well, that was a pity. (Laughter.) Had you but requested me
to your *Cicerone*, there's not a brother lion in the town to
which I had not introduced you. (Loud laughter.) I beg
pardon—there is one place to which even my influence would
not have obtained the *entree*—you were emphatically *tabooed*
from the walls of the *Royal College*. (Loud cheers.) You have
uttered one statement about our students, partly true and
partly false, and I love to set your blunders to rights. (A
laugh.) You have said, there is no hope of the Presbyterian
youth of Ulster so long as "that loathsome Theologue, Doctor
Cooke, has influence over them." (Loud cheers.) Now, that
there is no hope of their becoming Repealers is, happily, one
truth; but that I have influence over them is utterly untrue.

No, Daniel, I will tell what and who has influence over them. The Bible and its principles have influence over them. (Hear, and Cheers.) The spirit that descended upon Knox, who "never feared the face of clay", has influence over them. (Loud cheers and Kentish fire.) His mantle has fallen around their manly shoulders, and they will never exchange it for the frieze coat of Repeal. (Vehement cheering.) Yes, had you approached the College, well and firmly was the determination taken to close the gates, and to defend it from pollution. (Loud cheers, in which the students present took a considerable part.) The anniversary of your visit would, to future generations, have produced a holiday; and the shutting of the gates of Derry against James would have stood, not in coequal, but in instructive contrast, to the shutting of the gates of our College against a similar intruder. (Vehement and prolonged cheers, Kentish fire, and "No Surrender".) My lord, I beg leave to move—

"That, looking to the numerous and solid advantages which have accrued to Ireland in particular, and the empire at large, from the effects of the legislative Union between the two countries, we have seen, with indignation and alarm, the recently renewed efforts to effect its Repeal."

And with barely one argument shall I support my motion— look at the town of Belfast. When I was myself a youth I remember it almost a village. But what a glorious sight does it now present—the masted grove within our harbour— (cheers)—our mighty warehouses teeming with the wealth of every climate—(cheers)—our giant manufactories lifting themselves on every side—(cheers)—our streets marching on, as it were, with such rapidity, that an absence of a few weeks makes us strangers in the outskirts of our own town. (Cheers.) And all this we owe to the Union. (Loud cheers.) No, not all—for throned above our fair town, and looking serenely from our mountain's brow, I behold the genii of Protestantism and Liberty, sitting inseparable in their power, while the genius of Industry which nightly reclines at their feet, starts with every morning in renovated might, and puts forth his energies, and showers down his blessings, on the fair and smiling lands of a Chichester, a Conway, or a Hill. (Vehement cheers.) Yes, Mr. O'Connell, we will guard the Union as we will guard our liberties, and advance and secure the prosperity of our country. Were you to succeed in effecting Repeal, we know our liberties were strangled for ever. (Tremendous cheers.) Were the agitator once elevated on the shoulders of ascendant Popery, the "death's head and cross bones" would be the emblems of his "great seal"—(cheers)—and refractory Reformers themselves would soon be handed over to the "tender mercies" of "de boys". (Cheers and laughter.) If, then, there be any Repealer in this assembly, as I suspect there is not—(renewed laughter)—but if such an one there be—I ask him, as I asked O'Connell—"Have *you* ever seen Belfast?" He answers, "I have seen it." Well, before the Union, Belfast was a village; now it ranks with the cities of the earth. Before the Union it had a few coasting craft, and a few American and West Indian ships—and that open bay, which now embraces the navies of every land, was but a desert of useless water. (Hear, hear, hear.) The centre of our town was studded with thatched cottages, where now stands one of the fairest temples to the genius of industry and commerce. (Hear, hear, hear and vehement cheers.)—Our merchants, then unknown, are now welcomed in every land, and the energies of their industry, and the profits of their toils, are only surpassed by their honourable character—(loud and vehement cheers)—the basis of their prosperity, and the charter of its continuance. (Continued cheering.) In one word more I have done with my argument—Look at Belfast, and be a Repealer—if you can.

(The Rev. Doctor then retired amid the most enthusiastic cheering, and loud shouts of approbation, which continued for several minutes.)

R. B BLAKISTON, Esq., of Orangefield, in rising to second the motion said, that, when he looked upon the brilliant and influential assembly which now met his eye, he could not but congratulate the meeting on the display of Conservative strength they had made, and on the failure of the Repeal pantomime, which had been attempted to be enacted, in this

town, a day or two ago. (Cheers and laughter.) The Agitator
had attempted to diffuse his doctrines here; but they had found
no echo,—or, if they had, it was like the celebrated Killarney
echo, which when the words "Repeal of the Union" were
uttered, repeated only the last one, "Union". (A laugh.) In this
quarter of the world, he thought they had sufficient proof,
that the Agitator's followers were few and uninfluential; so
much so, indeed, that an old saying in the South would not
be inapplicable to the party—"What a fine *tail* our cat has got!"
It recalled to his recollection a species of animal which he
used to see in England during his earlier days—eight of them
harnessed, at once, to a cumbrous waggon, and they without
a bit of tail at all. After a few other remarks Mr. Blackiston
sat down amid rapturous shouts of applause.

The resolution was then proposed from the Chair, and
passed unanimously.

The Rev. H.S CUMMING, of Ballymena, who was warmly
received, on rising, with a hearty response from the body of
the house, to a call for a "cheer for the Conservative ladies
present", proposed the next resolution:

"That we heartily rejoice in the deep and universal impression
that pervades not only all denominations of Protestants in the
kingdom, but a respectable proportion of the Roman Catholic population, that Repeal is but another name for Rebellion, and a flimsy
cover for the contemplated dismemberment of the empire; and that
we are determined, most cordially, to co-operate in frustrating the mischievous and destructive project, and for preserving that settlement of
property which Repeal both threatens and endangers, and that civil
and religious liberty which it would ultimately and infallibly destroy."

He proceeded to say, that he would not only act in
accordance with his own wishes, but would best consult the
interest and convenience of the immense assembly before him,
by merely reading the resolution which had been entrusted to
him. A prominent principle in the resolution was, that Repeal
was but another name for Rebellion. He was anxious not to
be misunderstood on this point. He had ever thought that an

opponent was entitled to courtesy, and that we ought not to attribute motives to any man which he refused to admit. He might not have understood the meaning of the committee in adopting this language, but he took it to be that there was a large body of men in Ireland determined, by the use of every justifiable means, to resist the Repeal of the Union; and if there were, unhappily, another portion of the inhabitants resolved to effect it, such a state of things might eventuate in so deplorable a catastrophe, that upon the latter class must rest the blame and the guilt. This he felt bound to say, to prevent misapprehension. (Great applause.)

REV. DANIEL M'AFEE rose amid loud cheers. He said he felt, at that late hour of the day, it would not be proper in him to trespass on the attention of the meeting. He did come prepared to say something with reference to Mr. O'Connell. What he was prepared to say, he was fully prepared to demonstrate by documents he had brought with him for the purpose. He would, perhaps, take another medium of laying them before the public. The Rev. gentleman concluded by seconding the resolution. (Tremendous cheers.)

SIR A. BROOKE, M.P. for Fermanagh, rose to propose the next resolution and said, he felt, at that hour of the day, no apology was necessary for not delaying the meeting with any observations of his, particularly after the splendid specimens of oratory and argument which had been advanced, and which they had heard and listened to with such unbounded pleasure and approbation. After what had been said by Dr. Cooke, that indomitable champion of civil and religious liberty, it would be impossible for him to add one single argument in addition to what had been already advanced to-day. He was connected with one of the most loyal counties in Ireland, and he would feel himself disgraced if he had not come forward that day to countenance, by his presence and his voice, the objects for which they had been called together. With the exception of the counties of Down and Antrim, he believed there was no other county exceeded Fermanagh in the array of Conservative gentry which it could bring forward.

The honourable baronet then alluded to Lord Ebrington's denouncing the Repeal agitation, and said, he could have prevented it, but he dare not—(hear)—as he was well aware that the Government was supported by the agitator. His lordship had left the country and had gone to England, and the consequence was, that the Repeal agitation had progressed and succeeded to a very great extent in the South of Ireland. He would not detain them any longer, as the day was so far gone; he would, however, congratulate them, with all his heart, on the very splendid display they had made that day. The honourable baronet sat down amidst loud and protracted cheers, after moving the following resolution—

"That we have seen, with sincere satisfaction, a recent expression by the Lord Lieutenant, of his official disapprobation of this renewed agitation of Repeal, and that we deeply regret that any circumstances should have prevented his Excellency from following up that declaration by active measures, similar to the vigorous steps taken to suppress a like treasonable agitation in 1833".

HENRY RICHARDSON, Esq., of Somerset, briefly expressed his concurrence in the objects of the meeting, and seconded the motion, which was unanimously carried.

CHAS. FOX, Esq. late M.P. for Longford, with a few spirited observations, moved the following resolution:—

"That we feel it incumbent upon ourselves, to come forward, thus collectively, in order to assure her Majesty the Queen, of our loyal attachment to he throne and person, our resolution to aid her in preserving, inviolate, the integrity of her dominions, as established by the Act of Union, in 1800, and that an humble address, embodying these sentiments of our devotion and fidelity, be adopted by the meeting, and presented to her Majesty".

SIR HERVEY BRUCE rose and said, after the eloquent speeches they had heard that day, he would not detain them by offering any observations on the resolution. He felt happy to see so many gentlemen there from the county Derry.

(Hear, hear.) He was sure the gentry of the county would always sustain the high character they had so long and so creditably borne. (Cheers.) He would say no more than that he felt great pleasure in seconding the resolution. (Cheers.)

MR. LINDSAY, High Sheriff of Tyrone, proposed the 12th resolution, and said, he felt highly flattered in being called upon to propose the resolution which had been entrusted to his care; but at that late hour of the evening he would not trespass upon the time of the meeting, after the many able and eloquent speeches they had just heard. He could only say, that he most cordially concurred in the objects for which they had been assembled—objects of such vital importance, not only to this country, but to the empire at large. He regretted exceedingly that Lord Claud Hamilton and Mr. Corry were, owing to circumstances, prevented from attending that meeting; but he could assure them that their hearts were with it, and although they were not present with them there that day, they would, at all events, be at their post next week, watching over their interests in the House of Commons. (Hear and cheers.) For himself he could only thank them most sincerely for the kind attention with which they had listened to him, and begged to assure them that he would at all times and on all occasions be happy to join his brother Conservatives in any thing that might tend to the welfare and prosperity of Ulster; and he could assure them with perfect confidence, that his brethren of the Conservative county of Tyrone would be as ready and zealous as himself in doing everything in their power for the good cause. (Cheers.) He would now read over the resolution, and he was sure it could not be better entrusted, than to the care of the noble lord who so ably and efficiently presided over that meeting, and the noblemen and members of the lower house who have signed the requisition by which this great and noble meeting had been convened. (Hear, hear.)

"That the address now read be adopted, and that the Most honourable the Marquis of Downshire, the other Noble Lords, Members of her Majesty's most honourable Privy Council, and Members of the House of Commons, who have signed the requisition for this meeting, be requested, at their earliest convenience, to present the same to her Majesty."

This resolution, after having been seconded by JOHN ROWAN, Esq., Merville, was put and passed.

The DEAN of Ross proposed a vote of thanks to Dr. Cooke, and spoke in the highest terms of that Rev. gentleman. He expressed in the course of his address, his sanction of the "banns of matrimony" proclaimed at Hillsborough by the Rev. Doctor, in 1834.

Lord ADAM LOFTUS seconded the resolution. Passed *nem. con.*

Captain JONES, M.P., moved, that Lord Downshire do leave the chair.

The motion was seconded by SIR R. BATESON, M.P., which passed unanimously.

THOMAS GREGG, Esq., was then moved to the Chair; thanks were then voted to the former Chairman, by Colonel Gage, seconded by John M'Neile, Esq., and passed.

The Marquis of DOWNSHIRE in returning thanks, said, he had no doubt whatever, but that, with the blessing of Providence, so influential a meeting as that was would be productive of the best results. (Hear, hear.) The sentiments expressed at that meeting,— comprising, as it did, the rank, wealth, and respectability of Ulster, would, he was certain, find their way to the foot of the throne. (Loud cheers.) Before dispersing, he would just say to the Protestants of Ireland, continue to act as they had been doing hitherto—(Hear, hear)—consider it your duty never to bring disgrace on the Protestant name. (Cries of hear, hear and cheers.) They had that day exercised a constitutional privilege, in expressing their views with a reference to Lord Stanley's Registration Bill, and the question of the Repeal of the Union, and he had no doubt that those sentiments, when circulate through the length and breadth of the land, would have their due weight. (Cheers.) The noble marquis concluded by thanking the meeting for the high honour they had that day conferred on him. (Tremendous cheers.)

At the conclusion of these observations, this immense assemblage separated.

THE DINNER.

ON Friday, 22d January, at six o'clock, a grand entertainment was given in the Music Hall, to James Emerson Tennent and George Orr Dunbar, Esqrs., Members of Parliament for the borough of Belfast, by a number of their constituents. The party in the Hall itself amounted to between 400 and 500 individuals of the highest respectability. Another party, for whom accommodation could not be afforded in the principal room, dined in a lower apartment, and afterwards joined the assembly. Robert F. Gordon, Esq., presided on the occasion.

REV. THOMAS WALKER asked blessing.

THE CHAIRMAN then rose and gave, "the Queen",—"The Princess Royal",— "Prince Albert"; each of which was received with enthusiastic cheers.

THE CHAIRMAN again arose and said, that the next toast he had to propose was, "Her Majesty the Queen Dowager"; and he was sure it was unnecessary to accompany it with one single observation. (Tremendous cheering and several rounds of the Kentish fire.)[96]

Tune—"Hark, the purple stream!"

"The Duke of Wellington, the greatest captain and the first statesman of his age." (Great applause, and the Kentish fire, amid cries of "The Duke, the Duke—long life to him".)

"Sir Robert Peel and the Conservative members of the House of Commons".—(Immense cheering, one cheer more, and the Kentish fire.)

THE CHAIRMAN arose, after the cheering had subsided, and said, the next toast he had to propose was the toast of the evening. This was the health of their Representatives. (Tremendous cheering, waving of handkerchiefs, &c.) "I cannot", continued the Chairman, "but express the high honour I feel at being asked to preside over this assemblage. My heart is warm in the cause of Conservatism, and in its success I have the greatest happiness. (Great cheering.) The toast I have proposed requires little to be said to it. Your representatives you have known in their infancy, and in their public conduct, you know besides what they deserve at our hands. (Continued cheering.) I only ask you to look at the great divisions in the House of Commons, and can there be shewn one instance in which either of them were absent? (Cheers.) And in questions affecting our own town, late and early they were ever at their posts. (Hear, hear.) For some months every session I have found it necessary to be in London; and as I observed the conduct of our representatives, being engaged in the mornings in committee, and in the evenings attending to the debate, I must confess that I felt it a happy privilege to be one of those who returned them to Parliament. (Applause.) But I am convinced that at the present, their services are but partly appreciated by us. (Enthusiastic cheering.) It is when ages unborn will see the position in which we have been placed, that those will be rightly honoured who have taken a lead in the service of our country. (Loud cheers.) When this generation has passed away, our descendants will observe the nature of that bondage, under which this nation has unhappily laboured for years, and of that thraldom of Popish tyranny from which we are striving to free it. (Great applause.) Look to our happy homes and green vallies, as fruits of our labours. (Hear, hear.) The smiling hills around us are monuments to the honour of Conservatives; and, in the words of the poet:—

> "When Kings in dusty darkness lie,
> Have left a nameless pyramid:
> Those heroes, though the general doom
> Have swept the mighty from their tomb—
> A mightier monument command
> The mountain of their native land."—(Cheers.)

MR. EMERSON TENNENT, before returning thanks to the meeting, could not resist the impulse to fully acknowledge his obligations for the terms in which the Chairman had introduced that toast, in a speech characterized at once by the feeling of a gentleman—the taste of the scholar—and the sentiments of the patriot. (Hcar, and loud cheers.) It would be

either affectation or insensibility in any man to say, that his
heart did not swell with gratitude and pride, under the honours
which had that evening been conferred upon him. It was a
common thing in the small talk of friends to condole with
Members of Parliament upon the labours of their situation,
and to speak as the Chairman had done of their late hours,
and to days of confinement in committee-rooms, and public
offices. The office of a member of Parliament was, it was quite
true, when fairly and faithfully discharged, one of labour and
of toil: but one evening such as they were now enjoying,—one
shout of approbation, such as he had just heard, more than
repaid him for all his years of exertion, and anxiety. (Cheers.)
One of the toasts at the repeal dinner the other day was, "two
honest and working members for Belfast". He was certain there
was not a man in that room now present who would not unite
even with the Repealers in drinking that toast; and when Mr.
O'Connell came to redeem his promise, and sent the Repealers
a present of a representative,—whether he sent them a Mr.
Raphael or a Mr. Dillon Brown,—he would soon be taught
that no member but a "working" one need show himself as a
candidate for Belfast. (Cheers.) In the next session of
Parliament, as in the last eight or ten, Ireland seemed again
likely to be the battlefield of the contending parties; and Lord
Stanley's Bill and the Repeal agitation would in all proba-
bility, inherit the attention lately bestowed upon Tithe Bills
and Municipal Corporations. (Cheers.) On the former, he
(Mr. E. T.) would be found, as heretofore, at his post in every
skirmish, and prepared to defend justice, and the honest
elector, against perjury and the usurper of his rights. (Cheers.)
Whilst on the latter, if there be one representative in the
House of Commons whom duty, inclination, and conviction,
would more than another impel to resist the Repeal of the
Union to the death, it must be the members for Belfast. If any
man doubts the benefits of the Union to Ireland, let him only
land at the quays of Belfast, and drive through every winding
of its manufacturing streets; and if he fails to discover there
the fruits of the Union, it must be from the same cause that

prevented the Irishman from discovering the wood—the thickness of the trees. (Laughter and cheering.) No human being of ordinary intelligence can doubt the blessings that Ulster has derived from the Union, who sees the forest of masts that are moving in her harbour, or counts the multitudes of her factory chimneys that rise in every direction, like the lofty columns of some still unfinished "Temple of Industry". (Loud cheers.) It is well known to every manufacturer that the grand secret of producing cheaply and successfully is not dependent on a mere average of wages, or in the price of fuel, or in the first cost of a machine; but upon the extent of his market, and upon the quantity which he calculates on supplying. With hand labour the case is different, but in a contest with machinery, the man who can dispose of 500 pieces of goods whatever be the reasonable difference against him in wages or fuel, can as certainly calculate on underselling the man who can dispose of but 50, as he is sure to be in time undersold himself by the one who can sell 5,000. Now, one glorious advantage which Ireland has derived from the Union is, that it has thrown open the almost limitless markets which England supplies, to be stocked by the industry of Ireland. (Loud cheers.) But that is an advantage she could only enjoy so long as she is an integral part of her own dominions. Undo the Union, and England would have no more interest in identifying Irish manufactures with her own, than she would those of any rival on the continent. (Hear, hear.) But then we shall be told by the red-hot patriots, that Irish manufactures would still make their way into their accustomed markets, as they do now, upon their inherent merits. No such thing. They would be kept out by the same tariffs and duties that exclude those of other countries, unless specially admitted by commercial treaties. But no petty nation can ever make a treaty on the same advantageous terms as a great and powerful one. Treaties are reciprocal—the party who *asks* advantages must have some to *offer* in exchange for them; and what has Ireland to offer, in coming for instance, to ask admission for her linen yarns to France? (Hear.) England, when it was talked of lately, in

France to impose an almost prohibitory duty upon them, holds her shield over Ireland, and threatens retaliation upon French produce. What retaliation could Ireland threaten, if the Union was repealed, and the shield of English interference withdrawn? None. She must have unresistingly submitted to her fate. (Cheers.) He (Mr. Emerson Tennent), had lately been visiting a country, which Mr. O'Connell, in his speech on Monday last, had instanced as one in which the patriots had "*Repealed the Union*". He alluded to Belgium, which separated itself from Holland in 1830. But Mr. O'Connell could not have selected a more unhappy illustration.—(Hear, hear.) Belgium was a manufacturing country; and, before the revolution it had in Holland and her colonies no less than fifteen millions of consumers. It was in vain, when the revolt was threatened, that the manufacturers of Ghent and the shipowners of Antwerp protested against it as the destruction of their trade; the priests and the patriots could not understand such arguments,—they proceeded; they repealed the Union with a vengeance; and, in one day, they reduced the customers of Belgium from fifteen millions to something less than *four!* The consequence is that her machinery may produce, but she has no markets in which to sell; and her shipping is destroyed, because she has no colonies to which to carry her produce. (Hear.) She has, for the last few years been turning in despair to every quarter for relief, seeking treaties of commerce which no country will grant, because Belgium can only take advantage from them, but can offer none in return. (Hear, hear.) Her population are manufacturers without markets, and merchants without commerce. France shuns her, Germany refuses every effort at alliance with her; and, at the present moment, nine-tenths of her population are anxious for a restoration of the Union, and a return of the blessings they enjoyed under the protection of Holland. So much for Mr. O'Connell's example for Ireland—so much for the prospects of Irish manufactures under a Repeal of the Union! (Loud cheers.) Now look to the prospect of Irish *agriculture*! At the present moment England consumes of our corn and cattle, our wheat and oatmeal, what amounts year by year to the enormous sum of between 10 and 12 millions sterling. (Cheers.) Were we a separate and independent nation, England might then just as well take this amount from the continent as from us; and if she could get it on more advantageous terms she would do so in one instant. (Loud cheers.) This must be one of the calculations of Mr. O'Connell. He must know in his heart that the manifold advantages which the Irish farmer derives from the English consumers would not survive the Union an hour—(hear, hear)—and hence in order to disembarrass himself of that argument against him, he wishes now to abolish them by anticipation. This can be the only object he has in view in opposing the corn laws in the House of Commons; and he (Mr. E. T.) defied the ingenuity of man to reconcile the effects of the Repeal of the Union with the continuance, for a single day, of that preference which the Irish produce now enjoys in the markets of England, all the blessings of which would expire with the first breath of separation. (Hear, hear, hear and loud cheers.) The most formidable feature in the present agitation for Repeal, is the negative indifference of the Government, who have as yet taken no one positive step to discourage or check it. (Cheers.) Their situation is, it is true, one of extreme embarrassment, to men who feel themselves indebted for their power to an unlawful source. (Hear, hear.) To interpose vigorously and effectually for its suppression, to declare authoritatively the fomentation of Repeal to be treason to the Queen's authority, and to punish it as such, would be at once to sever all connexion between them and Mr. O'Connell, and to convert his support in the House of Commons into an instant opposition, the effect of which would be fatal to their official existence. (Hear, hear, and long cheers.) Some years ago a trial took place in the South of Ireland, the issue of which created some astonishment at the time. A man was tried for murder, under the most clear and convincing circumstances, the crime was almost admitted, and the evidence was irresistible, so much so, that it was with surprise that the Court found that the jury wished to retire at

all to consider of their verdict; but they were still amazed
when they found that they could not agree upon it owing to
the obstinate resistance of one man, who held out against the
other eleven; and ultimately at the close of the Assizes, the
jury was discharged, and the proceedings quashed. Some time
after, this tenacious juror was met by an intimate friend, who
could take the liberty of asking him in confidence, "how he
could possibly, in the face of such evidence, entertain a doubt
of the prisoner's guilt?" "Doubt", said he, "I had none". "And
how, then", continued his friend, "could you hesitate to unite
in a verdict of guilty?" "*Ah, then*", cried he, with incredulous
impatience, "*and would you have me go hurry the last life in my
lease!*" (Cheers and laughter.) He (Mr. E.T.) could not but feel
that Lord Melbourne and Lord John Russell stood precisely
in the situation of this politic juror; they might condemn the
malefactor, it is true, again and again, even upon his own
confession, but the lease of Downing street will expire with
the verdict. (Cheers.) But there is also another equally galling
source of embarrassment—the pain and shame of turning
round to punish as traitorous criminals, the very men upon
whom, for the last four years, they have been showering the
selected favours and honours of the crown, with a full
knowledge of their sentiments and feelings upon Repeal. They
have already had to transport for life one convicted traitor
whom they had made a magistrate at Newport:[97] and the
country cannot forget, that it is not their fault that the Arch-
Repealer of Ireland is not at this moment a JUDGE![98] (Loud
cheers.) The present Lord Lieutenant, warned by the dilemma
in which the absurd escapades of Lord Mulgrave have
involved the Government, has wisely taken a more moderate
course in selecting the parties for Ministerial favour, and has
announced, that no professed Repealer need look for one
particle of the patronage of the Crown. But, unfortunately,
this threat can affect only one, and that a very limited section
of the Repealers. He meant the hungry cormorants of the
Irish bar, who have been looking for assistant barristerships,
and commissions of enquiry, and the charge of Crown

prosecutions; and it is a good illustration of the sincerity of the apostles of Repeal, to witness the talismanic effect which one single threat of this nature has had upon the pure spirits of the patriot bar. In the former agitation of 1833 and 1834, they were its very springs and levers—counsellor this, and counsellor that, and counsellor t'other, were the speakers at every parochial assembly; and, by means of their harangues, they stepped from the cold flags of the Four Courts, to the comfortable offices of the Attorney and Solicitors General, and even to the Bench itself. The Repeal agitation was then the high road to promotion, and the very reputation of having made an oration against England, was sufficient with Lord Mulgrave to throw open to the orator the very highest offices of the State, from the President of a Sessions-Court, to a seat at the Privy-Council. (Loud and long continued cheering.) Lord Ebrington's timely threat has operated like magic upon this patriotic class in Ireland. Not a single "counsellor", high or low, has since it ventured to open his lips at the Corn-Exchange, or to move a resolution in all Connaught. When Croesus was about to perish by the swords of his enemies, the legend tells us, that the agony of his son, who was dumb, overcame the bonds of his malady, and his voice burst forth in shouts to spare the life of his father. (Hear.) But the voice of Lord Ebrington has had a different effect upon the sons of Ireland, and amidst all the agonies of their parent, it has suddenly struck them *dumb*: and nothing but a little of the wealth of Croesus himself would induce one of these sons to open his lips in her favour.—(Great applause.) And here he (Mr. E. T.) might be excused if for one moment he pointed to the noble contrast which the Conservative section of the Irish bar exhibited, as compared with this conduct of the liberal and patriot lawyers. (Hear.) It is notorious that, with very few exceptions, the talent and learning of the Irish Bar is almost exclusively Conservative. (Hear, hear.) The Government, aware of this and conscious of the utter incapacity of the Radical and Repeal barristers to fill high legal offices as they fell vacant, spared no temptation, and would have spared no

reward, to seduce one single Conservative gentleman to join
their ranks, and release them from the scorn of filling office
after office with their own incompetent hangers-on. (Cheers.)
With *one solitary exception*—(and *that* he was sorry to say, an
eminent one)—the whole Conservative Bar had spurned the
bribe, and proved themselves—

> *True* as the dial to the sun,
> Although it be not shined upon.

Lord Mulgrave's brief reign in Ireland did in this respect a
service to the Conservative Bar, such as long years of ordinary
government could not have rendered them. *It proved their metal.*
Like gold in a crucible, they have issued bright and unspotted
from the fire; and, when it shall please Providence to remove
from us the scourge of Whig domination, their successors will
have already learned, that on the high honour and integrity
of the Irish Conservative bar, as upon its talents and its
learning, they may rely with firm and unbounded confidence.
(Loud cheers.) In like manner, Lord Ebrington has tried the
metal of the Repeal counsellors, and he (Mr. E. Tennent) was
satisfied they might with propriety wish Mr. O'Connell and
his friends any thing other than joy upon the result of the
experiment. (Laughter.) But this threat of Lord Ebrington
could effect but a circumscribed and contemptible section of
the people of Ireland. It had kept the "counsellors" out of the
arena, but it could not influence the priests, or the exciteable
peasantry—and hence it was, that the agitation was now
sweeping like a pestilence through the land, and invading like
a cholera, even the hitherto peaceful and contented province
of the north. He (Mr. E. Tennent) saw around him, however,
in that assembly, and in the meeting of yesterday, a "board of
health" such as would be vigilant for the safety of the public;
and like the awful visitation of 1832, he ventured to predict,
that the moral cholera of the day will speedily pass away and
leave no trace behind, except the shudder of its remembrance.
(Tremendous cheering.) It would be omitting the part of

Hamlet, to allude to Mr. O'Connell's visit to Belfast, and to forbear an expression of admiration at the chivalrous and gallant bearing of the great champion of Protestantism in Ulster—Doctor Cooke. (Loud cheers.) He (Mr. E. T.) felt by that cheer, that he awoke a chord that would long vibrate in their breasts without a repetition of the touch. One only observation he had to offer, upon the manner in which that challenge had been met,—not by Mr. O'Connell, for *he* met it precisely as every individual felt and prophesied he would— but by the organ of the Roman Catholic party in Belfast, the *Vindicator*, which announced, that it had a BUTCHER *ready for Dr. Cooke, so soon as he was disposed to discuss the question.* (Loud cheers.) There was something awfully significant in that intimation—it was this, so long as you are disposed to let us have all our own way, our priests and our leader are quite sufficient to carry on the "peaceful agitation"; but we have *other parties* in reserve so soon as it comes to an opposition. Our clergy and Mr. O'Connell are sufficient to *declaim* upon Repeal, but take timely warning, that it is as BUTCHERS *we mean to discuss it*, so soon as you or the Government are disposed to take active steps to resist us. (Loud cheers.) This and similar demonstrations of violence on the part of the Repealers and Roman Catholics, was the result of the insane and disgraceful servility with which the present ministers had flung themselves at the feet of the movement party, and consented to hold office by their sufferance. This had given the Roman Catholic priesthood of Ireland an over-weening sense of their own importance as the direct sustainers and sole support of a British Ministry, and it is the intoxication of this unexpected elevation that is now exhibiting itself in their vulgar and intolerant pretensions at ascendancy. (Tremendous cheering.) The grossness of their ambition is however, working its own correction—the intelligent Liberals of Belfast, have already taken the alarm and withdrawn from their contaminating alliance. Belfast was the last place in Ireland in which that unnatural connexion had survived between the advocates of practical liberty and the slaves of theoretic as well as practical intolerance. In every other part of Ireland the Protestant Liberals have been making common cause with the Conservatives against their common enemy. Belfast has been the last, but they will yet be compelled to make their election.— When some one was speaking of some of Napoleon's marshals, who, after his return to Elba, followed at first the example of Macdonald, and hesitated to join the standard of the Emperor, but came in by degrees, and attached themselves to the army along with Ney, Talleyrand coolly remarked, that the only difference between those who had come first and last was the "watches of the one party went a little slower than those of the other";—(loud cheers)—and he (Mr. E. T.) felt satisfied, that the day was not far distant, when such might be said of the Liberals of Belfast—their watches are going a little slower than ours at present; but the priests and Mr. O'Connell will speedily move the regulator, and bring them up to us. (Loud cheers.) He (Mr. E. T.) would not farther intrude upon their patience, either by references to his past conduct, as their representative or minutiae of his intentions for the future. (Loud cheers.) He could only say, that so long as he had the honour to fill the exalted office their partiality had conferred on him, it would be his earnest desire to preserve the same undeviating course which had won him the high honours that showered on him that evening. [The hon. gentleman resumed his seat amidst loud cheers.]

MR. DUNBAR, on rising, was greeted with loud and long-continued cheering, accompanied with rounds of the Kentish fire, given in the most enthusiastic manner. When silence was restored, he said—Mr. Chairman and gentlemen, never have I addressed any assembly under feelings of greater excitement than at the present time, for there is no man who could remain unaffected by such a display as that now before us—and especially by the more than cordial manner in which the sentiment given from the chair has been received. Gentlemen, I also feel, that I labour under another and a peculiar difficulty, in coming before you immediately after my eloquent friend who has just spoken—for seldom have I heard a disquisition so able—and turn what way I may, I feel myself puzzled to lay hold of a topic which has not been brought forward by him. If I should take, for instance, Lord Stanley's bill, I would be at a loss to know what could be said in addition to his observations delivered on a late occasion that is not familiar to every one; and, if I advert to the great and powerful Daniel O'Connell, you will not tell me that I can reduce him to smaller dimensions than those into which he has been contracted by the wand of the mighty Magician of the North. In truth, gentlemen, my colleague has left me little to say on general questions, but I may take this opportunity of stating, that I will never hesitate to give an account of my conduct to my constituents, and that I am ready to do so in regard to all matters that have arisen since I last addressed them! But this I find is altogether unnecessary, as I have substantial reasons for believing that you do not require it. (Hear, hear.) During the recess of Parliament, I have universally met with the outstretched hand of welcome in every direction, and this could not have happened had I given one vote of which you did not approve. (Cheers.) I hold myself ready to give, at a moment's warning, a full and true account of my public conduct— (cheers)—as I am conscious that I have never abused my trust; but I do not think it necessary to enter upon any vindication of myself, until I have experienced some symptoms of dissatisfaction. In regard to a Repeal of the Union, after the powerful statement of my friend, I need only to ask any Protestant, can he have the slightest doubt as to the intentions of the parties by whom that scheme is promoted? But, were Protestants even mad enough to join them, can any man believe that England, too, would be mad enough to lose her right arm without a struggle? It is vain to disguise it—Repeal is only a stepping-stone to separation from England, and the religion of Protestants sits not upon them like a borrowed cloak, which they are ready to throw off at pleasure; and, it is matter of congratulation to find that many of the men who opposed us on other questions are with us on this; and, I have no doubt, that the whole body will come forward to join us, should Repeal be again agitated in our town, while to Derrynane itself will be extended the glorious cry of "No Surrender". (Immense cheering for several minutes.)—I only ask you to call to your recollection the state of your town during the past week, and does it not recall the dreadful scenes of '98?—Troops, cannon, and other warlike preparations were made, such as have not been paralleled since the disastrous period referred to; and it may be recollected, that the Protestant leaders of that time afterwards admitted that, had they been successful, they would have had to fight the battle over again with their own allies, and so it is at the present time. (Hear, hear.) The Repeal agitation is essentially a conflict between the North and the South; and we must either resist it, or permit ourselves to be put down by a dominant sectarian ascendancy. (Cheers.) Our Protestant Liberals have misunderstood our opinions as Conservatives; but the more they know of us the less will our respective differences become—it is impossible for my colleague and myself to please all our constituents; but this I can say, that no two members are better watched—I am proud that it is so, and I glory in it, because I have never yet given a vote which I am unprepared to defend. As one of the prominent topics of the day I may, in passing, notice the Corn Law question; and to the advocates of a repeal of the protecting duties I would submit the query, how would they provide for the evil, supposing a war to break out, and all interests in the country to be left at the mercy of a foreign government for a supply of grain? The powers thus destroyed can never be recovered, and therefore it is utter madness to permit the introduction of foreign grain, which can be raised at a rate of productive cost infinitely cheaper than we can do at home. (Cheers.) The greatest consumers are our own countrymen—and if this market is done away with, the best consumption of our agricultural commodities is destroyed. (Cheers.) It is, no doubt, a most difficult thing for any government to adjust, in a satisfactory manner, the differences between the manufacturing and farming interests; but it is clear that we cannot, without the utmost

peril, be left dependent upon foreign nations for one of the
prime articles of subsistence. So much depends upon this
question, that I could not avoid taking notice of it; but in
coming here this evening I scarcely expected to be called
upon for a public speech, and I see amongst us "chiels takin'
notes, an' faith they'll prent them"—laughter and cheers)—
though I had much rather that they had come without their
appropriate arms. There is, gentlemen, disunion amongst our
opponents, and my intention is not to say a word that may
hurt their feelings; on the contrary, I had rather conciliate
them—but it is to be borne in mind that Radical and
revolutionary attempts have not been confined to this town,
or even to Ireland. (Hear, hear.) In England itself Chartism
prevails, and if we can, by using moderation, secure the services
of our opponents—at all events, not offend their prejudices—
a great point will be gained; and though troops have lately
been sent down to preserve the peace, yet in a little time it
might truly be said that Belfast is the most Conservative town
in the kingdom. (Immense cheering.) The Liberal Protestants
in this town have been badly treated by their former associates; they joined with them in struggling for what were
called their rights, and what is the debt of gratitude that has
been paid? (Loud cries of "Hear, hear, hear".) Were the
Roman Catholics ever deserted by the Liberal Protestants?
No; and an ably-conducted press, too, sustained their cause—
yes, I say it is ably-conducted, though I have occasionally
received some rubs from it—and I hope that the whole party
will yet live to be convinced that Conservatives are not the
dishonest dogs that they thought them.—(Loud cheers.) In the
mean time, let us say nothing to offend them, and perhaps
they may yet join us. (renewed cheers.) We do not ask them
to give up any of their political sentiments—no such sacrifice
is necessary, and I do not therefore despair of seeing many of
them joining us yet. In regard to the press, I do not wish to
make complaints; but I have been represented as joining in a
coalition with Lord Belfast, for the purpose of ousting my
honourable colleague, but it is untrue—it is, in fact, a

damnable lie, and one which I am sure no man can seriously believe. (Prolonged cheers.) Why should I join Lord Belfast, or what could I possibly gain by it? Who placed me in my present position except the Conservatives, and could I expect their assistance or countenance if I should join any one who was not a man after their own hearts? (Loud cries of "Hear, hear".) Le the base insinuation then be treated as it deserves, and I may remark, that I have never yet met with one individual who believed it. On character and character alone I stand, in contradiction to a calumny so unworthy. To you I am indebted for the high position in which I have been placed; and, while I live, that debt of gratitude which I owe you can never be obliterated. (Enthusiastic cheers.) My utmost exertions, I assure you, shall be put forth in your cause, and the cause of Conservatism in general; and at any moment you require it, I am ready to give you an account of my entire conduct. Should the day ever come that I shall cease to enjoy your confidence, that moment will I replace my trust in your hands, as unspotted and unsullied, I hope, as the hour I first received it. (The hon. gentleman sat down amidst tremendous plaudits, and rounds of the Kentish fire.)

The "Army and Navy",—Song, "Rule Britannia", which was received with all the honours. When the cheering had subsided,

Lieut.-General COULSON rose and said, Mr. Chairman and gentlemen, in the name of Lord Hill, the Commander-in-Chief of the Army, and as, I believe, I am the senior officer present, I rise to return you thanks for the manner in which the toast just proposed has been received. (Hear, hear, and loud cheers.) I would call your attention for a moment to the latter, and I am sure you will all agree with me in saying, that they have exhibited on a late occasion sufficient evidence that, under all circumstances, the British Navy will sustain its character and fame, and will brook no insult. That navy has shown Europe that, though their great commander, the gallant Nelson, is no more, the same spirit which animated his breast animates theirs. (Hear, hear.) With reference to the army, I will merely add, that they will always be inspired with that fervour and devoted loyalty to the throne which has ever distinguished the British soldier, and which had in former times led them on conquering and to conquer, under the command of the greatest captain of the age, the Duke of Wellington.—The gallant General sat down amidst loud cheers and several rounds of the "Kentish fire".

The CHAIRMAN next gave—

"The Lord Primate and the Established Church." (Immense cheering, and rounds of the Kentish fire.)

REV. THOMAS WALKER, Curate of St. Anne's Church, having been loudly called upon, said—Mr. Chairman and Gentlemen, I return you my cordial and hearty thanks for the manner in which you have received the toast of the Lord Primate and the Established Church. It would ill become me to speak in commendation of that princely man, but this I may be permitted to say, that his heart beats as warmly as any here in the cause of Protestantism. (great cheering.) For myself, as a minister of the Church, I can say, that I am equally with yourselves attached to the Protestant cause, while it is happily not necessary that I should so much as attempt to establish the fact, that the Lord Primate and the Established Church deserve the confidence of every Conservative. (Loud applause.) Some of you may differ from his Lordship, and from the Church, in regard to Church government and discipline, but on the great point of maintaining Protestantism in opposition to Popery, we are all agreed. (Tremendous cheering.) We are one in our determination to stand by the principles for which our fathers died—the principles of the Reformation; for, as a venerable bishop of our Church once said,—"if the Reformation were worth establishing, it is worth maintaining". (Renewed cheers.) This, Mr. Chairman and gentlemen, is the first time that I have appeared at a public meeting such as the present; and if I am asked the reason why I have done so, my answer is, that I have come forward to pay a compliment to the gentlemen on either side of our worthy Chairman—to both of our borough members conjointly; and I am thankful that Belfast has sent such men to Parliament. (Prodigious cheering.) Farther, gentlemen, the present is a time when every man who regards God as the foundation of his true happiness, is bound to come out, and to express his true sentiments. (Hear, hear.) I trust not to mere political flattery—and let no man so trust—but God's declared will in reference to the salvation of sinners, and the unrestricted use of the Bible in Christian education, are the only sure foundations of civil and religious liberty to every individual in her Majesty's dominions—(hear, hear and loud cheers)—and these are the principles upon which we take our stand. (Cheers.) Mr. Chairman and gentlemen, I will not farther trespass upon your time—(cries of "go on")—as I am to be followed by my brother Cooke—(tremendously enthusiastic and long-continued cheers)—and by his side we are prepared to stand in the maintenance of our common cause. Gentlemen I return you sincere thanks for the exceedingly kind manner in which the toast of the Lord Primate's health, and the Established Church of this country has been received. (Renewed cheers, accompanied by the Kentish fire.)

The CHAIRMAN again arose and said, that in proposing the next toast he need not occupy the time of the meeting with any remarks. These were unnecessary. He himself had filled a flowing bumper to give the health of Dr. Cooke. (Deafening cheers, accompanied by waving of handkerchiefs and rounds of the Kentish fire, which were again, and again renewed.) Silence being restored,

The Rev. Dr. COOKE then proceeded:— Mr. Chairman and gentlemen, it is so short a time since I last addressed so large a part, nay the whole of this assembly, that I do not feel warranted in occupying any considerable portion of your time at present. (Go on, go on.) But, *apropos* to a dinner—Mr. O'Connell declares he is a greater faster than I am. Well that remains to be tried. (A laugh.) But, if he have an appetite for penance, this I can say for him, that, in the three short days he has spent amongst us, we have laid on him more true blue Protestant penance—(a laugh) –than his father confessor has

ventured to impose during the last three years. (Great cheering.)
In imposing this penance I rejoice to have had some share;
but I claim no more merit for committing him to the *lock-up
house*—(a laugh)—in Donegall-place, than the mere parch-
ment upon which is written a conviction for breach of the
game laws, or the paper upon which a magistrate endorses
the *mittimus* of a culprit to the jailer. (Cheering.) Yes, let it not
be concealed, that with the exception of the Romish priests
and their followers, all Ulster felt the insult of O'Connell's
invasion; and, while they did not dread, they saw all the
danger of the 50,000 *sans culottes*, and the hour and a half processions, and the pocket-fulls of shouts—(laughter)—with
which either himself or his *tailery* threatened to honour "our
village". (Cheers.) It was under these circumstances I endeavoured to turn him from riot to reason—(cheers)—from mob
oratory to logic—from fiction to fact—(cheers)—and, by the
evidence of his moral imbecility, to demonstrate that his
reliance was solely upon physical force. (Hear, hear.) When I
called upon Mr. O'Connell to discuss the question of Repeal,
it was not as a politician dealing in the expediencies of government, or the financial calculations of pounds, shillings, and
pence; I was emboldened to challenge him, in the name of
the word of God and of his truth, in the name of our common
and concentrated Protestantism; and, by the blessing of God,
we have administered to him a lesson he will not readily forget.
And yet, I fear I am wrong in that assertion. His memory is
failing fast. (A laugh.) What a pity he had left school before
the days of the learned Baron Von Feinagle, so famous in the
department of memories![99] For, would you believe it, his
memory is so clean gone, that though a few days ago, he
recollected to have read, in a late number of the *Ulster Times*,
an authorised statement—a statement authorised by Dr. Cooke
himself—that he did not intend to challenge him"; and
though, upon this *clear* "recollection", he civilly pronounced
me *twice a liar*; yet I say, would you believe it, the poor man's
memory is so clean gone, that when, on Monday last, the
Sub-editor of the *Ulster Times* waited upon him, offering the

file of the papers, he could not "recollect" in what number he had seen it, so modestly declined attempting the search. (Hear, hear.) Yes, Daniel was too busy to vindicate his veracity—(laughter)—so rolls over the task to his friend, the *Vindicator*, who will scarce well perform that task till he has once established his own. (Cheers.) But no matter—when O'Connell called me "*liar*", the "gulls shouted"—a name that will stick, because they have earned it—I will not retort upon him the unmannerly name he has so frequently applied to me; but, if he do not vindicate his veracity, the world will say he deserves it.— (Loud cheers.) Now, I will freely confess to you, that though through life I have had my own small share both of "good report and of bad"; and though I perhaps feel that my faults and my infirmities were justly entitled even to more of the latter than I have ever experienced, yet still I feel no taste for being evil spoken of. I have no grumblings after voluntary martyrdom. I should much rather have any man's and every man's good will and good word. Yet I do most sincerely thank Providence that I have never yet received a good word from you, Daniel O'Connell. (Loud cheers and laughter.) No; that is a degradation never yet inflicted; and I have one reasonable evidence that I am becoming a better man, as I find that Daniel's tongue is daily becoming worse. (Cheers and laughter.) Daniel's friends are pleased to accuse me of challenging their patron saint through an ambition of notoriety. Well, he is indeed a wise man who knows his own heart; and I shall, therefore, make no assertions in favour of my own humility. But this I will say, that the man who is ambitious of letting loose O'Connell's tongue upon him, together with the hurricane of the whole pack at his tail—(cheers and laughter)—has a curious ambition of notoriety; and very much akin to the ambition of the poor hare, which is said to covet the neighbourhood of the beagles, for the pleasure of being hunted and eaten. (Loud cheers and laughter.) No, Sir, I would not assert any thing in favour of my motives; but I can fearlessly say, my record is with Him that "pondereth the heart". (Hear, hear.) But one motive I may be permitted to disclaim, and one to assert. I disclaim all idea of credit to myself, and I assert that, under Providence, I depended on the concentrated loyalty and Protestantism of the Province— of all who hold Rebellion and Repeal to be purely convertible terms, and, like "Daniel and O'Connell", merely two different names for the same "lovely monster".[100] (Tremendous cheering.) But having, yesterday, inflicted upon you nearly as much penance as upon Daniel himself, I do not wish again to try the metal of your patience. (Cheers, go on, go on.) Well, since it is your good will, let me suggest another topic of thought. And allow me to say, that I never can think so well as when conscious that I have a good thinker near me, from whom I can borrow a pound or a shilling's worth of thought— (a laugh)—and, in this way, I believe I am so much in debt, that is useless to think of repayment—so must just go on to borrow as long as my friends are generous, and, if they fail me, I shall slyly work my fingers into Daniel's own budget; and do not despair of extracting something to set us all a thinking. (Cheers and loud laughter.) Yes, we have all reason to thank Mr. O'Connell for his visit, for he has compelled us all to have recourse to the history of the past. I am not sure that it is always correct to say, that

"Coming events cast their shadows before".

I feel rather inclined to say, that

"Former events leave their lessons behind".

And the history of our fathers tells us what their sons may expect, if God do not nerve and arm us for its prevention. (Immense applause.) But what are our only arms? They are, first, the arms of Protestant union, that cannot be dissolved— (cheers)—secondly, the arms of truth, that cannot be gainsaid; of resolution, of determination, that cannot be shaken— (cheers)—with the loud, but unfaltering, voice of warning to our beloved Queen, to beware of the traitorous designs that are hatching in this land against the integrity of her empire, and the lives and properties of her Protestant subjects—(hear,

hear)—and, specially, I mean, the arms of a free, a fearless, and unrestricted press. (Great applause.) Upon what arms have our enemies hitherto relied? No doubt, in a large degree, upon the "death's head and cross bones"—a species of Poonah painting well suited to Daniel's extemporaneous genius— (hear, and a laugh)—but which, as Protestant Christians, we can neither study nor imitate. (Hear, hear.) But I do not hesitate to say, their main reliance has been upon simple and unadulterated boasting and lying. (Hear, hear.) O Daniel! thou professed Apostle of civil and religious liberty, what is your liberty, but the liberty of boasting of what you would do, and lying of what you have, or have not, done, when safely ensconced in the Corn-Exchange? (Cheers.) You challenged me to discuss Popery in the newspapers: relying upon God and his truth, I at once accepted the challenge—instantly the craven lowered his wing. (Groans and hisses.) Next, when safe in the old shed, down street—(a laugh)—I beg your pardon, in the "immense pavilion"—(bursts of laughter)—"erected for the dinner"; that is, by the *hocus pocus* men who knocked it up some years ago, for the exhibition of other animals, but who, by virtue of their art, clearly foresaw to what other uses it would come at last; and, therefore, in Maynooth logic, "erected" it expressly for the dinner. (Hear, and a laugh.) Yes, Mr. O'Connell, when fairly ensconced in this venerable hall—emblem of the foredoomed system you are pledged to cling to and uphold—with crumbling bricks, tottering to their fall; with rotten wood, terror-stricken at its own gravity; the whole shapeless mass skewered up with crooked timbers, emulating and outdoing every curve and angle in Euclid's elements. (loud laughter.) When there, you thrice, in one breath, challenged me to a "six-and-twenty hours'" discussion of civil and religious liberty. Again I accepted your challenge— and again you have shrunk from the meeting. (Hear, hear.) But the press will brand your braggart challenging—your own dupes will at last discover the intellectual cowardice it is intended to conceal—(hear, hear)—and the next thing I expect to hear is, that you have "registered a vow" never to change

words with "the loathsome Theologue"—(loud laughter) as
the only screen that Rome can provide for the bully she
employs to lie and revile, but whom she dares not trust in
argument with the objects of his falsehood and revilings.
(Loud cheering.) Thrice, Mr. O'Connell, have I attempted to
compel you to argument upon subjects of your own choice;
and thrice have you escaped me with the slipperiness and
tortuosities of an eel. (Loud laughter.) But even an eel can be
held, if you grasp it by the neck; and into whatever mud he
may dive, and whatever twistings he may practice, I hope yet
to be able to clutch him so far above "the tail"—(laughter)—
as to compel him to discover that he is a mere political eel, if
not an animal of the same form—far more lovely, but far more
dangerous. (A voice, "A serpent, I suppose".) Remember,
then, Mr. O'Connell, that thrice, in one breath, you "*challenged*"
me to a discussion upon "civil and religious liberty". I took
you at your word. But what is your word worth? I'll tell you
what it is worth—and let the reporters faithfully send it
forth—it is just worth a "shout of the gulls"; and it would not
buy a pennyworth of any other earthly commodity. (Great
laughter.) O'Connell's promises remind me somewhat of the
Irish Boniface, somewhere near Skibbereen, to a hungry
traveller, taking guage of his larder, he fairly and confidentially
announced "every delicacy of the season", the traveller chose
roast beef. Boniface disappeared to have it served up; but
speedily returned with a sorrowful apology, that the last rib was
just gone. The traveller next selected an elegant veal cutlet.
Boniface again disappeared, and again returned, announcing,
with rueful visage, that the veal, too, was devoured. A mutton
chop, a roasted capon, followed in like succession, until, at
last, the hungry traveller exclaimed, "what, what is left?" When
"mine host" confessed to as fine a rasher of bacon as ever was
singed in Clonmel. The traveller was glad to get it; and, if I
can get but a "rasher" from Daniel, I protest I shall be
equally contented. (Loud cheers and laughter.)

You are aware that this honourable "gentleman", this pol-
ished scholar—this sublime orator, has been exhibiting his

genius with a pun upon my name, eking to it to keep his capacity in use, what he knew to be a falsehood—and seasoning it
with just as much of "death's head and cross bones" as he
dare employ as a lawyer, without becoming liable to an
indictment at the Quarter Sessions. Well, I shall not imitate
him in all these points—for I cannot if I would, and I would
not if I could—(hear, hear)—but in the sublime department of
punning, I owe him a Roland for an Oliver, and beg to tell
him what he knows right well, that my "cookery" outrivals
Ude in dressing a calf's head.—(Immense cheers and laughter.)

In speaking to-day to my honourable friend, General
Coulson, upon Daniel's talent for retreat, he reminded me
how that was of the utmost importance even to the most
successful commander; but advised me just to watch for the
moment when the "hero of the hundred retreats"—(laughter)—
should fairly outmanoeuvre himself. My friend was right; and
I think the time is come—(hear, hear)—I challenged him to
discuss repeal—he retreated into Purgatory. (Cheers and
laughter.) I could not follow him there. But when he next
appeared above-ground—(laughter)—he challenged me to
meet him on the ground of "civil and religious liberty". And
scarcely were the words out of his mouth till—"fly jack and
begone"—(a laugh)—and away with the whole "stock, lock,
and barrel" of Repeal (Mr. Dillon Browne's "*forty-guinea rifles*"*
inclusive) to Donaghadee—where, it has been conjectured or
reported, a sly Highland piper, who had watched the embarkation, struck up the appropriate air, "*We'll gang nae mair to yon
toon*". (Great laughter.) And believing, as I do, that whether the
piper so played or not, Mr. O'Connell will fulfil the words, I
now tell him, through the press—that *Exeter Hall*, and the
time of the *Easter Recess*, or *Ascot races*, will, if he chooses to *keep*

---

* The existence and *price* of these famous *Repeal Rifles* were made known by
one of the *Repeal party* having forgot them in the *well* of a jaunting-car—
and announcing the fact to detain *her Majesty's Mail* for their recovery.
They were recovered, and the *percussion caps* thrown off from them, and
some cases of *pistols* (quere. "ANCIENT PISTOLS?") after the "*peaceful
conquerors*" had passed through Newry, and bidden "farewell to Ulster".

his word, afford place and time, either to realize his challenge, or afford another, but unnecessary proof, that he is either a truth-speaking honest man, or a boasting braggart and a skulking coward.

Hear me, Mr. O'Connell—you challenged me in Belfast— I challenge you in the face of the empire. (Cheers.) I know you are confident in your abilities—but you feel the rottenness of your cause.—(cheers.) *You* argue for civil and religious liberty! Like the "Amen!" in the throat of Macbeth, the very words would engender strangulation—(cheers)—and would so vividly conjure up before you the foul mysteries of the Confessional, and the horrid racks of the Inquisition, that you would shrink from the cause you had purposed to advocate, and become the convert of that Protestant liberty you have hitherto laboured to destroy. (Cheers.) Do, do, Mr. O'Connell, undertake to demonstrate that Rome *"ever has been, ever can be, or ever will be,* the patroness of "civil and religious liberty"; and you will do more if you succeed, to establish Popery, than Leo X by his bulls, Zetzel by his indulgences, or Cajetan by his diplomacy;[101] or more, if you fail to overturn it, than Luther by his Bible, Cranmer by his martyrdom, or Knox by his courage! (Cheers.) But will you meet me? Will you keep your word? You will not. (Cheers.) And why will you not keep your word? Do you dread to meet me? You do not. But the priests dare not trust you. I am wrong—they dare trust *you,* but they dare not trust *Peter Dens,* the *Douay Bible,* and a "bitter *bad"* *cause.*—(Continued cheers.) But they say you will return to Belfast to complete the victory you have so gloriously begun! Well, I heartily wish you joy of your victory; and I will tell the *Pavilioners* when you return on another Repeal expedition— you will return either at the *"Greek Kalends"* of my learned friend beside me would say—or as I, an unlearned Irishman, would say—*"at Tibb's eve",* that is, neither before Christmas, nor after it. (Loud cheers and laughter.)

Unhappily for yourself, Mr. O'Connell, but happily for us, you have appealed to history. And it is but just to those unacquainted with authorities to say—that when you appeal to *Taylor*, you appeal to an authority very much on a par with the memoirs of Captain Rock,[102] the Belfast *Vindicator*, or the word, promise, or challenge of Daniel O'Connell, Esq., Member of Parliament for all Ireland. (Loud cheers.) And though I would not speak of Sir Henry Parnell,[103] as classified with any of these, yet when he has incautiously built upon Taylor's sand, the building he has raised, however good the mason and masonry, must tumble to the ground. Now, as my friend Daniel has begun to deal in history, I shall either be his customer or his merchant. As his customer, I have examined some of his wares already; and, as his merchant, I shall deal "liberally" with him. (Hear, and a laugh.)—To three periods of Popish power, with tolerance and cherishing of Protestantism which he then asserted—I yesterday helped to a fourth, and, by the aid of a friend then present, I was also enabled to suggest a fifth. (Cheers.) Now, let me read an extract concerning one of these periods, and which I am enabled to lay before the public, through the kindness of my friend Mr. Macrory,[104] by whose indefatigable research in Presbyterian records, it has recently been brought to light:—

"Attested and compared copy of a petition of Anna Griffith, relict of Mr. Thos. Murray, minister of Killileagh, in Ireland, stating, 'that her husband was most cruelly murdered and crucified on a tree, by the most unchristian rebels, with two other gentlemen hanged with him, the one on the right hand, and the other on the left; her two sons killed, and cut to pieces before her eyes; her own body pitifully bruised, maimed, and wounded in sundry parts: her tongue half cut out; her body carried away, and kept in prison, and inhumanly used by the rebels, from whom, at last, by God's merciful providence, she escaped; all which was testified under the hands of the best nobles and counsellors of this kingdom'; and humbly praying them to extend their charity to her, which was granted." *5th August, 1642.*

And this is popish charity! Aye, this is the charity of the second period, when power was obtained by Daniel's "precursors"—(cheers)—and if, since that, any change has come upon them, let the martyred ministers of our land bear witness—let the sheeted dead appear to yield their testimony. (Great cheering.) For myself, if I saw that Repeal was merely political, then I should not appear to oppose it, but let politicians battle with it as they might. But, as ministers of the Gospel, we are to be "watchmen" ever at our posts; and the blood of those committed to our charge must be upon us, if we neglect, in any wise, our duty. (Great cheering.) Let, then, our ministers taking the past as the mirror of the future, prepare for the time that is coming. (Hear, hear, hear, and loud cheering.) We are not to listen to the gentle voice of the wolf, when it puts on the dress of the old grandame to entice the child within to open the door. (Cheers.) This Mr. O'Connell has done all in his power to effect. (Hear, hear.) He has taken up the old grandame's dress, and as far as he could he would wheedle the Protestant, Presbyterian, and Dissenter, down to my good and Rev. friend, Daniel M'Afee. I should say rather *up* to him, for Mr. M'Afee is an older correspondent of his than I. (Great cheering.) And then, taking another step further, he would go on his knees to the Orangemen, and, if he thought necessary, drink buckets of Boyne water to conciliate them. (Much laughter.) Then some farther steps he'd take, would be, first, to tell lies; second, he would get Tom Steele to believe them and swear to them; and, lastly, he'd present Dillon Brown to Belfast. (Tremendous groans and hisses.) Of all Daniel's presenting, since first he made a present—(a voice, "what kind of a present?")—this is greatest. And since he is so ready and willing to dispense with his friend, and, as we do not want him, and will not have him, I shall tell him how to dispose of his *protégé*. There's a certain Mr. Cavendish wishes greatly to meet him, and his great desire is to persuade him to certain preliminaries, in order to enable him to take a part in the *pistol scene* in the farce entitled, "A new way to pay old debts". (Great cheering.) We are not disposed to receive Mr. Dillon Brown, and so dismissing him, I will also, with your leave, dismiss myself. (Great cheers, and cries of "Go on, go on.") If I must then, let me re-echo the sentiment of my kind friend who has preceded me—(Mr. Walker)—if Protestants be not mad, they will be united.—(Great cheering, waving of handkerchiefs, and cries of "Hear, hear".) With Churches holding the "unity" of the spirit's testimony, surely we may fully realize the "bond of peace". (Loud cheers.) And I am neither afraid nor ashamed to say, that to this union we are called by common Protestantism and by common danger. (Hear, hear.)—I recollect of some one who sent an ambassador to a wise neighbouring king, to request of him a lesson on government. The wise king said nothing; but taking the ambassador into his garden, he beat down with a rod every tall flower in the parterre, and so dismissed him. Arrived at home, he related what had occurred, expressing his opinion that the reputed wise king was little beyond a fool. But his master thought differently—so, immediately commenced cutting off the aristocracy, or the tall flowers, convinced he could easily manage the short ones. (Hear, hear.) And now ye Lansdownes, ye Devonshires, and Angleseys, who have aided to hilch the "bad man" to his present bad eminence, does he not plainly tell you, you shall not be permitted, under his *regime*, to hold estates in both kingdoms? (Hear, hear.)—My Lord Lansdowne would sell—but who will dare to buy? Kerry shall be a fief of the imperial Derrynane. (Cheers and laughter.) His grace of Devonshire shall be delivered from the troubles of Cork, and the echoes of Lismore shall respond to the mellifluous squeak of Richard Lalor Shiel—(Cheers)—and my Lord Anglesey shall make a "*present*" of the picturesque mountains of Carlingford to the "companionable" Mr. Dillon Brown. (Cheers.)

The next step will be to praise, to the echo, "the sturdy Presbyterians of Ulster". Oh, how dearly Daniel loves the Presbyterians! (Loud cheers and laughter.) But how long that humour might last I shall not take upon me to say. You recollect the case of a friend—"a very dear friend"—of O'Connell's, some four miles from Belfast.—(Laughter.) Oh! he was all that was good, better, best, with Daniel, as long as it suited his purpose. (Hear, hear.) But Daniel's good opinion, like the short-lived flower, one colour in the morning another in the evening—or, to be more dignified and classical—his good opinion, "like lobster boiled—(laughter)—from black to red began to turn"; and now, if there be one Presbyterian whose image more haunts Daniel's waking dreams than the "pale-faced man" before you—(cheers)—it is a certain tall gentleman, some six feet four, whom Daniel, by word or letter, never wishes to recognize; but whom he sometimes thinks of as a resident near the picturesque village of Dunmurry.[105] (Cheers and laughter.) Now, after the Presbyterians have been sufficiently praised, the next step would be to take them into a kind of confidence and counsel. (Hear, hear, hear.) These bishops, it would be said to them, are of no use; neither are these curates nor rectors—let us just unite to give them the "wheel about"; and then we'll just have old Ireland to ourselves, and the half of Ennishowen for a potato garden. (Loud laughter and cheers.) But the Presbyterians are not such "gulls" as to be deluded thus. (Tremendous cheering, waving of handkerchiefs, and cries of "never, never, never".) They know what would be their fate; they remember the Cyclops in the cave. Daniel would fatten me till my pale face became rosy as his own, and, like another Ulysses, I should be spared till so fattened, that I might be eaten last. (Hear, hear.) The Liberals, too, would fall. Once the highest flowers were knocked off, the lowest would not long be spared. (Great applause.) I've but one more point to notice, and I have done. It is said of Constantine the Great, that in one of his marches, in vision he beheld on the sun a cross, and bearing this motto, "*In hoc signo vinces*". (Hear, hear.) So, also, seizing on the cross of Christ, you'll conquer—not by intellect, or intelligence, or zeal, but by the spirit of our God—our fathers' God. (Applause.) But, the cross represents union, while it seals the reconciliation between God and man. We'll stand, like Luther, so long as this Protestant kingdom stands, upholding that doctrine which he declared to be the sign of a standing or a falling Church—the doctrine of justification by faith, with humble hearts and uplifted hands. "By the Cross of Christ crucified to the world", and by the spirit of God "rendered meet" for a better inheritance, an enduring kingdom. And if the enemy should ever repeat his invasion, the Protestants of Ulster will stand united, as the parts of that sad, yet glorious emblem of our religion to which I have referred; and we shall meet him again, as our rock-bound shores meet the waves of the Atlantic; and though again he may come in with lies, again must he go out in blasphemy.—(Loud cheers.)

The CHAIRMAN then gave—

"The health of the Rev. Daniel M'Afee", which was received with the most tremendous cheers, and the Kentish fire.

The Rev. Gentleman then came forward and said—Mr. Chairman and gentlemen, I assure you I feel at a loss for words to express the gratitude I feel to all present, and to the independent electors of Belfast. I feel a difficulty in giving utterance to the language of my heart, for the very high honour you have conferred upon so humble an individual as myself. I feel delighted on the present occasion, surrounded as I am by men whom I consider an honour to any representative, and representatives who are honoured by such a constituency. I will not trouble you with any special apology for being present this evening; it is the first time I have ever yielded to go to such a meeting as this, although I have often been invited. I came, however, for this purpose, to show myself here as a Wesleyan minister, not as a representative of that body, but as a specimen of the whole, and to state that they were all united for the benefit of our common country. (Loud cries of "Hear, hear".) He alluded to Lord Stanley's bill, and the perjury that he has known to be committed in the south of Ireland—to the visit of Mr. O'Connell to Belfast, and illustrated the effect Dr. Cooke's challenge had upon him, by an anecdote founded on a fact, which took place during the miracles of Priest Hohenlohe.[106] A woman had been brought to the hospital in a fever case, and she was to be cured by a miracle. The apothecary who had charge of the hospital, being an intelligent man, suspected that she was an impostor, and he told her the manner in which they cured fever was, by thrusting a needle under the nail of the finger, and if that did not prove effective, then it was to be thrusted up a little farther, and, in case that did not do, then it was to be thrusted up to the knuckle, and then there would be no doubt of a cure. The next morning came, and the apothecary proceeded to sharpen his needle: when he had done so, and was in the act of putting it in the woman said, "Oh, Sir! I'm better." The apothecary then caused her to dress herself as quickly as possible, and horse-whipped her out of the place. (Hear, hear and laughter.) In the same way, Daniel O'Connell was brought here by the priests, and put in his sick room, when Dr. Cooke, acting as apothecary, applied the needle to his nail, but he did not horse-whip him. (Cheers.)—Daniel at first said, grant us Emancipation, and all would go on well—that was all they wanted. Then he said, grant us Reform, and we will ask no more. (Hear, hear.) He rejoiced to know that the Liberals of Belfast were beginning to have their eyes opened to the objects of that party. The Rev. gentleman then went on to prove that all their doctrines, infallibility, transubstantiation, and purgatory, led to the grand object they had ever in view, namely, Catholic ascendancy. After reading for the meeting an extract from a work called the "Pedigree of Popery, or the genealogy of Antichrist", he concluded a lengthened speech, which we have only been able merely to notice, by saying, that the object of Repeal was to gain ascendancy for such errors, and that Dan's object was to filch the money out of the people's pockets. He never expected such a measure would pass. He trusted the late visit which we had from him here, would be the last he will ever make to the North. (Tremendous cheers.)

The CHAIRMAN then proposed "the health of the Most Noble the Marquis of Donegall".

Lieut.-General COULSON, on being called on, rose and said—He regretted that the honour of responding to the health of that nobleman did not fall on some one more competent to perform that pleasing task. The gallant General alluded to the glorious triumph that had been obtained in Belfast over the aspiring tyrant who came here for the purpose of agitating the Repeal question. He could assure that large assembly, that Lord Donegall was as much opposed to that measure as he was the advocate of Lord Stanley's bill, and there was sufficient evidence of his Conservative feelings and principles, in the fact of his entrusting his proxy, on all occasions, to the greatest general and most profound states-man of the age—he meant the Duke of Wellington. [The remainder of the gallant General's remarks were lost amidst the bursts of applause that ensued the mention of that name.]

The CHAIRMAN then gave,

"Colonel Bruen, Mr. Alexander, and the Conservative electors of Carlow."

MR. JOHN ALEXANDER said—Mr. Chairman and gentlemen, I beg to return most sincere thanks for the honour you have done to Colonel Bruen and the Conservative electors of the County of Carlow. Believe me, no man deserves better of his Conservative brethren than the gallant Colonel, who has ever proved himself our uncompromising advocate. (cheers.) His heart and his purse have ever been open to support our glorious cause. In him we have always had a firm and steady supporter, able and willing to defend us. (Hear, hear, and cheers.) In Carlow we have been placed in circumstances of particular difficulty; attacked by Popery and her assistants, superstition and perjury; but, by a determination to do our duty, by steady perseverance and union; and by a close attention to our registries for the last eight years, we have now gained one of the most glorious and decisive triumphs on record. We have defeated the Priests and their candidate, and left them behind in one the vast majority of 167.[107] (Loud cheers.) In Carlow, like our forefathers at the memorable siege of Derry, (for I boast of having descended from one who took an active part in the doings of that eventful period), like that band of patriots, we have imprinted on our banner the glorious motto of "No Surrender", written in characters too plain to be misunderstood. We have nailed our banner to the mast, and clinched the nail on the other side, determined to conquer or to die. (Cheers.) Again I beg to return my best thanks for the honour you have conferred on Colonel Bruen and the Conservative electors of Carlow, and for the compliment bestowed on myself, in connecting my name with a body of men, than whom there is not on earth a more resolute, more high-minded, or more disinterested. (Cheers.)

The CHAIRMAN then rose and said, he would give the health of "The Most Noble the Marquis of Downshire, one of the best Landlords in Ireland". Received with tremendous applause, and several rounds of the "Kentish fire".

"Major Armstrong, High Sheriff of Fermanagh, and the strangers who have honoured us to-night with their presence."

Major ARMSTRONG briefly returned thanks.

The CHAIRMAN then rose, and gave the health of the gentleman who had been so successful in preparing and paving the way for that splendid meeting.

JOHN BATES, Esq., in returning thanks, said, he felt that on that occasion he had some reason to find fault with this excellent friend, the Chairman, as when he came there he did not anticipate that such a mark of distinction would be conferred upon him. There was no one fonder of Conservative friendship than he was; yet, they would believe him when he said that it was not to gain their applause that he had taken the part he did in convening that great assembly—it was a higher motive—one of duty. They had entered upon it reluctantly, but, at the same time efficiently.

MR. E. TENNENT, M.P., then proposed the health of the Chairman, who had so efficiently performed his duties on that occasion. (Tremendous applause and Kentish fire.)

MR. GORDON returned thanks, and then gave "Our next merry meeting". Considerable applause ensued, and it now being twelve o'clock, the meeting dispersed in the most orderly manner.

LETTER TO LORD STANLEY,
ACCOMPANYING THE PETITION.

THE following letter, which sufficiently explains itself, was forwarded to Lord Stanley, along with the Petition, agreed at the Conservative Meeting, of which a full report has already been given:—

"Belfast, Feb. 20, 1841.

"MY LORD,—I have been directed, by a resolution passed at the Great Northern Meeting, held in Belfast, on the 21st ult., to request that your Lordship will present to the House of Commons, the Petition agreed to at that meeting, in favour of the principles of your Lordship's Irish Registration Bill; and I have the honour now to transmit that Petition to you for presentation.

"In order that a fair estimate may be formed of the importance of this Petition, it is necessary that I should state to your Lordship some facts connected with it.

"The meeting at which it was adopted was a public one, convened on the Requisition of 1607 of the Nobility, Clergy, Gentry, and Merchants, connected with the North of Ireland. The Requisition avowed the opinion of those who signed it to be in favour of "the principles of Lord Stanley's Registration Bill". The meeting was held in the largest building in Belfast. It was admitted by the Conservative and Whig Press, that there were more than 4,000 persons present. Every part of the building was densely filled, and not less than 2,000 gentlemen were unable to make their way into the assembly.

"The Petition which will be handed to your Lordship was unanimously adopted at that meeting, and has since been signed by 86,170 of the Nobility, Clergy, Gentry, Merchants, and Yeomanry of the Northern Irish Counties.

"No Petition has ever been presented to Parliament which represented as much of the wealth, character, intelligence, and independence of the country. It would be difficult, even if time permitted, to make an estimate of the wealth of the whole body of the Petitioners, or of those who attended the meeting, or of the great body of merchants and manufacturers who signed the requisition, but I have selected the only class of the requisitionists which admits of calculation, in order to support my statement, viz., the Landed Proprietors:—

"With a view to procure an accurate estimate of the annual value of the landed property represented by those who signed the Requisition, I addressed a circular letter (of which I beg leave to enclose a copy) to one landed proprietor, of the most information and accuracy, in *each* County. I have received replies to this circular from *eleven* out of the *twelve* Counties over which the Requisition extended, with the required information; and I have now the honour to enclose the result from which your Lordship will see that the value of *landed property alone* in the North of Ireland represented by those who have *signed the Requisition* is £1,665,600 per annum, without including the landed proprietors who did not sign the requisition, but who attended the meeting and signed the Petition.

"To the requisition were attached the names of 41 Peers and Noble Lords, 14 Right Honourable and Honourable Gentlemen, 18 Baronets, 32 Members of Parliament, 11 High Sheriffs of Northern Counties, 6 Lord Lieutenants of Counties, 98 Deputy Lieutenants, 355 Justices of the peace, 257 Clergymen of the Established Church, 45 Presbyterian Ministers, and 26 Clergymen of the Methodist Communion.

"The Petition emanates from this great body of Irishmen, and is, in addition, signed by men of all classes in society, embracing Conservatives and Whigs, Episcopalians, Presbyterians, Methodists, and Roman Catholics, all of whom have had the best opportunities of forming a correct opinion on the subject; and while their views and interests on other questions differ, they all concur in approving of the provisions of your Lordship's Bill.

"I have the honour to be, my Lord,

"Your obedient servant,

"JOHN BATES.

"The Right Hon. Lord Stanley, M.P., London.

THIRD LETTER OF DR. COOKE.
ACCEPTANCE OF MR. O'CONNELL'S
CHALLENGE FOR 26 HOURS DISCUSSION
OF CIVIL AND RELIGIOUS LIBERTY.

IN our preliminary narrative, page 60, we have stated, that, at the Pavilion dinner, Mr. O'Connell offered to give Dr. Cooke, "not *two*, but *six*, or even *twenty-six hours*" of public discussion "on any subject connected with civil and religious liberty." This offer was well understood by the audience to be little better than a "rhetorical flourish", resorted to for the purpose of covering Mr. O'Connell's previous defeat; but, lest any seeming ground of glorification should remain to his discomfited adherents, Dr. Cooke willingly accepted the terms proposed, thus leaving the Repeal faction without the shadow of an excuse for their political cowardice. Accordingly the following admirable letter, addressed to Mr. O'Connell, appeared in the *Ulster Times* of the 28th of January. In point of energetic vigour of style, and felicity of argument, it is barely excelled by the communication in which Dr. Cooke's challenge to Mr. O'Connell was originally conveyed.

TO DANIEL O'CONNELL, ESQ., M.P.

SIR,—This is probably the last letter with which I shall trouble you. I beg you, therefore, do not burn it as you did my first. Rather treat it like my second, and read it *twice*—as, I trust, it contains some matters important to yourself and your country.

But, before proceeding farther, I must set myself right with the public.

In the Dublin *Monitor's* report of the speech in which alone you attempted a reply to my challenge to a discussion of Repeal, I find these words—"He invites me to a conference, and the mode he takes of conveying that invitation is, by writing me *the most insulting letter he could possibly pen*. I had read

about five lines when I flung it into the fire. I am sorry for it;
for had I thought it was of value, I would have kept it as a
curiosity." I am happy I can gratify you with a copy—not that
I believe you either like it or care for it—but that the public
may judge of the nature and extent of the "*insults*" I was guilty
of penning. For the accuracy of the *copy*—indeed it is rather
the *original*—I pledge my word; and I am grateful to that
Providence by which such an important document has been
preserved—that from the charge of offering an unmannerly
insult, I may stand exonerated before the public:—

"*Belfast, 5th January, 1841.*

"SIR,—As you have determined to carry the Repeal
agitation into Ulster—and as I hold it to be the duty of every
loyal subject to give it all the legal opposition in his power—
I beg to inform you, that I purpose to challenge you to a
public discussion of the question in all its bearings, political
and religious.

"The challenge I intend to appear (God willing) in the
Belfast *Chronicle* of to-morrow; and I send you this notice that
you may have the earliest knowledge of my design.

"I have the honour to be
Your obedient servant,

"H. COOKE.

"To Daniel O'Connell, Esq."

Now, there's the wondrous "*curiosity*" you wish you had preserved—
there's "*the most insulting letter I could pen*". Let the public judge of my
insult, and your veracity;—but, no matter, "the gulls shouted", and,
on the faith of your testimony, I was written down "*unmannerly*",
while you were echoed the very "*pink of politeness*".

Perhaps you will say, you referred not to my private, but to my
first public letter. If so, I shall submit the point of *etiquette* to any
tribunal of gentlemen that ever you may appoint; and if you find

three gentlemen in the kingdom who will say that, in that letter, I "insulted" you, I pledge myself to the most public retractation and the most humiliating apology. I'll do more. Now, that the affair is not before "the gulls" for a "shout", but before the public for decision, point out, in my challenge, what you denounce as "*most insulting*", and I shall explain, retract, or apologise, as the nature of the case may require.

But, to come to a more important point.

I have always, Mr. O'Connell, suspected you mistook your profession. Nature intended you for the army. Never was the "*cedant arma togae*" more unhappily verified than in you. Why do I think so? I'll tell it you in a story, for the truth of which there are living vouchers. A little before the year '98, a respected country gentleman received a commission to raise a corps of yeomanry for the defence of the country against the impending rebellion. On applying to a worthy farmer to join his company, the reply was a question—"will it be foot or cavalry?" The Captain answered—"foot". "Ah! " relied the farmer, "I would join you if they were cavalry". "And why, my good fellow, would you prefer the cavalry?" "Ah!" rejoined the farmer, "*they're best for a retreat like*". Now, it is on your powers at "*a retreat like*" that I found my opinion that Nature intended you for a great General. For, as one of the chief qualifications of a good General, is always to secure the means of retreat, I will venture to affirm that, since the days of Nimrod, in the *retreating* department, you stand fairly without a rival. But, let me warn you, Mr. O'Connell, that, though you foiled me once—though you utterly baffled the whole army of PROTESTS thrown in your rear by the *Belfast Newsletter*—still I don't despair of making you my prisoner. At all events, of one thing I am certain—that I will *cut off your retreat* upon every way but one— a road you know right well; and by which, if again you retire, I leave you "alone in your glory".

But, to exhibit your "*retreating*" powers to the public—You threatened to invade Ulster to argue *Repeal*. You threatened to appear on its military frontier with an agreeable cortege of 50,000 men—the most of them notoriously *sans culottes*—the men who had, a few years ago, been shut out of the same town (Newry) by the turning of the pivot bridge, and the muzzle of the cannon.[108] You did not tell us how many might accompany you to Belfast; but you gave tolerably plain indication of the *will*, that with so many, is *law*, when you told "the gulls" in Dublin that you could, or wished you could, "*fill a pocket handkerchief*" with the consolidated shouts that would greet you at the Linen-hall—a vaticination of yours that may hereafter rank you with that brother prophet, who, for love of the *Moabitish rent*, came to curse Israel, but whom Providence overruled, in spite of his covetousness, to bless them.[109] And though you should, in your usual style, call me by the name of the animal that rebuked his "madness" I will not be deterred from administering that castigation, so long as your gigantic talents are perverted to disturb the peace of this province, undermine the integrity of the empire, and threaten the stability of the Protestant religion.

Now, it was to arrest your mad career of mobbing, and speeching, and shouting, that I challenged you to a deliberate discussion of the Repeal question, before an impartial and orderly assembly. For doing so, you said I "*insulted*" you, and of my *insult* the public now can judge. You called me every ill name you could invent or recollect; and, because I dreaded you would accuse me of wishing to convert a political question into a polemical controversy, and therefore promised to *exclude religion*; as a consummate tactician, you turn my flank, and effect your *retreat* with a skill that would have made Xenophon stare, at the head of the ten thousand[110]—and the "gulls shouted". Well, some one has said of a great General—"He has beaten us so often, that, at last, he will teach us to beat him";—and, to compare the small with the great, so thought I, in my simplicity. *I took you at your word.* I offered to discuss religion, by asserting in the newspapers, as you wished, the *errors and heresies* of the Roman apostacy. *I stand to my word still*—and on the same condition—viz., that you obtain for me one column, or two, or more, weekly, or less frequently, in one or two *Southern Romanist papers;* and I now add to my proposal, that for every *Romanist Southern paper* you furnish me, I secure to you THREE NORTHERN PROTESTANT PAPERS.

Now, my dear Roman Catholic countrymen—and though I denounce the traditions and heresies whereby crafty men have deluded you, you are dear to me—consider, I pray you, for you are admirers of courage, whether physical or mental—consider, I pray you, the cowardice of that man who dares neither to meet me *fairly and openly* on politics or religion. Let your priests and a hireling press say what they will, there is something within you that tells you my proposal is fair, and, if Mr. O'Connell again *retreat*, not merely from me, but from *his own word*, what can you conclude but that he dreads my exposure of the rottenness of his cause? And what, Mr. O'Connell, is your next retreat? Why, in Belfast there is not a word whispered about my *cutting off your retreat into religion*; but you are ready, you say, at *any time*, and, I must presume, *at any place*, to discuss with me the questions of *civil and religious liberty*, for TWENTY-SIX HOURS. And at this second edition of your challenge "the gulls shouted". Now bear witness, ye 30,000!!! Repealers, who, for the greater convenience of hearing, were so miraculously squeezed by the *patent Vindicator press*, into a space that never heretofore did, and never again will, contain twelve hundred men, women, and children—bear witness to Mr. O'Connell's challenge and pledge, and to my third, and, I trust, successful attempt to *cut off his retreat*. Mr. O'Connell, with joy do I accept your challenge, and I undertake to demonstrate, from your Councils, Bulls, Extravagants, Decretals, Theological and Moral Institutes, and Biblical notes, as well as from history—binding myself to quote only from Romish authorities—that the religion of Rome has ever been, and still is, not only adverse to, but absolutely destructive of CIVIL AND RELIGIOUS LIBERTY. I take up your Romish gauntlet—there lies my Protestant glaive. Won't you lift it, Mr. O'Connell? What! gone again?—another retreat?—and why not? Dr. Cooke, you're a "*loathsome theologue*"; I hate your insulting pen; I abhor your "Ulster brogue"; I'll have none of your "Cookery"; don't think to "bully " me *into keeping my word*; don't think on your own dunghill to crow over me, you sleepless "Cock of the North". Patience, patience, Mr. O'Connell—a truce to all this *genteel talent* at nomenclature. I thank you heartily for the sublime pun with which you have illustrated your own wit, and for every scholarly and gentlemanlike name with which you have not insulted, but honoured me; and especially I thank you for the last—"Cock of the North". Yes, I accept the *soubriquet* as an omen for good, though, like your vaticinating brother, you meant it for evil. It was a cock that reminded Peter how thrice he had hovered on the very threshold of

apostacy and ruin, and thus warned, he went out and wept bitterly.
And, while the work of the bag-carrying Judas was going on, the
salvation of the penitent was assured. And I, Mr. O'Connell, contemptible as you affect to believe me, have been privileged to utter
a warning, that even not a few of the vacillating "Liberals" have
heard, while our sleeping Protestantism has been aroused to a sense
of danger, and the defence of those liberties and institutions, which
the Judas hand of Repeal would sell to our enemies for a "shout of
the gulls", or another bag of the "rent". Yes, Mr. O'Connell, I thank
you for all the "*insulting*" epithets you have applied to me; for you
honour me, when you treat my humble name with the same civility
with which you treat a Stanley. But, especially for the last attempted
insult, I thank you, for it not only reminds me of the salutary
warning of the "Bird of Dawn", but also of the poetic power with
which the great Master of Nature has invested it; and when I think
of how God was pleased to own my humble labours in concentrating
the might of Ulster, and terrifying the wizards of Repeal, it reminds
me of the sulphurous exit of the Ghost in Hamlet, which

"*Faded* at the crowing of the Cock'
For then (you know) no spirits dare walk abroad;
No planets strike, no witch her power to charm—
So wholesome and so gracious are the times".

But your pitiable partizans here, taking their cue from their
leaders, talk of my "crowing on my own dunghill".—I pardon them
the uncomeliness of the figure; but even of that, I will not leave them
the possession. No, Mr. O'Connell; it is not in Belfast I desire to meet
you. And though I shrink not from Dublin—the Rotunda, or the
Corn-Exchange—London and Exeter-Hall should be our ground of
meeting. You'll *retreat* upon business, I know. You shall not. I'm behind
you again. There are the *Easter recess* and the days of (I think) *Ascot
Races*; on either of these occasions, I offer to meet you; and that no
obstacle may be pleaded, I shall depend on the very few friends I
can muster in London, to bear the whole expense of the meeting.
You know, and I feel your every advantage over me—but you know
and I feel the boundless advantage of my *cause;* and, by the blessing

of God, upon my feeble arm, I trust to tear away the cloak of hypocritical and mercenary patriotism, in which you are enveloped, and to expose, to the horror of the nation, that horrible system of studied falsehood and mental slavery, of which you are the pensioned missionary.

Yes, Mr. O'Connell, there is nothing I more cordially desire than to expose that system of "enormous lying" by which Romanism and Repeal are supported. Yet, at the same time, I am thankful to God, that your party are serving the cause of Protestantism by every additional volley. The chief of our "Liberals" are getting their eyes opened, when they read the transcendental falsehoods which the Priests' organists here are every day playing—and yet absolutely continuing, without a blush, to walk the streets in open day. 30,000 Repealers!—the "immense pavilion *erected* for the dinner!!—your graceful entry and triumphant exit!!!" Tut, these are all but trifles to what I might gather. And, indeed, they are but trifles to the "out and outer" capacity of your own son, Charles O'Connell—at least from the name, so I take him to be. He says in a late oration in Dublin, and which, from the peculiar raciness of "*genteel invention*" he must, as I take it, have learned from yourself. He says, you had to be protected by an army from the "Orange mob, the bloody blackguards" of *Sandy-row!* "Oh! where was Roderick then?"[111] Where was Tom Steele, with the 30,000 Repealers?!!—Terrified for the millions of *Sandy-row!*—a little street, of a few houses, to a considerable degree occupied by Roman Catholics, and the whole about as extensive as a back-lane in Brentford! But, then, this eloquent son of yours affirms you had to be "guarded *through*" this redoubtable, this most warlike *Sandy-row*, at an early hour in the morning. I'll tell Charles a secret—neither you nor he had a foot in Sandy-row—neither of you ever saw it, during your whole sojourn. Should this eloquent *eulogy*, which Mr. Charles O'Connell has pronounced on the more than Grecian prowess of our modern Marathon, ever be read by any citizen of London, and should this, I hope, my last letter to you, ever be read there as the commentary—what will he think, when informed, that when Mr. O'Connell and Co. stood to enact the Repeal pantomime in Belfast, they were somewhat about as near Sandy-row, as a man at Charing-cross is to the White-horse in Piccadilly—and what will he think of the necessity of a mighty guard throughout *Sandy-row*, when told that he O'Connell in his *triumphant exit* from Belfast went as much towards *Sandy-row* as a man goes towards Piccadilly, when he gallops from Charing-cross directly over Westminster bridge!! Charles, Charles, you are your father's son—but I suppose "the gulls shouted".

You were "guarded through Sandy-row", says the veracious Charles O'Connell. I will tell you through what you were guarded— Sandy-row lies to the west of "our village", and you spanked away utterly unheeded, with only the loud laugh of one single Belfast merchant, and at whom the exalted Thomas Steele most valiantly shook his clenched fist, by way of conciliation; and you passed by the corner of Cromac and May-street, where your "cherishing" friends had demolished the windows of one Protestant dwelling, and by the *visit of a two pound brick-bat*, had nearly killed a female member of my own congregation in another.

Believe me, Mr. O'Connell, I do not state this by any way of excuse for the stone thrown into the Music-Hall, and which is said to have injured one of the "lovely and the good"; but I do it to put an end to your tragical bluster, and to remind the nation, and especially our Protestant brethren, that the life of a Protestant female is still as precious as that of a Romanist.

Mr. O'Connell! Mr. O'Connell! I must speak to you in indignant seriousness. If there be one thing that more than another should harrow the conscience now, or that more than another will burn in it hereafter, it is, and it will be, the fearful thought and recollection of having poisoned principle at the fountain-head, and, by neglect, example, or encouragement, contributed to the ruin of your own children. See with what reckless audacity you have taught your son to practice your own art of invention! Repent, ere it be too late. Retread the maze of imposture into which you have not only run yourself, but in which you are inextricably involving your beloved offspring! I have called you a "great bad man!" Beware, or you will soon become a little one. The towns of *Kilworth* and *Annan* have afforded you two ominous warnings. I am not superstitious. But I tell you again to beware—the hand of Providence, and not of accident, prostrated the animals before you; and, be sure, these events are but the "*precursors*" of the prostration of your character and your

influence, if you return not by repentance to the utterance of truth
and the practices of peace. I remain, an inveterate enemy to your
principles and practices, but a sincere friend to your immortal soul,

H. COOKE.

Belfast, 27th January, 1841.

THE O'CONNELLITE VERSION
OF
THE FLIGHT FROM BELFAST.

WE cannot bring this publication to a conclusion, without
a brief mention of the almost incredible fabrications to which
the Repeal party have resorted, for the purpose of covering
Mr. O'Connell's ignominious retreat from our Northern
Metropolis. Of course, in Belfast itself, and throughout the
North generally, in consequence of the extensive circulation of
the Anti-Repeal newspapers, no deception upon a large scale
could have been successfully practised; but the manoeuvres
which we are about to notice were intended for districts into
which

"———————— no daylight enters,
But cats, bats, and badgers for ever breed."

The *Vindicator*, under the direction of the Priests, set the
first example of this monstrous system of lying, by representing
the Repeal demonstration as one of the most magnificent dis-
plays of its kind which had ever occurred. And here let us interpose a cursory remark upon the morality of the case. Even
Priests profess to admit, that the *telling* of a known falsehood is
criminal; but it does not appear that a similar law is extended
to the writing, printing, and *publishing* of falsehood, when the
tendency of the latter is likely to be advantageous to the cause
of "Mother Church". To our laic apprehension, however, it
would seem that the deliberation, with which the publishing
of untruths is necessarily accompanied, aggravates immensely

the immorality of printed as compare with spoken lies. But we forget—the offenders have in their own hands the keys of future bliss, and can let in themselves and their satellites on their own terms—hence, veracity may naturally be expected to be a cheap virtue in the Repeal market; and so it truly is.

Mr. Charles O'Connell, it will be recalled by our readers, was one of the parties who accompanied the Repeal Missionary on his retreat to Donaghadee, and on the following Monday, Jan. 25, he attended a meeting of the Repeal Association, in Dublin, at which he gave, in the form of a speech, one of the most curiously apocryphal narratives, of the exit from Belfast, that have ever amused an intelligent public. He was quite sure that the Orange mob, which interrupted Mr. O'Connell's oratory at the public meeting, was composed of "shirtless, waistcoatless", individuals, while he could not undertake to say that they were provided with nether garments of an indispensable nature; but such was the ferocity of the "bloody blackguards", as he called them, that a strong escort of Police was requisite to protect Mr. O'Connell from their violence, during his passage through Sandy-row on his way to Donaghadee. It happens that the moment he left the Royal Hotel he turned his back directly upon Sandy-row, and was never once within its dreaded precincts; but this is a point which Dr. Cooke has touched with admirable effect in his third and concluding letter, to which we refer our readers.

One of the excuses put forward by the *Vindicator*, and the other Repeal organs, for Mr. O'Connell's refusal to meet Dr. Cooke in a public discussion, was the necessity imposed upon the former of attending a great meeting of Reformers at Leeds, on Thursday, the 21st January; but the fact is, *he did not attend that meeting at all.* Some convenient obstacle arose on the way between Portpatrick and Leeds—*accidentally*, of course[112]— and Mr. O'Connell did not enter Leeds until twenty-four hours *after* the time appointed for holding the meeting! The obstacle aforesaid was *prudent* as well as *accidental*; for so exasperated were the English populace at his political misconduct, that their indignation exceeded, if possible, that of the Protestants of

Belfast, and, had he made his appearance at the period expected, he would have been literally drummed out of the town.

The following resolution, which was unanimously adopted
at a meeting preliminary to the general one already alluded
to, is a powerfully significant indication of the contempt which
his paltry shrinking from Dr. Cooke's challenge had generated
in the minds of the intelligent operatives of England:—

"Resolved—that this meeting, constitutionally representing the
working classes of Great Britain, is heartily in favour of a Repeal of
the Legislative Union between Great Britain and Ireland; while they
will not stir, aid, or join in any plan for its accomplishment, recommended by Mr. O'Connell, who, while he has made it a source of
personal wealth, has endeavoured, by all the artful means in his
power, to deter England from acquiescing in the measure; and who,
though he blusters, vapours, and repeats his oft-told rigmarole to his
staff, has just now refused to meet Dr. Cooke, in fair discussion, on
the question, thereby proving either that he feels his inability to
defend it, while he must be aware, that, if successful, such a triumph
would be worth ten thousand meetings, where none are allowed to
dissent from him under pain of political excommunication."[113]

Here is one of the most splendid testimonials that Dr.
Cooke, or any other public character, has ever received. The
authors of the resolution above quoted expressly declare
themselves to be Repealers—to be men after Mr. O'Connell's
own heart; and yet they honestly record their contempt of his
moral cowardice, and their high approval, on abstract grounds,
of the fair terms proposed by Dr. Cooke. This voluntary
declaration, on the part of avowed opponents, which declaration the intrinsic power of truth alone could have induced,
is infinitely more valuable than the collected harvest of
"golden opinions" which the learned Doctor has deservedly
won from all the rest of the community besides. It might have
been supposed that the strongly expressed opinions of the
Repealers of Leeds, who must have known far less respecting
the realities of O'Connell's agitation visit to Belfast than the
Irish population themselves should naturally be expected to do,

would have neutralized the inventive energies of the party; but the event turned out to be far otherwise. Accordingly Mr. O'Connell, after his arrival in London to attend the parliamentary session, deliberately sat down and wrote, to the Dublin Repeal Association, an official account of his own mission to the North, in which the following, amongst other monstrous fabrications, were attested under his hand and signature:—

1. That more than 1,200 gentlemen, each having *paid* half-a-guinea for his ticket, entertained him at the dinner in Belfast. The truth is, that free tickets were *pressed* upon Liberal Protestants; that Roman Catholic employers induced their dependants to procure tickets; and, after all, there were not 900 men present at the dinner.

2. That "more than 600 of the lovely and the good" graced the gallery with their presence. There may have been 200 females present, including fish-vendors, public-house keepers, and red legs from Hercules-street; but this is a subject, in regard to which the principle usually called gallantry bids us to be silent. Some of the *dresses* were wonderfully passable, considering the *rank* of the wearers.

3. Almost the only truth contained in this letter is the important admission, that the dinner "was substantially a *Repeal* demonstration"—but it was, "at all events, a demonstration of *kindliness* to, and calculated to *animate* and *cheer* on the *Repealer*." A capital reward this to the half-dozen of Liberal Protestants who attended the dinner on the faith of its being a *Reform*, not a *Repeal* demonstration!

4. It is pretended that the Pavilion could not have held the assembled Repealers. A commonplace enough excuse this for cheating, and continuing to cheat, the public out of the price of the admission tickets! It can be demonstrated that, at the time of adjournment, the Pavilion would have held, as Dr. Cooke states, fully 500 persons more than were actually within its walls.

5. It is asserted, by Mr. O'Connell, that the Repealers attended the open air meeting, in "tens and twenties of thousands", though the noise created by the Anti-Repealers was so great as to render inaudible every syllable that he uttered, even to his nearest friends on the platform. There were not, at any time, 10,000 persons present, and of these not more than *one-third* were Repealers.

6. Mr. O'Connell states, that the resolutions printed in the *Vindicator* and reprinted, as having been proposed to the meeting, were carried by overwhelming majorities. We have already said, and every man of every political creed in Belfast knows, that, neither a speech nor a resolution could possibly be heard at the Repeal meeting, and the consequent impudence of the O'Connellite agitation is therefore unparalleled.—As a body, the Anti-Repealers purposely abstained from mustering their forces, lest a riot should be created; but, if abominable falsehoods of this grossly villanous description are to be put in circulation, let the equitable proposal of the *News-Letter* be adopted, and let the parties try their respective strength at a public meeting called for that especial purpose. If any thing can teach the Repealers the duty of telling truth, this will, and let them adopt the suggestion, if they dare.

7. Mr. O'Connell, in the letter referred to, has the exemplary courage to say, —"There never was the *least intention of a* PROCESSION on my journey through any of the towns from Newry to Belfast, nor in Belfast itself." This paragraph is ingeniously worded, and, to those who do not look closely into it, would convey the impression, that Mr. O'Connell's visit had been originally intended to be the most quiet, unobtrusive thing imaginable. No procession was to be hazarded in any of the "towns from *Newry* to Belfast": but the truth is suppressed, that, in the principal towns from Dublin to Newry, processions had been arranged, as we have already stated in the introductory narrative, while, in Newry itself, the Repeal party had made preparations for a display upon a scale of absolute grandeur. The *Newry Examiner*, an O'Connellite journal, in its publication of the 6th January, in reference to Mr. O'Connell's advent, says—

"There will be a grand Repeal demonstration here. A *procession* will meet Mr. O'Connell, and escort him into Newry."

Again, in the *Examiner* of the 16th January, it is stated in relation to the same event—

"There will be a glorious demonstration here, in despite of paltry Whigs and truculent Tories—the greatest ever witnessed in Newry. *Thirty thousand* brave men shall rally round the deliverer of Ireland, and make the welkin ring with shouts of welcome to Ulster's frontier town."

In his letter to Dr. Blake, Mr. O'Connell used the following expressions, in regard to his arrival in Newry—

"I can be in Newry by nine o'clock, at farthest; and *giving my friends there an hour and a half for their procession*, be able to leave at half-past ten. As a matter of merely literal, technical, pettifogging veracity, it is true, that Mr. O'Connell cannot be legally convicted of encouraging a procession in any town farther North than Newry; but is it credible that he would have refused in Banbridge or Dromore that which he so proudly anticipated in Newry, or can it be supposed that the example set in the one case, would not have been at least attempted in the other? That this was the primary intention of the faction, we have the conclusive authority of the *Newry Examiner* for stating, as the fact was, in this journal, carefully announced beforehand, that 4,000 Repealers would welcome Mr. O'Connell into the Orange town of Lisburn, and there present him with an address! But this is a point to which we have already referred in our historical introduction. Why were the avowedly arranged processions in Drogheda, Dundalk, &c., abandoned, and why all this new-born anxiety to repudiate the very idea of a processional demonstration?

8. After the astounding and palpably wilful falsehood to which reference has just been made, we may well be excused from all further examination of the details of Mr. O'Connell's letter; but it contains one other statement, which cannot be passed over without some notice of its infamous character. Mr. O'Connell has actually the worse than brazen audacity to insinuate that the mob who broke some windows of the Music-hall, and injured, in a slight degree, one of the ladies in attendance at the Soirée, as we have already, with sincere regret, stated in our historical narrative, were acting under the instigation of Dr. Cooke![114] This is absolutely too bad even for Mr. O'Connell—he would not himself, on grounds of secular expediency, be a party to any such proceeding—and why should he covertly try to cast odium upon an opponent whom he knows to be neither ungenerous, nor destitute of proper feeling, to say nothing of Irish chivalry on this occasion? To formally contradict the vile insinuation alluded to, would be, on the part of Dr. Cooke, an act of highly blameable condescension, as his character is too strongly established to need any testimony in regard to a matter so obvious. Mr. O'Connell must have been sadly confounded, when he ventured to task a man whom he dared not meet, with conduct which his

worst enemy will inevitably set down as an invention hazarded only in a moment of utter desperation. Were Dr. Cooke capable of the villainy insinuated, he is too able a tactician to be guilty of it; but what will be thought of Mr. O'Connell's hypocritical thanksgiving to the Deity, that the Repealers had been too innocently forbearing to commit any outrage, when the fact is reiterated, that the brickbat which had nearly killed a respectable lady member of Dr. Cooke's congregation, is preserved, and can still be exhibited at the shop of the publisher of this narrative? Violence on any side we deplore; but it is intolerable, that Mr. O'Connell should intimate charges of which he knows it is morally impossible that any intelligent opponent should be guilty. That Dr. Cooke is not devoid of intelligence, is proven by the fact of Mr. O'Connell's flying from him, while the secondary inference is too plain to require elucidation, and, accordingly, we will not affront Dr. Cooke by its immediate deduction, not only from the premises, but from the direct evidence of his nonplussed calumniator.

The service which Dr. Cooke, by his seasonable challenge to Mr. O'Connell, has rendered, not alone to the Protestants of Ireland, but to the British empire at large, and even to such Roman Catholic gentlemen as happen to possess property, cannot be too highly estimated. A suitable testimonial to Dr. Cooke has been accordingly projected—a subscription Committee has been appointed; and, since the cause is one in which *all* classes of British subjects are interested, we are proportionately happy to announce, that the "*Repulser*" of the "*Repealer*" is not likely to be permitted to retire to the modest discharge of his onerous clerical duties, without a becoming testimony of public approval. For this object, a central Committee, as already stated, has been established in Belfast, and local branches are in course of rapid formation throughout the three kingdoms, so general is the gratitude felt for the national services of Dr. Cooke, on the recent occasion. If there be any one indifferent to this subject, let him, in the words of the dramatic poet,

> "Think what a blow he deals the noble cause,
> We now stand up for"—[115]

THE NORTHERN LIGHTS
OR,
SKETCHES AND SONGS ALL ABOUT REPEAL.

HITHERTO, delighted reader, under our guidance, hast thou been conducted through the veritable history of the redoubtable Repealers in Belfast. With thy permission we feel we have a right to pause for a moment, and survey the ample scope we have for self-congratulation. WE ARE NOW AN HISTORIAN. We have earned immortality. *Exegi monumentum.* We have recorded the touching scenes of the three days of Repeal in Belfast—equal in interest to the days of the French Revolution; and our History of Repeal and Retreat shall henceforward rank with the *retreat of the ten thousand*, and our name shall now be enrolled with that of the illustrious historian thereof. We are now equal to Herodotus or Hume, Robertson or Rapin, Gillies or Gibbon, Schlegel or Smollet. Henceforward shall we repose under our historical garlands; we shall be hailed as one of the benefactors of our species; our authority shall be undisputed; and our historical performance shall be one of those "which men will not willingly let die".

But, while we have thus soared to our dignified immortality, we are not strangers to human feelings; and, therefore, we are not uninfluenced by that gratitude of thine, O reader, which we are confident we deserve, and which, in its depth and extent, maketh even more exquisite the superabundance of our exaltation. Had we nothing wherewithal to rejoice ourselves but even that gratitude which we have already earned, of a verity we should have ample compensation for the labour we have cheerfully undergone for thy sake, in the collection and comparison of authorities, the discovery and arrangement of rare and curious documents, and the sundry and special toils we have borne in bringing to a successful termination our historical performance. We say, therefore, emphatically, that we can calculate with certainty on thy gratitude. Without resting, however, on what we have already done, we intend to do more; so that, for this additional and gratuitous exertion on our part, we expect—nay, we are confident that thy benevolence to usward shall ascend to the superlative degree. We have hitherto entertained thee with the strict reality of the above-mentioned days—and perilous, withal. We now relax from our philosophical severity, and we condescend to regale thee with the Romance of the History of that ever-to-be-remembered epoch.

If, peradventure, reader, thou hast occasionally turned thy attention to the history of Literature, thou must have found, that civil and political commotions have almost invariably been the means of giving a corresponding impulse to the mind of the time. We could quote, if necessary, the eras of Augustus and Elizabeth, and that of the French Revolution, as proof. On the same principle we should expect that there would be a corresponding forth-calling of intellect, in consequence of that political commotion which hath of late taken place, and which hath been so faithfully recorded. Such hath been the case. The talent of the North was roused; a new impulse was given to the mind; vast and gigantic conceptions struggled to obtain vent; poets who erst were unconscious of their powers, appeared in a multitude; lyrics and elegies were flung forth; nay, an epic was meditated, whose subject was Repeal—whose hero was Dan—whose episodes were soirees—whose moral was loyalty—and whose catastrophe was defeat.

In entering then on the pleasing task of transmitting to posterity a *libamentum* of the literature of that wonderful time, there are divers remarks which we would desiderate to offer. We would wish it, therefore, to be gratefully remembered that, the labour and skill in collecting were astonishing; and, though it boots not enquirers to know, the sources of investigation were ample and peculiar. In sitting now in our solitary dignity, encircled with the multifarious exhibitions of intellect scattered around us, we desire also to register the additional honour in which we feel ourselves clothed, in thus being permitted to hold sublime converse with those master minds by the instrumentality of their productions. We are labouring under the pressing consciousness of our responsibility in venturing to make a selection. We are burning to disclose the History of these immortal relics, and the Biography of their authors; but above all, inasmuch as it lieth not within our power to do so, we wish to convince the world of their genuineness and authenticity. In order to effect this therefore, we adventure on a solemn statement, for the truth of which we stake our reputation. Be it known then to all and sundry whom it may concern, that, with respect to the poems hereunto annexed, various sources of emendation have been explored, numerous MSS. have been collected and collated, so that the text of these immortal productions may be now depended upon as almost, if not altogether, agreeing with the autographs themselves. After this grave declaration, and necessary withal, we rest satisfied, that the world will feel henceforth at ease, that thousands of learned conjectures will be unnecessary, that the Editors of coming centuries shall be saved a world of trouble, and that hence forward *in secula seculorum*, this will be regarded as the only correct and genuine edition of *The Repeal Anthology*.

The first in time and therefore in place is "*O'Connell's Warning*". As soon as Dr. Cooke published his manly challenge to Mr. O'Connell, among those who were Anti-Repealers the opinion existed, either that Mr. O'Connell would decline, or that if he would accept the challenge, his defeat was certain. The latter seems to have been the opinion of the author of this piece. In consequence, it appeared a few days afterward in the *News-Letter*, from which it was copied into some of the other papers. It is evidently intended as a Parody on "Lochiel's Warning".

O'CONNELL'S WARNING

FRIAR.

O'CONNELL! O'CONNELL! beware of the day
When Northwards you go for expected display:
For your certain discomfiture bursts on my sight,
And your clan of Repealers are scattered in fight,
Who burn to restore to our Island its crown,
Woe, woe to old COOKE, for he tramples them down!
The "*loathsome*" old "*theologue*" gloats o'er the slain,
And the sons of Repeal are now trod to the plain.
—But hark! through the wide preparation for war,
What note to the Southward flies fearful and far?
'Tis the challenge of COOKE—'tis thy omen of fate,
If Northward you move from thy Darrynane gate.
You may go to Belfast, but disaster is there,
And Repealers are showing their signs of despair.
Weep, sons of Repeal, to captivity led,
Your hopes of Repeal in the North are now dead,
And the flag of defeat o'er O'Connell shall wave
—O'Connell subdued by that heretic slave.

O'CONNELL.

Go, frighten old RITCHIE, thou woe-preaching seer—
If my trip to Belfast so terrific appear,
Draw, dotard, around thy old wavering sight,
This frieze-coat to cover thy phantoms of fright!

FRIAR.

Ha! Laughest thou, O'Connell, my vision to scorn?
Old beggar of Kerry, thy bags shall be torn!
Say, dreadest thou not to go wantonly forth
The Eagle to meet in his home of the North?
Still, the shafts of all foemen despising, he rode,
Resistless, and scattering destruction abroad;
And now he will pounce from his eyrie on high,
Encounter him not, for thy spoiling is nigh.

Why riseth yon tent? Why so eager and fast
Do thy worshippers hurry thy trip to Belfast?
'Tis thy tocsin of woe, for you hence shall be driven,
Like leaves down the vale, by the tempest of Heaven!
Oh! foolish O'Connell, untrained for the fight,
Though Kerry-men think thee the peerless in might,
COOKE's lightning is waiting to blast and to burn,
Return to thy dwelling, be wise, and return,
For no foe hath before him, unconquered, yet stood,
And he'll vanquish both thee and thy frieze-coated brood!

O'CONNELL.

Old dreamer! avaunt! I shall muster a clan
Of sturdy Repealers whose object is one.
They are vastly profuse of their lungs and their breath,
And shall roar for Repeal till the hour of their death.
And woe to the "THEOLOGUE!" woe to his cause,
When the crowds at the Linen-hall open their jaws;
When their frieze-coated chieftain harangues long and loud,
From the royal balcony, that wonderful crowd,
All gathered and trained for that goodly display—

FRIAR.

O'Connell! O'Connell! beware of that day!
For dark and despairing my sight I might seal,
And keep from you now what I cannot conceal:
'Tis the gloom of our friends in Belfast gives me lore,
And your coming defeat casts its shadow before.
I tell thee that Ireland's valleys shall ring
At the news of this doom I unwillingly sing.
Ay, crushed by the might of antagonist wrath,
Thou shalt hasten away on thy desolate path.
Now, floundered and vanquished, he sweeps from my sight;
Hush, tempest of Eloquence! mock not his flight! —
The discussion is ended, and out from the doors
He is fled, and his party in silence deplores!-
But where is he gone—the defeated—oh! where

Shall he fly from the storm of pursuing despair?
Say, mounts he the car on which hitherwards borne
In triumph he came, but departed in scorn?
Ah, no; for a quicker departure is near—
He hastes to the steam-boat, which waits at the pier.
Its third bell is tolling—Oh! mercy, dispel
The hisses of those who the victory tell!
Accursed be the gathering at Leeds! Can he meet
Those men who shall hear and shall mourn his defeat,
Whose unwelcome sighings shall burden the gale? –

O'CONNELL.
Down, heartless forboder! I trust not the tale,
For ne'er shall O'Connell a destiny meet
So black with dishonour—so foul with retreat.
Though Cooke should defeat me, like others before,
And the cause of Repeal should be heard of no more,
O'Connell replenished with rent-gathered gains,
While the gullible taste of the people remains,
Can to Darrynane's dwelling contentedly go,
All shielded and safe from his every foe;
And leaving but one *duel*-stain on his name,
Soar shriven from earth, and then—what about fame?[116]

While such, however, seems to have been the opinion of
that party, those of another class were loud in their boastings,
and sanguine in their expectations, touching the descent of
this Repealing *Avatar*, and the consequences which would follow.
It was calculated by them, that his visit to the North would
give a new impulse and conglomeration to the Avalanche of
revolution. The whole body at once seemed animated with
new mental powers; and, from the additional noise of the
Sabbath-evening oratory of Anne-street, down to the roar of
the Repeal chaunts in the Barrack-street tap-rooms, we have
something like an index to the golden dreamings with which
they looked forward to the millennial glories of Repeal. By the
kindness of a friend, we have been able to rescue from

oblivion, a lyric of that *ça ira* class. It was sung not in one of
the taverns of our town; but in a remote *shebeen*, where Bill
Flanagan, Murtagh O'Brady, Paddy M'Graw, Torlogh Mullan,
had been discussing the glories of Repeal, and the dignity to
which all and each of them might be eventually raised. After
divers solicitations and sundry preparations of throat, voice,
and gesture, Torlogh roared out a ditty, whose structure reminds
us very much of an old snatch we used to hear at school,
which was

"Auld bauld Baulder M'Gregor lost his dagger,
On Friday, among the rain;
If ony auld bauld beggar find auld Baulder M'Gregor's dagger,
Let him restore auld bauld Baulder M'Gregor's dagger to him
again."

In a style of verse somewhat similar, and with all the eupho-
niousness of the Munster brogue, he sings to the air of "*The
Groves of Blarney*", a new song called

THE BLISSIN'S OF REPALE

ASSIST ye Muses, my wake invintion—
Inspire my ganius while now I pen,
The agitation through Erin's nation,
Her Parliament to restore again.
'Tis it, most surely, that 'ud be curin',
What we're endurin', for many a year;
No Tithes nor Taxes, 'ud be to vex us
Likewise no Rints, as yees soon shall hear.

Och! were I Caesar, or great Belshaisar,
Or Nebuchadnaisar, who wrote of Troy,
Its I'd be traitin and celebratin'
The greatness thin that we'ud enjoy.
Musha! pace and plinty, an' sweet contintmint,

Would be beyant all yees ever knew:
Faix we'd be vyin' with ould King Bryan,
Who bate the Dane's all, both black and blue.

Sure O'Connell's sayin' to be delayin',
To get Repale does be mighty wrong;
And if we want it, it must be granted,
Bekase, says he, we're eight millions strong.
Och! *wirra strue*, we'd thin appear in
The fame we're hearin' we had av yore,
Whin we were a nation of exaltation,
And our ould king's goolden sceptres wore.

Whin we're obtainin' an' after gainin',
The cause Dan's seekin' of great Repale,
Bad luck to Judge, or to Lord or Parson
Will thin be troublin' ould Granua Waile.
Whow! tare an' ounties, how we'll be shoutin',
When back the Parliamint again we'll bring;
An' whin nixt saisin', we will be raisin'
The great O'Connell for to be our King.

An' thin, ye Pattherns an' days av fightin';
Which we delight in, again 'ud be;
And our sweet clargy, the Heaven reward them,
They would be guardin' us from heresy.
In peace wid live in, an' would be givin',
Ourselves to coort, an' to drink and fight;
Wi'd have good atin', an' fun an' tratin',
And sweet divarsion, from morn till night.

We'd keep our Nation, in a situation,
As from all furriners for to be free;
They've been our ruin, an' our ondoin';
Since first they entered our counterey.
But thin the land, in which we are standin',
They would abandon widout delay;
Och! by the powers, 'twould thin be ours,
For we 'ud banish thim beyant the say.

Now for conclusion to my effusion,
An' for to finish what I have penned:
May the great Saint Austin, likewise Chrystostom,
And the Pope of Rome, upon us descend!
May the Virgin Mary, who lives in glory,
Grant unto us that we nivir fail!
An' may Saint Pether be our directhur—
An' thin, by gorra, we will have Repale![117]

Dan, it will be remembered, had threatened to come thirty thousand strong, and to terrify the North by physical display. His march was to be like that of a Sovereign and a Conqueror through his provinces. The shout of reception was to be caught up at Newry, and to be prolonged, in one unbroken torrent of exultation from town to town, and from multitude to multitude, until at last the thousands who were to meet him at Belfast would utter forth one immortalising yell of triumph, and give the finishing touch to his political apotheosis. But alas! alas! The hopes of earth and of earthly agitators are vain. They are "as the morning cloud", &c. His oration was turned into mourning; his welcomings into hisses; his blarneyings into silence; and Dan—King Dan—the Liberator—was obliged to come quietly into Belfast, rejoicing in the title of Mr. CHARLES, and professing the honourable calling of a—Ventriloquist. Hereupon, he of Banbridge—an immortal BARD—did write "ane richt pleausant song", the whilk did make its compearance in the *Evening Mail*, and goeth to the air of *"Here's to the maiden of blooming fifteen"*.[118] Here it is, and with the leave of the good author we shall designate it—

THE MOUNTEBANK CROSSING THE BANN.

Oh, heard ye the inroad was made on the north?
Lord Ebrington's method of reigning?
Horse, foot, and artill'ry—police, and so forth?
  And Daniel's successful campaigning?
  And how Bully Dan,
  That popular man,
  In triumph—*in cog.*—sallied over the Bann?
  GRAND CHORUS.
  Dan—diddle Dan!
  That popular man,
We'll sing of his triumph in crossing the Bann.

Those rigid "black north'rns" are comical folk –
They relish no Popish attacks on
Their faith or their fortunes; and count it no joke
To be called "the SATANICAL SAXON".
  So they vowed to a man –
  That if they caught Dan,
They'd put him, as sure as a gun, under Bann.
  GRAND CHORUS.
  Dan—diddle Dan!
  That popular man!
Who triumphed *in cog.*, going over the Bann.

And some of them, too, have a sort of a feel
That the whole Corn-Exchange agitation
Contemplates sedition, and more—that REPEAL
Means—rightly explained—SEPARATION.
  So they swore—to [a] man—
  That, if they caught Dan,
They'd put him and his politics both under Bann.
  GRAND CHORUS.
  Dan—diddle Dan!
  That popular man,
Had a certain dislike to be put under Bann!

Then bethought Dan of a bit of a plan;
For, tho' he loved "piping and droning",
He had no sort of taste for a Heretic Bann,
With its consequent "grunting and groaning".
    So he sent on his man
    To announce that—not Dan,
But the mountebank Charles was approaching the Bann.
    GRAND CHORUS.
    Dan—diddle Dan!
    Mister Charles is the man
Whose mountebank tricks will get over the bann.

Whose carriage in green is now crossing the Bann?
It is CHARLES's—the ventriloquiser.
There's someone inside—and *in cog*. It is Dan,
And the Bandbridgers never the wiser.
    And thus it was Dan,
    By a mountebank plan,
Escaped for the nonce being put under Bann.
    GRAND CHORUS.
    Dan—diddle - Dan!
    That popular man,
Disguised as a mountebank, got o'er the Bann.

We now arrive to the Mount Olympus of the proceedings—THE DINNER. Be it remembered, then, that "the
man wot does" the *Vindicator*, called the place of the feed a
PAVILION, and represented it as decorated with such gorgeous
magnificence that we did wonder by what Aladdin's lamp
process it could be converted, all at once, from an old
shingled tabernacle, where erst were exhibited the tricks of
"Punch and Judy" to the "unwashed artificers", for threepence
a-head, into a hall, pillared and festooned, and partitioned in
a style of oriental glory. It was all a dream, which stole over
the imagination of the veracious caterer, and which, in all
charity, we must believe, when in a state of somnambulency,
he unconsciously scribbled, as he roamed through his room,

like a child at a feast, ridolent of wine and rollicking in his glory. Dr. Cooke called the Pavilion *Ricketty Hall*; and, acting on this hint, one of the scoffers, in a moment of tickled excitement, did touch off the following witty stave, y'cleped:—

RICKETTY HALL.

I'LL sing you a wonderful song, and it's all,
From beginning to end, about Ricketty Hall,
Whose history, banquets of late, and so forth,
Have haloed with glory the land of the North.

Ricketty Hall is no mansion which rears
Its head with the hoar of some hundreds of years;
Ricketty Hall is no old fashioned place,
Where long has resided a chronicled race.

When this mansion magnificent erewhile arose,
Near the Lagan's wide stream, it was made to enclose
The beasts of the forest, whose gambolings drew
Many crowds to behold and admire them there too.

But that era passed by, and another one came,
Though somewhat less savage, yet nearly the same;
For "groundlings" there gathered, to witness the rage
Of the heroes who fretted their time on its stage.

But, *Io Triumphe!* the greatest of all
Of the scenes which took place within Ricketty Hall,
Was the feast of Repeal, and its feeding and fun,
In the year eighteen hundred and forty and one.

From the South to the North the intelligence passed,
That Dan would be fed in the town of Belfast:-
So, as wild beasts at gorging time, many agreed
That Dan to advantage would look at his feed.

So many a *Raggedness* gathered to see
The feasts gastronomic of this great M.P.;
And how, after repletion, he'd waggle his tail,
And blarney, and bellow, and roar of Repale.

Like the lions of Amburgh, the fasting-famed Dan,
And the whole of the hungry menagerie began;
Yet, when feasted and gorged, not like Amburgh's they grew,
For they shouted, and spouted, and growled until Two.*

So hurrah! for great Ricketty-Hall, and each scene
Of wild exhibition, which therein has been!
And a toast for my wonderful song, which was all,
From beginning to end, about Ricketty-Hall.[119]

Such was the feed in Ricketty Hall! But then Belfast was
not only to be gorged into Repeal, but a soiree was to complete the revolution; therefore did the "lovely and the good"—
the fishwives and the handmaidens of Hercules-street, and
divers of a similar description—assemble in all the gaudiness
of their borrowed finery, and present such a conglomeration
of beauty, that the heart of the chivalric Dillon Browne did
melt under the warmth and light of such a galaxy of con-
certed splendour. There were caitiff Knights without, however,
whose hearts were steeled against such delicate susceptibilities,
and who had no sympathies with those throbbings of love, or
breathings of Repeal. Therefore was Dan disturbed—
therefore was Dillon Browne disturbed—therefore was Repeal
disturbed. Oh! there was parting in hot haste—there were
runnings to and fro—there was Dan hasting to his hiding-
place—and there were the "lovely and the good" hurrying
away to their domestic duties. Hard-hearted indeed was the
clever wag who could indite such a piece of sarcasm anent
such tender scenes. Read it and judge. It is called

* Two o'clock, Printer's Devil.

THE DEPARTURE.

No shout was heard, no Repealing yell,
As Dan from the Soiree hurried;
For the trembling frames of the junta tell
How their hero was sadly flurried.

They stole him in, 'neath the shades of night,
To his prison, quick retiring;
And they swore him out, in the morning light,
In wisdom worth admiring.

No gay procession moved along,
In our Northern town around him;
But he passed as he came, unseen, unsung,
In the frieze-coat that tightly bound him.

A few short prayers were quickly said,
But they could not banish sorrow;
For the thought of COOKE, was in his head,
And much he feared the morrow.

We thought as we heard his oration read,
He had slept on a thorny pillow;
But he lied like a knave, in all he said,
For he tossed like the ocean billow.

Loudly they talk of their money that's gone,
And Repealers begin to upbraid him;
But he'll blarney them yet, and the rent they'll pay on,
For lies can no further degrade him.

But draughts of tea had scarcely done
Their trembling hearts inspiring,
And the evening scarcely half was run,
When Dan was seen retiring.

Slowly and sadly they led him forth,
By the backward door so lowly,
Counting his beads, and cursing the North,
And the "*Theologue*" unholy. [120]

Yes, as that immortal bard singeth, "the thought of Cooke was in his head, and much he feared the morrow" and no wonder indeed. Turn to the pages of our veritable history, and read the thrilling scene which took place at the Linen-Hall, when the Apostle of Repeal had to encounter the loyal opposition of the sons of Brown-street[121] and Sandy-Row,[122] and Ballymacarrett. Some one from the banks of the Ballow, (may his name be immortal) in his own style right wittily celebrated that scene. Read the song of him of Ballow which we copy from the *Chronicle*.

"THE BATTLE OF THE NORTH"
"Paulo majora canemus".

Of Daniel to the North
Sing the *glorious* posting down,
And how boldly he stood forth
In its first and proudest town,
To meet the sturdy foes of Repeal!
With staunch members of the "*Ass–*"
To support his burly mass,
Daunt, strong in triple brass,
    And Tom Steele!

But like grampuses aground,
Writhed the leader and his men,
When an evil-boding sound
Of Dan's *namesake in the den*
Reminded them—a sound which did not chime
With their hopes of vict'ry's wreath,
While the crowd look'd stern as death
And the BRAVE O' held his breath
    For a time!

Then the pride of Ulster flushed
To anticipate the scene,
And Dan had hardly brushed
With his cuff his smart caubeen,
And giv'n the "hem", prelusive, when a yell
From ten thousand loyal throats
Stopp'd the issue of his notes,
And the *trader in frieze coats,*
    Heard his knell!

Again, again, again!
And the shouting did not slack—
While fiercely, but in vain,
The Repealer urged his pack,
To check the stunning tempest with their cheers,—
But at length there came a pause,
As if friends of either cause,
Claim'd a respite for their jaws
    And their ears!

Out spoke O'Connell then,
As he rolled him left and right,—
"You're in darkness, Ulster-men!
And I'm come to bring you light,—
But you carry no *extinguishers,* I hope;
Dear friends, you must forego
Mad Luther, Knox, and Co.
And kiss the blessed toe
    Of the Pope!"

Right merry grew the crowd,
When they heard him thus propose;
And the peals, both long and loud,
Of wild laughter that arose,
Proclaimed—that Northern sense had won the day!
And the doughty Prince of knaves,
With his retinue of slaves,
Like the tide's retiring waves,
    Slunk away!

Now joy, old Ulster, raise
At this triumph of thy might;
And, amidst the banquet's blaze,
While the goblet shines in light,
And you glory in the flight of your foe; -
Then toast your PEERLESS TOWN,
With its street y'cleped "Brown",
And that place of high renown,
    "Sandy-row!"

Brave hearts, to Britain tied,
That no slavery can brook;
Who have battled side by side
With O'Connell-quelling COOKE,
Bright shine the light of freedom on your home!
And still may Ulster smile,
As a favoured GOSHEN, while
Thy darkness plagues our Isle,
    LYING ROME![123]

Equally pleasant and touching was the following from a man of Athens, and which appeared in that right-well beloved and loyal paper *The Derry Standard*. It is entitled

ANOTHER CHANT FOR THE BIG BEGGARMAN BY AN IRISH ATHENIAN.

Burly Dan took a notion to visit Belfast,
Where the Priests had all clubbed for a glorious repast,
And Daniel took with him his "fiddler"[*], Tom Steele,
To hear the "gulls" shouting, "Hurrah for Repeal!"
"If I *blarney* the North, I'll die easy", says Dan,
And the fiddler he winked at the Big Beggarman.

[*] The soubriquet bestowed upon Tom Steele while in Belfast—it is supposed from his resemblance in figure to the celebrated Paganini—perhaps from his peculiar talent in drawing the *long bow*, while playing second fiddle to the Chief Musician.

For the sake of a whole skin, Dan travelled *incog*,
And the fiddler sung out as they came to each bog;
There was one *bog* at Banbridge, and one at Dromore,
And at Lisburn another, behind and before,
And the "boys" would have made a new Boyne of the Bann,
Had they met with the serfs of the Big Beggarman.

His "speech" at the "meeting" was all a dumb show,
His head up and down, and his arms to and fro,
The sounds he was met with were "down with *Repale*",
"No Surrender", "the Doctor", "Dan shew us your tail",
"Three cheers for the Union", "three groans for King Dan,
The bully and coward—the Big Beggarman".

Had you stood to the fight—although drubbed you would be,
Your way had been smoother to Donaghadee;
But your cause was not worse than the bent of your mind,
And the words of your doom are, "THE CHALLENGE DECLINED",
So hurrah for the Doctor! And down with King Dan,
The Irishman's robber, the Big Beggarman![124]

But who remembers not the escape of Dan? The whole history of the entire proceedings of the Repealer in Belfast was happily epitomized by Dr. Cooke into one short expressive sentence: *"they lied him in and they swore him out."* Such is the burden of the following song—a lyrical chant which will enrapture the lovers of poesy, and animate to additional vigour the hearts of the brave. Its author called it

A NEW SONG,
To the old tune—"Which nobody can deny".

THEY lied him in and they swore him out,
Which nobody can deny;
They turned his horses round about,
And winked at the "gulls" to raise a shout,

But silent sadness reigned throughout,
Which nobody can deny, deny, which nobody can deny.

They hurried him in, and they closed each blind,
Which nobody can deny;
But the noise of the jaunting-cars behind
Disturbed the great Disturber's mind,
That repose he sought, in vain, to find,
Which nobody can deny, deny, which nobody can deny.

The armed police by his coach did ride,
Which nobody can deny.
Below the bridge did Lagan glide,
While the tollman flung the gates so wide,
For they said a prisoner was inside,
Which nobody can deny, deny, which nobody can deny.

Dan felt the freshness of morning air,
Which nobody can deny;
And, turning to Steele with a hungry stare,
"If Sharman's at home we might breakfast there;
But the *Jewel* ne'er axed us, I declare",
Which nobody can deny, deny, which nobody can deny.

They scampered along to Newtownards,
Which nobody can deny;
But the corners were posted with *"great rewards"*,
And the boys looked so queer from the cabbage-yards,
That Dan merely nodded his passing regards,
Which nobody can deny, deny, which nobody can deny.

And next they came to a swelling brook,
Which nobody can deny,
"A brook", cries Steele, with a frightful look
But the angry waters echoed "COOKE",
And Dan to his Paternosters took,
Which nobody can deny, deny, which nobody can deny.

And now a crowd came slowly near,
Which nobody can deny;—
Dan's knees, like Belshazar's, shook with fear,
And he hastily drew his pistols near,—
When, behold! A funeral did appear!
Which nobody can deny, deny, which nobody can deny.

Both sat depressed as men could be,
Which nobody can deny,
Till Steele espied the open sea-
"Huzza!" said he, "for Donaghadee!" –
"Hurra!" cried Dan, "and Grammachree!"
Which nobody can deny, deny, which nobody can deny.

Now rattle the wheels along the street,
Which nobody can deny;
But not a voice was heard to greet,
While Dan, like a fox in a winding sheet,
Twisted his tail between his feet,
Which nobody can deny, deny, which nobody can deny.

And now the steamer has left the quay,
Which nobody can deny;
While a Highland piper thus did play-
"*I'll gang nae mair to yon toun!*"—nay;
For Repeal, in Belfast, is lost—lack-a-day!
Which nobody can deny, deny, which nobody can deny.

Reader, hast thou ever trembled at the incantations of the "weird sisters?" Flatter not thyself that the days of witchery are gone. Talk of the nineteenth century indeed! No!—they play their "fantastic tricks" still in divers places and sundry ways, in this "visible diurnal sphere". Are you still sceptical with respect to such a truism? Look to the opposite picture, and lo! Thou art confounded. In the late tragi-comic Drama of Repeal, they have played their part, which is thus visibly represented, in—

A NEW SCENE FROM MACBETH,
(NEVER BEFORE EXHIBITED
ON ANY NORTHERN STAGE.)

SCENE FIRST.—ACT LAST.—*A dark Room in the Vindicator Office—In the middle, a pot boiling—The Gulls shouting.*

ENTER THREE WITCHES AND HECATE.

1W.   Thrice the "gulls" have loudly roared.

2W.   Thrice and once Tom Steele hath snored.

3W.   Daniel cries "'tis time, 'tis time".

1W.   Skin the eel, but save the slime.
    Round about the boiler go:
    In, the fell ingredients throw,
    Pails of water, three times three,
    From Struel, Derg, and Urachree;[125]
    And when it foams, all hissing hot,
    Then fill up the magic pot.
    Cast in first, of Papal Bull,
    Hoof and horn, and tail and scull;

2W.   Cinders three, from Scullabogue,
    Hobnails nine, of Whiteboy brogue;

3W.   Tongue of dog, and snout of pig,
    Curl of Dan's official wig;
    And when it foams, all hissing hot,
    Sing around our magic pot.

All.   Double, double, toil and trouble;
    Fire burn and cauldron bubble.

Hec.   Cool it with Heretic blood;
    Then the charm is firm and good.
    Turn the cock and off it goes—
    Drink, ye "gulls", and drown your woes.
    Fly, ye post-boy, lash your nag—
    Speed the *Vindicator's* bag;
    Tell of "bloody Sandy-row",
    And the great "Pavilion" show;
    Of the "lovely and the good",

Repeal Cookery.

Who in *shoes and stockings* stood!
Of the brave Repealer throng,
Mustered "sixty thousand strong";
Of the shouts at Linen-hall,
Caught in dishcloths neat and small.
Stop not, herald! Haste away!
Till you reach fair Ballintrae,
Then, in potions deep and strong,
Pledge the cup with Maister John.

We deeply sympathise with our readers in the sorrow
which will settle down on them when they find that this
enjoyment is nearly done. Our songs are dying to an echo;
our pleasing task is nearly over; our communion with them in
the world of Poetry is nearly done. Verily, we feel mournfully
sentimental, when we give our last chant, called

THE CHIEF OF REPALE.

The chief of Repealers came down from the South,
To let the North breeze cool the *lie* in his mouth!
And, save his assurance, he license had none
To blarney the boys from Coleraine to Shinrone.
From the rocks of the Causeway to far-famed Kinsale—
Oh! who has not heard of the Chief of *Repale!*

He stayed not at Newry, nor yet at the Bann,
And the hot smoking breakfast was eat without Dan!
But, ere he arrived at Malone turnpike-gate,
The gallant repented his coming so *late;*
For he missed the loved shout of the "gulls" on the gale,
Bidding—welcome, O'Connell, high chief of *Repale!*

So slyly he stole into Kerns's hall,
While waiters, and helper, and shoe-boys and all,
Were solemnly cautioned, by word and by look,

To say nothing of him—not even to (the) COOK,
Lest she might, in her wrath, slip a pill in his *kail*
That would finish, for ever, the Chief of *Repale!*

I long loved "*fair Ulster*", my suit you denied,
And you laughed me to scorn in your stiff Northern pride;
And now I'm come here with friend Charley to dine,
With the "*lovely and good*" to drink one cup of wine,
For I want your fair Province attached to my *tail*,
Don't you wish I may get her, quoth he of *Repale!*

The eve of the dinner beheld gallant feats:—
There was placing of dishes, and scouring of plates;
There was crushing, and pushing, in Donegall-place,
But few got a glimpse of his broad Kerry face;
For he knew his fool measure hung high in the scale,
Over-poised by the Northerns, opposed to *Repale!*

But away to the dinner, where gallant M'Dowell,
In the high seat of honour presides o'er the whole;
Where Keenans and Dorians, O'Neills and O'Rourkes,
Are eagerly handling their knives and their forks,
And Dan's "wee dog, *Charlie*", sits wagging his tail,
As he looks on his master the Lord of *Repale!*

When Daniel had swallowed his share of the food,
He kissed his broad palm to the "*lovely and good*";
And the blarney that flowed from his tongue was as pure
As the stream from the Liffey, the Shannon, or Suir;
He never before knew that blarney to fail—
But, alas! It was wasted great Chief of *Repale!*

Arrah! pray is this Ulster? is this the black North?
There is no other North that such stars can send forth?
Though the hearts of the Southerns are hot as a coal—
But yours!—you'd excuse me, Sir Chairman M'Dowell,
If I in attempt to describe them should fail,
For I fear I'm unequal, quoth he of *Repale!*

But why should the muse dwell on all that was said,
Small blame to you, Dan, when the reckoning was paid,
By these would-be Repealers sprung up in the North,
To call all your wit and your eloquence forth,
And shower it around you, wholesale and retail,
To stuff the "gulls" ears with the sound of *Repale!*

Oh! was it a dream that O'Connell was here?—
The shout of the "gulls" hath now died on the ear,
And the "*brilliant and good*", in their chambers are pent,
And the cheers, and the groans, and the hisses, are spent;
And Daniel has left us to weep and to wail,
Wirra strue for O'Connell high Chief of *Repale!*

He came as the wind comes, and nobody knows,
The place that it comes from, and whither it goes;—
And silent and secret they took him away,
For his errand was hopeless, and he might not delay.
Then, hurrah for fair England; with steam and with sail.
They'll have swift ships that follow, quoth he of *Repale.*[126]

Reader, hast thou ever luxuriated in that pleasant book and profitable withal, the sayings of Sam Slick? We presume thou hast, and hast seen how he exposeth the vagaries of the "most free and enlightened nation on the face of the earth". Wouldst thou desire to hear his opinion about Repeal? Here it is then. Ask not how it has been received; but read carefully, and admire prodigiously the

NOTIONS OF SAMUEL SLICK, OF SLICKVILLE, ABOUT THE REPEAL MOVEMENT.

"He put me in mind of about the meanest thing on airth—an old worn-out 'coon-dog barking up the wrong tree".—*Autobiography of Colonel Crockett.*

"WELL, Squire, getting' along by steam does beat all, that's a fact. We have had a considerable deal of talkin about the wonderful works of steam-ingines in the newspapers already; but a notion strikes me, that in a year or two, it will take some of our first-rate Congress men to do justice to them, by makin' speeches about what steam can do every once in a while; and you know, Squire, that some of them fellows ought to be pretty considerable judges of *that* at least. However, this don't much convene with what I'm goin' to tell you. Well, squire, I was sitten by the fireside, last night, and havin' been down to see cousin Woodberry, during the day, and travelled a good deal about his location (and a plaguery nice thing he has of it). As I was saying I was somewhat tired like, and had fallen into a kinder doze, when, who should come runnin' into the room but a critter called Michey Mulvaney, that has been about my consarn for some little time. Well, if he didn't look the very picture of a curiosity—it's a pity. There he was as shaggy as a Kentucky bear, busy pullin' out a newspaper that he said had just come from a friend of his in Ireland, givin', among other things, an account of Repeal doings on the other side of the water. Well, I thought I would see what it was all about; for, says I to myself, if there's nothing else in it, there will be, at least, something worth larfin at, for them critters in Ireland do poke fun at one another now and again like all natur'. So I glanced my eye over the newspaper, and what should I stick at but the account of "O'Connell's visit to the North to agitate Repeal". I knew already, Squire, that this O'Connell was a chap who, as regards the matter of every kind of loco-focoism, as we say in America, had all his eye-teeth cut a considerable while; so says I to myself, let us see what the feller does want to be at. Well, I begun a readin' away like any thing, about the 'journey', and the 'demonstration', and the 'Soiree' to the 'lovely and the good'; and, in short, about a consarn that, thinks I to myself while reading it, it' like nothin' in natur' that I know, but a New England pedlar's bag of pewter notions, that it convenes for him to try an' make pass for silver, when he gets in among some of them

Ingin critters that don't know the differ. And sure enough, Squire, the Repeal speech of O'Connell did put one in mind of a thing that happened once when I was in the Clock line down east, and that I won't forget for one while. You see I happened to be down in one of them factory locations, an' as I was walkin' along by the side of a brick wall, what should I see pasted on it but a most a flashin' advertisement, very nearly as big as a flag of the United States, all kivered over with an account of a speech that was just goin' to be made by a critter called Jonathan Crane. Well, the people began to gather to hear the speech, and I went along with them; but, of all the fellers that ever made speeches, I expect this one *did* go a-head. He proposed that there should be a repeal right off the reel of the union between the married folks in them parts, and all, as he said, from a desire to benefit his fellow-subjects of the most free and enlightened nation on airth.— Well, what would you think, Squire, but the thing took amazingly among the most of them, and so it was voted that it should be put into practice right off, for fere that the notion might spile in the keepin'. The woman critters were sent to live by them-selves, and things went on pretty considerable slick for a day or two. But it lasted a short time, I tell you; for one night there did get up the most cussed racket among the women. Why, Squire, I happened to be located for the night in a shingle, but not far off, and such a blarting out of disturbance I never heard, exceptin' once, when I travelled among the Rocky Mountains, an' came upon a battle of 'coons, in a harricane. It *did* beat all natur'—that's a fact—and it shewed that if the women critters would not keep up the old union, they couldn't keep up the new one. There they were a scoldin', screachin', and clamin' one another like mad, and some of them swearin' that they would set fire to the whole consarn, if for nothing but to spite one another. Well, Squire, Jonathan Crane's man'uvre was knocked on the head in two twos, and the fire-edge of *this* kind of repeal wore off before it was well put on.— Now, the Repeal critters in Ireland, I expect, are playin' much about the same game. They want to break up a union that has brought

them the most of the prosperity and true happiness that ever
they have had. They want, like the cursedest fools ever I
heard tell of, to cut away their sheet-anchor, at the very time
that the storm may be ready to blart in their very teeth, and
throw them upon all dangers of a lee shore. He's pretty considerable of a longheaded critter that O'Connell after all—
and yet it isn't clear to me, but he'll maybe yet have to snicker
into his skin, and live upon the fat of his old earnin', if he can,
somethin', Squire, like an old skunk that I once knew trapped
by his tail in the crotch of a tree. I one time took to trappin'
them varmint before I begun the clock line, and I just set my
trap in that kind of slantendicular way, that *the bigger its tail,*
and *the more the critter flourished it,* the sooner it was taken. Well,
there are, I do see, some in the trappin' line in Ireland, that
go a-head too. There's a Preacher, Squire, that is pretty considerable at the business, and that is not easy to be outwitted
by the cunninest varmint that ever carried a tail—that's a fact.
Well, I read in the newspaper that this Preacher challenged
O'Connell to discuss the question of Repeal. That he offered
to meet him, face to face, for any time and any where, but
O'Connell was too knowin a critter to come within rifle-shot
of such a first-rate hunter. It's my opinion, Squire, that, if he
had done so, this Preacher would have gone into him like a
flash of lightenin' into a gooseberry bush. I expect he would
have catawampously chawed him up while you would say two
twos. It's a great thing, Squire, to have a good cause and a
good hand to plead it. It's a great thing to have a skilful hand
to set the trap, and to set it where the real varmint may fall
into it. I tell you what, squire, that Preacher chap was up to
clock-makin'—he set his time-piece by the sun, and stopped
the main-spring of O'Connell's movements.[127]

Thanks to the Penny Postage, Rowland Hill, and to our
worthy friend John Hill, who has favoured us with the following letters of his Scottish correspondent James Anderson,
of Ballintrae. We have been always anxious to hear his sentiments on men and things in general: and therefore are we

proud in being enabled to give our readers his opinion touching the late exhibition of Repeal, nathless it should be in that dialect, which to some may be difficult to decipher. Be so good, however, reader, as not to pass slightly over our friend's lucubrations; and we promise, that when you have done, you will be at a loss to decide between the superiority of the masculine vigour of the sentiments, or the Doric simplicity of the style.

FROM JAMES ANDERSON, OF BALLINTRAE, TO MR. JOHN HILL, BOOKSELLER, BELFAST.

DEAR JOHN,—Dinna ye think that a woman is maistly wiser nor a man? I can tell ye, lad, its my opinion at ony rate, an' I'll gie ye the reason—I ne'er gae wrang while I follow Leezy's advice, an' I sometimes blunder when I tak' my ain. Noo, after a', that I think her wiser nor mysel'; but the women-bodies is someway sae accustomed wi' keekin' in corners, an' sweepin', an' washin', and darnin', an' sic like, that naething can miss their een; an' then, I'm thinkin', mairower, that whate'er bit wits they hae, is mair exerceesed nor a man's, wha aften depends mair on the streength o' his arm, nor on the soundness o' his head. Noo, I'll tell ye, John, what has led me intil a' this pheelosophy. Twa-three months syne, I was purposed to sen' ane o' our wee chaps to the schule, and was expressin' my thanks for the neighbourhood o' sae learned a dominie, whan Leezy says to me, ne'er mind the dominie; but tell me what kind o' ushers has he got. Dinna ye mind the Laird o' Grumphy? Didna his very servant-lasses look as sour as vinegar? An' didna his very tykes strain their jaws and weary their thrapples wi' perpetual girnin' an' barkin', an' gif a' about him was infecked wi' his ain ill nature? An' dinna ye mind the big hoose i' the park, whar baith master an' servants, the leddy an' the weans, a'thegether, seemed sae happy, and was sae kind? Ay, man, wadna the muckle tyke frae Newfoundlan' wag his tail, an' leuk up i' yer face wi' a welcome amaist as wise leukin an' as kind as gin he had been a human creature?—Look ye, then, till the ushers, Jamie. Sic tyke, sic maister, sic ushers, sic dominie; noo, what's the moral o' a' this clishmaclaver? Bide a wee, Johnnie, an' ye sall hear. Ye ken baith yoursel' an' my frien's i' the high toon o' Carmony, hae been lang urgin' me tae come our on a veesit. Weel, at last, ye ken, I did come; an' what baith o' joy an' sorrow we had in our meetin' I'll no repeat it here. We had joy, Johnnie, for we were levin, an' some o' us Providence had prospered far beyond our expectin' or deservin'; an' we had our sorrows Johnnie, for they were gone wha wad hae shared in our joy, an' we had a feelin' o' laneliness in our company, because there was some in our thoughts that was na at our table. But it's the way an' the will o' Providence, wha wisely an' mercifully mixes the sweet with the bitter—the ane for our comfort, an' the ither for our correction—an' he is aye the happiest man wha taks o' baith wi' humility an' thankfu'ness.

Whaes me, Johnnie; I dinna ken how it happens, but there's a pleasure in bein' sad. But I'm rinnin away frae my story, which was fairly to confess that, for a' the guide will I bear to yoursel' an' Carnmoney folk, ye wadna at this time hae seen my face, but that I wussed to get a syght o' the great O'Connell, an' judge o' *Repealers* an' *Repeal* wi' my ain lugs an' een. I intended, as Leezy advised, to judge o' the "maister by the ushers—an' try what O'Connell wad be at by a blink o' the bodies at his tail". Besides, yer auld neebor, Maister John Sinclair, fairly banned me, intil a promise that I sud go—for he swoor, and he swoor again, that O'Connell was the greatest man on the yirth—that he wad hae a body-guard o' 90,000 men frae Connaught; an' that he wad carry Repeal in Parliament, as easily as he could shoot a patrick or a moorfowl. Weel, gang I did gang—an' wadna trouble ye wi' what I heard or saw at the great street meetin', had O'Connell's body-guard allowed me to stay; but, as I weel remember, ye war glad to make yoursel' scarce, as the chiel, wi' the muckle nieve admonished ye, sae I think it weel tae gie ye twa three notes o' what happened after yer retreat. Weel, ye'll think it odd, Johnnie, but it's true that whan I leuked at O'Connell mounted on the riggin' o' the hoose, an' a' the Priests an' Maister Sinclair aside him, the first thing came intil my head was a picter I had seen o' an elephant wi' a muckle creel on his back, an' a dozen or twa o' men in it. Niest I thought it a kind o' emblem o' Repeal itsel', and what they ca' "Papish ascendancy"; for, as to the Repeal part, O'Connell an' his folk didna cum in by the door, but headforemost through the winnock, an' the "ascendancy" might weel be seen, for he wadna bide within ae hoos, but maun mount the riggin' o' anither. But what, think ye, I thocht o' niest? Just o' Tim Corr (ye remember Tim, man, wasna he the picter?) wi' his great muckle body, an' his ragged coat, an' his dirty face, an' his curley head, an' his breast as rough as a water spaniel, an' his long keat, an' his laziness—for he wad beg an' eat, but he wadna work—like some ither folk that O'Connell kens o'—an' then wi' a' his perfect daftness, the body had sic glimmerin's o' wisdom, that mony's the time I hae wondered how sae muckle sense could sometimes spring frae sic a fountain o' madness an' folly. Noo, the reason I thocht o' Tim was this:— Ye remember the '98. Weel, Tim, in his ain imagination, an' by common consent o' a' jokemakers, was a Crappy General. But, at last, cam pike-time; an' as a party o' pikemen was hurryin' along to the toon to fecht, Tim met them gaen the ither way. What! cried ane o' the Crappies, what! General, are ye no to lead yer men i' the battle. Na, na, he's no for that, quo Tim.—Why, General, quo the daffin Croppy, dinna ye see a' yer men afore ye? Ha, ha, quo Tim, wi' that curious dookin o' his head atween his shouthers that ye canna forget—ha, ha, quo Tim, he heard the de'il playin' a' tune, an' sees a' the folk dancin' till't. An' never sin' the world began was there a truer description o' the O'Connell fiddle an' the Repeal dance. An' noo, Johnnie, I propose, as they wadna let ye bide at the meetin', tae gie ye some inklin o' twa or three o' the dancers.

My Queen's head will carry nae mair paper, but ye'll sune hear frae me again.

Yours, in a' kindness,

JAMES ANDERSON.

Ballintrae, N.B., 1st February, 1841.

To Mr. John Hill, Bookseller, in Donegall-street, Belfast.

LETTER II.

DEAR JOHN,—Did you ever read "Tam o' Shanter"? If sae, ye'll remember how he saw among the witches,

> "A Winnock bunker i' the east,
> Whuar sat auld Nick in shape o' beast.
> A touzie tyke, black, grim, an' large,
> To gie them music was his charge;
> Wha screwed his pipes, and gart them skirl,
> Till roof an' rafters a' did dirl."

An' blieve me, Johnnie, whan I thought o' Tim Corr an' the Deil fiddlin', an' a' the folk dancin' tae the music o' rebellion,—whilk ye ken is just a ceevil name for robbery and bloodshed,—an' whan I leuked at O'Connell encompassed by lang Bab, an' auld John, like twa prented picters o' death upon wires—an' whan I saw a' the ither clanjamfry mounted wi' him on the riggin' o' a hoose - an' whan I heard him screedin' up Repeal; but abune a' whan I heard him playin' till the tune o' leeberty, equality, toleration, an charity—just imported frae Rome; an whan I saw the loupin' an' flingin' o' the creaters he had set a dancin'—I couldna but suspec' he had borrow'd Tim's fiddle or Tam's pipes, sae terrible was the row, an' the racket he produced. Ay, ay, John, that was the row! An' what wi' Tam Steele shakin' his nieve at the Protestants, an' them laughin' back in his face; what wi' a great muckle Priest girnin' an' roarin'; an' what wi' O'Connell himsel—for I heard him wi' my ain lugs— threatenin' the Papishes if they wadna shout; an' what wi' the tootin' o' a lang tin horn that a chiel blew wi' a' the might an' main o' a coachman; an' what wi' the skirlin' o' whustles, whilk seemed innumerable; an' what wi' the offerins o' pennies tae O'Connell on the tap o' clifted sticks; an' the grainin'—whilk is a soun' maist horrible— an' the ridin' o' poleesh, an' the universal rampagin' an' stramish— never Johnnie, since the warl' began was there aught tae compare wi't unless, mayhap, the confusion o' tongues at Babel, o' whilk, I suspec', the Repeal tae be just a kind o' Eerish imitation.

The first o' the Babelonians that I sall mention was Mr. John Sinclair, frae our town o' Ballintrae. An' there was he sittin' on a muckle creepy, whilk they ca'd a chair, wi' his shouthers a' hurkled thegither like the half hoop o' an auld herrin' barrel, an' the haill figer o' the body, for a' the warld like a clockin hen upon a bauk. It just vext me to see the auld body—for he's a kindly creater—it just vext me tae see him makin' sic a' guse o' himsel'. An' then sic a freezin' as he got, perched upon the riggin' o' the hoose, on a cauld winter's day, like unto a scart, or sea-maw restin' on a rock after a day's fishin'. Ay, a sair, sair, freezin' he had tae stan'—for whan I could hear naethin' for the shoutin' an' guffawin, I just slippit roun' till the door o' the Inns, an' whan a gawsy-leukin' body that might be the head waiter, or sic like, pusht me out, I just mumbled ower a screed o' Eerish I had learned frae a' stane-breaker o' the name o' Flanagan, wha worked on the new turnpike frae the Port, an' in I got in a gliff, an' made my way to Maister John's ain lug. An' there he was sittin', wi his nose as blue as indigo, an as cauld as an icicle, an' his teeth chatterin' in his head like banes in a dice-box, or a runaway naig an' cairt on a new macamized high-road. The niest to lead aff the dance, was just as it sud bed, the Laird o' Tullochgorum [query, Killy-Gordon?] Weel, up he starts, as blythe as a birkie leukin' for a partner at a penny-weddin'. But whan he showed his head!—wow, John, but he was a perfect curosity. He was an auld wizened body. In fac, the Repealers seem to be a' auld and wizened—save and except O'Connell himsel', wha seems tae live on nae deaf nits. But, as I was sayin', this Tullochgorum was an auld wizened body, but for want o' a better, the clappit him up tae speak. An' when he gat forret to the edge o' the roof, he first stickit his twa nieves intil his twa hinches, and leukt for a the warld like ane o' Leezzy's skivert rabbits—syne he pappit his hans intil the pockets o' his breeks—syne drew ane o' them out, an' fastened it atween his knees—then threw back his head, and maist upset baith Maister John and lang Bab—then shot his head forret like a lint-beetler's mell—an' apened his mouth, an' ganched an' ganched maist awfu'; an' never i' my days did I see the model o' the body, except a brock in a barrel a fechtin wi' a terrier.

But the sicht o' sichts was his seconder, a chiel they ca'd lang Bab, wha stud ahint O'Connell, for a the warld like the Hollywud maypoul wi' a whin bush for a head on't. Sae lang, an' skrimpit i' the middle,

an' starved like, just as gif he had come frae doin' a month's penance
for O'Connell's lees, at Stroul, or Lough Derg.—An' maybe after a',
freen Johnnie, the thocht o' annointin, an absolution at the hinner
end, may hae mair influence than they just like to mention ower
some o' the freens o' Repeal. But och! och! man, what a broken reed
o' Egypt! After three score years an' ten, in whilk bannin was eked
to bannin, tae expec pardon for ten pounds worth o' mumbled
masses, an' a priest's passport through a heathenish purgatory.

Niest came a camstarie o' a chap, ca'd Dillon Browne, fre
Connaught, wha danced wi' a chiel ca'd M'Kitterty, frae
Newtonards,—ye'll mind "*Kitterty*", he was a droll body that, an' I'm
suspeckin this maun be some relation o' the family. I couldna leuk
on the body without thinkin' on an auld hoose, whar the maist licht
cams in through the cracks o' the roof. But losh man, had you seen
him! how he rair'd an stampit, an' whappit, an' slappit his loof again
his sides, an' shot out his nose like the heft o' a peggin' awl; an' sae
raved about blood an' thunner, and peats, that sic nonsense ne'er
was begatten, since or afore. Mr. John leukt bluer an' bluer—lang
Bab grained inwardly—an' O'Connell bit his nether lip wi'
vexation—while the chiels i' the street shouted "awa tae ye'r tape";
an' the puir body slank awa, like a tyke wi' his tail bitten aff, in what
our dominie facetiously ca's a "dogomachy".

But, man-o-man, neist came a priest they ca'd Welsh, frae
somewhar about the Island o' Raghery, as they tell't me. Nae mortial
o' a' the Repealers afore him could ever hear his ain voice wi' his
ain lugs; sae terrible was the racket; but when Priest Welsh let aff, I
question muckle if ever Roarin Meg gaed sic a brattler. I amaist couped
ower the roof wi' the fright; an' I suspec he maun hae been studyin'
his speech, either at the clunk hole o' Portstewart, or Macswines gun,
in a storm. Man-o-man, how he did rave about absentees!—sae
that, I suppose, when O'Connell becomes king, nae man will be
permitted tae hae lands in twa kingdoms—that will be fine! But ilka
ane maun spend a' his cash on his ain property. There must nane
hae estates in twa countries, for nae man can leeve in twa countries
at ance—that'll be better still. Then comes twa parishes, then twa
toonlan's, an', after that, I'm maybe thinkin', twa farms! Aye, aye,
Johnnie, lad, that will be the time whan priests will get pickins! In

fac, gin it war na for the *tenth command*, I believe I wad turn Repealer mysel'. But, maybe, Priest Welsh would just obleege baith himsel' an' ither expectants sae far, that, as he has struck out the *second* anent images, sae he wad strike out the *tenth* command anent covetousness; an' then, but not till then, wull I join him in a loud *hurra for Repeal!*

O' the march till Donaghadee, an' the terrible frightenin the Repealers gat wi' the funeral, I sall naething at this present writin. An' in respect o' the story o' the piper playin—"We'll gang nae mair to yon toun", there's a sma' error I man crave leeberty to correct. Atween you an' me, Johnnie, the truth o' the matter is just this: as the Repealers were coming out o' the inns, I just steppet doon alang side o' them, whuslin in a low kind o' way the tune ca'd the Rogue's March—the whilk Tam Steele an' Dillon Browne baith seemed tae recognise, an' baith grun their teeth an shuck their neives at me; but I just whustled on till I saw O'Connell aboard the packet—an' then I changed my note an' and screeded out right loudly—"We'll gang nae mair to yon toun". That's just the fac o' the matter. But there was nae piper. O' the vage an' the carriage business at Portpatrick, wi' my puir deliberat opinion o' O'Connell himsel, ye sall hear mair sune.

Yours, in a' kindness,

Ᏼ JAMES ANDERSON.

Ballintrae, N.B., 2nd Feb., 1841.

To Mr. John Hill, Bookseller, Donegall-street, Belfast.

THE TAIL PIECE.

NOTES

1 McComb confuses Phelim O'Neill (*c*.1605–53) leader of the original 1641 Rising in Ulster and associated by Protestant polemicists with the massacre of Protestants, with his relative Owen Roe O'Neill (*c*.1582–1649), the Confederate Catholic general and victor of Benburb (1646). Phelim's defeat at Lisburn took place in November 1641.

2 In 1826 Wolfe Tone's son published his father's autobiography, which includes a description of his visits to Belfast (which he nicknamed "Blefescu") in 1791 in connection with the foundation of the United Irishmen and in 1792 as agent of the Catholic Committee. The book was widely reported and discussed in the Belfast newspapers.

3 One of O'Connell's favourite quotations was "Hereditary bondsmen, know ye not/ Who would be free, themselves must strike the blow?" (Byron *Childe Harold's Pilgrimage*, Canto II, verse LXXVI).

4 In the period 1830–2 O'Connell made several attempts to win over Irish Tories to the Repeal cause, including adorning his hat with intertwined shamrocks and orange liles and toasting King William in the manner described. This reflected (*a*) genuine hope of winning support for repeal among Dublin Protestant artisans, who often combined Orangeism with belief that the Union was responsible for their declining socio-economic position (*b*) desire to put pressure on the Whig government to come to a deal with him. O'Connell's renewed denunciations of Orange bigotry, when the Orangemen had refused to support him and an accommodation had been reached with the Whigs, was cited by Orangemen and Tories as proof of his hypocrisy and treachery.

5 O'Connell's Dublin headquarters, site of the weekly meetings of the Repeal Association (as of the Catholic Association in the 1820s) was the former corn-exchange on Burgh Quay. (A new headquarters, "Conciliation Hall" was built on a neighbouring site and opened in October 1843.)

In August 1838 the Ulster Liberal politician William Sharman Crawford and the Non-Subscribing Presbyterian leader Rev. Henry Montgomery appeared at the Corn Exchange meeting which launched O'Connell's Precursor Society (intended to advocate reforms as a precursor to Repeal). Crawford called on O'Connell to break with the Whig

Government and form an alliance with British anti-Corn Law Radicals; he accused O'Connell of making a corrupt bargain with the Whigs. O'Connell interrupted the speech with such facetious remarks as "What brought you here, Sharman my jewel? What are you doing, Sharman, my man" and comments on Crawford's white waistcoat. The audience grew so restive that Montgomery's biographer suggests he and Crawford faced actual physical danger. (Charles Gavan Duffy *Young Ireland* (London, 1880), p. 9; R. B. McDowell *Public Opinion and Government Policy in Ireland, 1800–46* (London, 1952); DNB entry on Crawford.)

6   William Crolly (1780–1849), parish priest of Belfast 1812–25, Bishop of Down and Connor 1825–35, archbishop of Armagh 1835–49, a longstanding associate of Henry Montgomery, was one of the more conservative Catholic bishops and opposed Repeal. His career is outlined in Ambrose Macaulay *William Crolly, Archbishop of Armagh 1835–49* (Dublin, 1994). McComb's hostility to Crolly is not merely the product of his general belief in Popish plots; a dispute in 1822–4 led to Crolly withdrawing Catholic children from the Brown Square school amidst accusations that school authorities were trying to convert them to Protestantism (Macaulay pp. 22–8).

7   Hercules Street, the westernmost extension of the Catholic Falls district, was inhabited by butchers. They were staunch supporters of O'Connell and frequently acted as strong-arm men at nationalist and Catholic meetings. Hercules Street was swept away in the 1870s by an urban clearance scheme which extended the centre-city Royal Avenue shopping district.

8   On 5 October 1839 the *Freeman's Journal* published O'Connell's *Letter to the Ministers and Office-Bearers of the Wesleyan Methodist Societies of Manchester*. Oliver MacDonagh describes its denunciation of "the filthy slime of Wesleyan malignancy" as "the solitary blemish on O'Connell's non-conformist record. He lapsed equally in charity and taste". (Oliver MacDonagh, *The Emancipist: Daniel O'Connell 1830–47* (London, 1989), p. 23, see also n. 21 below).

9   Burked = suppressed, suffocated; from the Edinburgh murderer Burke, who with his ally Hare threw themselves on top of victims and suffocated them to sell their corpses for dissection.

10   Samuel O'Sullivan, a well-known Church of Ireland clergyman, Orange chaplain and polemicist; a convert from Catholicism. This incident probably took place in 1835, when O'Sullivan joined R. J. M'Ghee and Cooke in denouncing the use of Dens' *Theology* at Maynooth, and demanding that O'Connell and Archbishop Murray of Dublin should explain their position on that book's justification of religious persecution. For further information on O'Sullivan and his better-known brother Mortimer, see Patrick O'Sullivan "A literary difficulty in explaining Ireland: Tom Moore and Captain Rock, 1824" in Roger Swift and Sheridan Gilley (eds), *The Irish in Britain 1815–1939* (London, 1989), pp. 239–74.

11   *Blackmouth*, derogatory term for a Presbyterian: *swaddler*, Protestant proselytiser.

12   *Lough Derg;* the famous site of pilgrimage and penance in Co. Donegal, widely ridiculed as superstitious by early nineteenth-century Protestant

writers including William Carleton and Caesar Otway. *Struel Wells*, near
Downpatrick in Co. Down, has a ruined monastic site associated with four
holy wells allegedly given curative powers by St. Patrick; it was a popular
pilgrimage site. McComb's 1861 *Guide to Belfast and the Adjoining Counties*
describes penitential practices similar to Lough Derg being undertaken
there, and their decline through Catholic clerical opposition.

13 A blowhole near Dunfanaghy, on the Fanad peninsula; under certain
   tidal conditions it makes a loud noise like artillery.

14 Tomas Ruadh O Suilleabhain (?1785–1848?), Iveragh hedge-school master
   patronised by O'Connell as poet and musician. He composed Irish-
   language verse eulogies to O'Connell in the style of eighteenth-century
   Jacobite poetry. An edition of his surviving verse was published in 1914.

15 The eighteenth-century Belgian priest Peter [Pierre]Dens was the author
   of a theological textbook used at Maynooth; in June 1835 Cooke and
   other Evangelicals, including R. J. M'Ghee (see n. 20 below) delivered
   speeches at Exeter Hall in London publicising Dens' justifications of
   the persecution of heretics and the power of priests to absolve penitents
   from solemn oaths. Catholic spokesmen (including Archbishop Murray of
   Dublin) claimed these passages were obsolete and denied they represented
   current Catholic teaching; Liberals like the Presbyterian tenant-right
   campaigner James McKnight pointed out that the Westminster
   Confession of Faith, imposed by Cooke as the standard of Presbyterian
   orthodoxy, also sanctioned persecution. (Jacqueline Hill, *From Patriots to
   Unionists: Dublin Civic Politics and Irish Protestant Patriotism, 1660–1840*
   (Oxford, 1997), p. 366; R. Finlay Holmes, *Henry Cooke* (Belfast, 1981)
   pp. 119, 129.)

16 From John Fletcher's (1579–1625), *Two Noble Gentlemen*. A version, "I'll
   mount upon the dog-star" by Thomas D'Urfey (1653–1723) was set to
   music by Henry Purcell (1658/9–1695).

17 *Sugaun*, a straw-rope. Brian Boru (d.1014) was the most powerful High
   King of pre-conquest Ireland, whose legendary attributes are celebrated
   in some of Thomas Moore's *Irish Melodies*; McAfee implies that he was a
   creature of fantasy and the predicted glories of Repeal are equally
   insubstantial.

18 O'Connell supported legislation outlawing child labour in 1832–3 and 1839,
   but in 1836, in the interests of his alliance with the Whig Government, he
   supported a government measure allowing the employment of twelve and
   thirteen-year-olds. This was widely criticised by former Radical allies.
   (Fergus D'Arcy "O'Connell and the English Radicals" in Donal
   McCartney, *The World of Daniel O'Connell* (Dublin and Cork, 1980),
   pp. 68–9.) MacDonagh, *Emancipist*, pp. 145–6 notes Tory accusations of
   bribery and defends O'Connell.

19 John MacHale (1791–1881), Catholic archbishop of Tuam and one of
   O'Connell's most prominent allies. His political and religious out-
   spokenness made him a hate-figure for many Protestants, some of whom
   denounced his flamboyant assertion of his archiepiscopal status as
   treasonable (because the appointment of bishops was a state function).

The official life of his Church of Ireland counterpart, the ultra-Evangelical Power le Poer Trench, is pointedly entitled *The Last Archbishop of Tuam*.

20 Robert James M'Ghee (1789–1872) leading Church of Ireland evangelical clergyman allied with Cooke.

21 Rev. Daniel M'Afee (1791–1873), well-known Methodist minister and controversialist, described by *Vindicator* as "raker together of filth" polemicised in defence of Arminian Protestantism against Calvinists and Catholics. His anti-Catholic writings (including the letters to O'Connell mentioned here, which appeared in the *Cork Constitution* in 1839 and sold 6,000 copies as a pamphlet) were collected in *The Anatomy of Popery, including letters to O'Connell* (Belfast, 1860). The letters respond to O'Connell's 1839 letter to the Wesleyan Methodists which attacked their attempts to proselytise Catholics, advised them to join the Catholic Church on the basis of its apostolic descent, and accused John Wesley of bigotry and antinomianism (the belief that those who possess true faith may disregard the moral law). M'Afee replies in a deliberately provocative style modelled on that of O'Connell; he invokes Scottish common-sense philosophy to ridicule Catholic sacramentalism, accuses Rome of breaching Biblical injunctions against fasting and celibacy, and calls Catholics antinomians for believing absolution cleanses from sin. M'Afee shows that O'Connell copied the accusation that Wesley helped to foment the Gordon riots from a polemic by Fr. Arthur O'Leary (1729–1802) against Wesley's opposition to Catholic Emancipation, while ignoring Wesley's refutation of the charge. [Wesley denied a proclamation bearing his name had been issued or signed by him; he did not accuse O'Leary of deliberate bad faith.] According to M'Afee, William Shanahan, a voter in the Kerry county constituency, was browbeaten by his wife and a priest into voting for O'Connell's nephew, Morgan John O'Connell, in the 1835 general election, after promising his landlord (John Hickson of Grove, near Dingle) that he would support the Conservative Knight of Kerry. It appears from M'Afee's account that Shanahan's eviction was for non-payment of rent rather than his electoral behaviour (hence O'Connell's refusal to assist him); Shanahan and his backers believed he should have been rewarded for his suppport. M'Afee opposed Catholic Emancipation. For his congratulations to Henry Montgomery for an 1831 controversy with O'Connell over Repeal, see Crozier *Life of Montgomery* p. 432. Further details of his career are in C. H. Crookshank *History of Methodism in Ireland* (Belfast, 1885), vol. 3.

22 The debate took place on 22 April 1834, when O'Connell introduced a Repeal motion into the House of Commons. Thomas Spring Rice (1790–1866), Limerick landowner, Irish Whig MP and supporter of Catholic Emancipation, Chancellor of the Exchequer 1835–9, ennobled as Lord Monteagle.

23 According to the *Vindicator*, O'Connell then said Cooke should have argued his case in the newspapers before demanding a debate. He listed the alleged economic ill-effects of the Union, stating that if Cooke disproved them he would really be "cock of the North".

24 See n. 5 above.

25 On 31 October 1831 there were widespread riots in Bristol against the rejection of the Reform Bill by the House of Lords. 100 houses were burned (including the palace of the Bishop, who opposed the Bill) and many civilians were killed by the military.

26 In the *Book of Esther* Haman, the minister of King Ahasuerus, seeks to exterminate the Jews because of his resentment towards the righteous Mordecai, but is killed with his family and supporters; his defeat is commemorated by the Jewish feast of Purim. Cooke insinuates that O'Connell's designs towards the Protestant "chosen people" resemble those of Haman, and God will defeat him also.

27 The poor hill country of North Louth and South Armagh, overwhelmingly populated by Catholics, was a stronghold of Ribbonism and agrarian violence; its inhabitants periodically clashed with Orangemen from North and Mid Armagh, cradle of the Order. The Catholics are called "redshanks" like the barelegged Catholic Jacobite soldiers of Lord Antrim, whose attempted arrival in Derry on 7 December 1688 was seen by Williamite Protestants as a Catholic massacre-plot. Their exclusion from the city by the Apprentice Boys marked the beginning of the Siege of Derry. The "deeds of darkness and of blood" associated with Forkhill were the mutilation of a Protestant schoolmaster and his family on 28 January 1791 during a period of sectarian violence, recalled by loyalist writers well into the twentieth century. (Marianne Elliott, *The Catholics of Ulster* (London, 2000), pp. 222–7). At Wildgoose Lodge, Co. Louth in 1816 eight members of a [Catholic] family were burned alive in their house by Ribbonmen; M'Comb probably knew William Carleton's short story "Wildgoose Lodge" (first published in *Traits and Stories of the Irish Peasantry, Second Series* (Dublin, 1833)), describing the atrocity in the voice of a perpetrator.

28 *Kailrunt*, cabbage-root—a reference to the *Vindicator's* threat to drive Protestant opponents of Repeal out of Ulster with a kail-stalk..

29 "Darrynane the younger" is the local workhouse or "union" constructed under the 1838 Irish Poor Law Act.

30 From "The Devil's Drive—A Sequel to Porson's 'Devil's Walk'" stanzas 12–13.

31 Charles O'Connell, MP for Co. Kerry 1832–5, O'Connell's son-in-law and remote cousin. In 1840–1 he experienced financial difficulties from "over-building"; O'Connell solicited a magistracy for him from the Whig government (MacDonagh, *Emancipist*), pp. 184–5. He was Resident Magistrate for Bantry from 1847 until his death in 1877.

32 Thomas Steele (1788–1848), minor Clare Anglican landowner, a trained engineer who participated in the Liberal revolt against Ferdinand VII of Spain 1823–4. He was an enthusiastic supporter of O'Connell and one of his principal lieutenants in the Clare election; O'Connell gave him the title "Head Pacificator" and sent him round the country during the Emancipation crisis urging the peasantry to refrain from violence in O'Connell's name. In later life his adulation of O'Connell and delight in the rhetoric and symbolism of the Repeal movement grew increasingly

eccentric and unbalanced. Soon after O'Connell's death Steele tried to drown himself in the Thames; he was rescued but died from the after-effects.

33 Robert Dillon Browne, Repeal MP for Mayo 1836–50, a relative of Lord Kilmaine, was a wild-living, impecunious country gentleman. Though a member of the Church of Ireland he was electorally dependent on Archbishop MacHale and therefore advocated the Archbishop's intransigent views on the interests of the Catholic Church.

34 The newly built St. Patrick's Church; the older St Mary's Church in Chapel Lane would presumably have been too small and shabby to accommodate O'Connell and his entourage. The *Vindicator* ridicules the idea that O'Connell should have made an exhibition of himself in the public street, and points out that the vast crowd who came to St Patrick's to see O'Connell almost produced a fatal crush. (*Vindicator*, 13 Feb. 1841.)

35 Peris; beautiful and benevolent Persian spirits who battle malevolent Devas (demons). One of the romances in Thomas Moore's *Lalla Rookh* describes the attempt of a Peri to obtain admission to Paradise. M'Comb insinuates that the spiritual benefits received by O'Connell are as intangible as the diet of the Peris.

36 A type of pistol.

37 John Wilkes (1725–97), a wealthy and somewhat disreputable London politician, became a radical hero in the late 1760s when prosecuted by George III's government for libel after accusing it of authoritarian tendencies fostered by crypto-Jacobite Scots favourites. Wilkes was repeatedly elected MP for Middlesex from 1768, and unseated three times by the government's parliamentary majority; his "Wilkite" supporters staged violent riots. In later life he supported Pitt the Younger, and allegedly joked "I hope you don't mistake me for a Wilkite".

38 From Burns "Tam O' Shanter".

39 From "Address to a Haggis". Kytes = bellies.

40 1812–75. The future Young Irelander, brother-in-law of John Mitchel, and Home Rule MP.

41 Samuel Butler (1613–80) "Hudibras"—a long verse satire, travestying *Don Quixote*, on Cromwellians and Presbyterians. M'Comb's references to *Hudibras* imply O'Connell is a disreputable plebeian and his hope of converting Northern Protestants to repeal is a quixotic fantasy.

42 In November 1837 O'Connell accused Irish trade unions of criminal violence and damaging Irish industries; in January 1838 he debated trade union spokesmen at public meetings in the Old Chapel in the working-class Dublin district of Ringsend. (Emmet O'Connor, *A Labour History of Ireland 1824–1960* (Dublin, 1992), pp. 22–3; MacDonagh, *Emancipist*, pp. 165–7).

43 I.e. to secure compensation when the old Corporation (a stronghold of Orangeism) was abolished under the 1838 Municipal Corporations Act.

44 Sir Abraham Bradley King (created baronet 1821), a prominent and munificent Dublin alderman, Lord Mayor 1812–13, 1820–1, an opponent of Repeal; he displayed orange colours on his mayoral coach in 1820 but

resigned from the Order in 1821 after Orangemen defied his prohibition of the ceremonial dressing of King William's statue on 12 July. O'Connell helped to obtain compensation for King when he lost his position as king's stationer in 1830. The letter from King was the one of 4 August 1832 (*O'Connell Correspondence* IV, 434, quoted in MacDonagh *Emancipist* p. 70); Hill, *From Patriots to Unionists*, pp. 319, 321, 331, 352n.

45 *Kentish fire*, stamping feet on the floor as a form of applause.

46 George Crolly (1810–78). Nephew (later biographer) of the archbishop of Armagh; as a Maynooth professor, accused of Gallican tendencies by Cardinal Cullen.

47 This is clearly a Burns parody (composed by M'Comb) with satiric references to Steele, John Sinclair, and Dillon Browne, the latter being mocked for his impecuniosity ("nabobs", returned Indian merchants and administrators, were proverbially wealthy). Nebbit = mouthed; birkie= lad.

48 Robert James Tennent was Liberal candidate for Belfast in 1832 and August 1835; he subsequently served as the borough's Liberal MP 1847–52. (The Conservative MP Emerson Tennent was his cousin.) Robert Grimshaw, linen merchant, was a leading Liberal activist and election organiser. (Ian Budge and Cornelius O'Leary, *Belfast: Approach to Crisis—A Study of Belfast Politics, 1613–1970* (London, 1973).

49 Samuel Butler *Hudibras* Part II, canto iii, line 1. The reference to the "rueful countenances" of the audience extends the Quixotic allusion. (Don Quixote was "the Knight of the Doleful Countenance".)

50 In Milton's *Paradise Lost*.

51 According to Cooke's biographer and son-in-law, J. L. Porter, several Anti-Repealers seated themselves in the tree with the sign, while their friends crowded around the trunk and prepared to resist any attempt to remove it. J. L. Porter, *Life and Times of Dr. Henry Cooke* (3rd edn, Belfast, 1875), pp. 359–60.

52 Ellen Courtenay claimed to have been seduced by O'Connell in 1817 and to have had a son by him. In 1832 she published a pamphlet setting out her claims, and subsequently accosted him on several public occasions. The scandal was exploited by O'Connell's opponents (who may have encouraged Courtenay to make her claims.) Most O'Connell biographers take Courtenay's failure to sue for maintenance in a court of law as vindicating O'Connell's claim that she was engaged in a politically-motivated fabrication. See Erin I. Bishop, *The World of Mary O'Connell 1778–1836* (Dublin, 1999) and 'Was O'Connell faithful? Ellen Courtenay revisited", *Eire-Ireland* (Fall/Winter 1996), pp. 58–75.

53 The Protestant handloom weavers of Ballymacarrett, a Protestant district across the Lagan to the east of Belfast (subsequently incorporated in the city by boundary extension) were vulnerable to economic fluctuations and suffered severe hardship in the 1840s. *Sowens*, a type of porridge eaten by the poor. The O'Connellites are throwing the accusation of "beggary" back at their opponents. (Christine Kinealy and Gerard MacAtasney, *The Hidden Famine: Hunger, Poverty and Sectarianism in Belfast* (London, 2000), pp. 9–10, 17, 20–1.

54 At this time O'Connell and several of his lieutenants wore specially made garments of Irish frieze as part of a campaign to get consumers to buy Irish goods.

55 A convention of Irish Volunteers, traditionally seen as a highpoint of Protestant patriotism and a significant milestone in securing legislative independence for the Irish parliament.

56 William Cooke Taylor, *History of the Civil Wars of Ireland* (2 vols, London 1831), I, 169–70. I owe this reference to Professor Sean Connolly. Taylor (1800–49) who came from a Church of Ireland family in Youghal, was a schoolteacher and Trinity College graduate who became a journalist and statistician in London. He was a founding member of the British Association and a strong advocate of political economy; his staunch defence of the new Irish National School system made him a protégé of the Church of Ireland Archbishop of Dublin, Richard Whately (and may contribute to Cooke's hostility to him). Taylor was a leading Anti-Corn Law League publicist; his *Notes of a Tour in the Manufacturing Districts of Lancashire: Letters to the Archbishop of Dublin* (London, 1842; reprinted 1968) defends the factory system against Tory and Chartist criticism and attributes industrial depression to the Corn Laws. Taylor returned to Ireland in 1847 as a government statistician and died of cholera in 1849. Taylor argued that class conflict arose from the fact that rich and poor were both ignorant of their best interests, and could be resolved through education. His history therefore sets out to debunk Catholic and Protestant views of the past. He emphasises the role of the Catholic hierarchy in upholding English rule before the Reformation (the passage quoted by O'Connell is immediately followed by the declaration that Mary's plantation of Laois and Offaly made her well-deserving the title "bloody Mary"). He complains that the benevolent intentions of British governments have been defeated by the short-sighted intrigues of settler oligarchies who prevented the growth of an Irish middle-class by "preferring a Celtic serf to an independent freeholder". Taylor ridicules Protestant complaints of Catholic bigotry and persecution by arguing that the Protestants behaved just as badly; so extensive is his satire on persecutors demanding freedom for themselves while attempting to justify its denial to their victims that the later sections of the book resemble a black comedy. He maintains that the massacres of 1641 were largely fictitious; that about 5,000 were massacred by each side, with Catholic atrocities carried out by uncontrollable mobs while Protestant crimes were the settled policy of a land-hungry oligarchy. Taylor defends the actions of James II's Irish Parliament with the exception of the Act of Attainder, and argues that the Irish Jacobites would have made terms with William after their monarch's flight except for the machinations of the Protestant gentry. He blames the Dublin Castle administration for driving the United Irishmen to rebellion, but details the horrors of Scullabogue along with the atrocities perpetrated by the government forces. Taylor concludes by hailing Catholic Emancipation as the belated vindication of the Union, and predicts that the blessings of parliamentary reform, coupled with economic development when English

capitalists recognise the incredible value of Ireland's southern harbours, will blend the two nations indissolubly.

57 William Parnell (1780–1821), grandfather of the Home Rule leader Charles Stewart Parnell, was a prolific polemicist in favour of Catholic Emancipation. *Heretical* should be *Historical*—the book appeared in 1807. R. F. Foster *Charles Stewart Parnell: The Man and His Family* (Brighton, 1976), pp. 16–29 outlines his life and views. Foster's suggestion that Charles Stewart Parnell knew of and was influenced by his grandfather's activities is confirmed by the journalist Michael MacDonagh in his reminiscences of an 1891 interview (*Irish Weekly Independent*, 11 Oct. 1941, p. 4).

58 *Bohea* and *Congou*—types of tea.

59 O'Connell's wife Mary died in 1836; their relationship was extremely close and loving. The quotation is from Sir Walter Scott *Marmion*.

60 Virgil Aeneid 1 v. 497–8.

61 Butler *Hudibras*.

62 O'Connell became a teetotaller for 18 months in 1840–1 after taking the pledge from Fr. Mathew. (MacDonagh, *Emancipist*, p. 1).

63 John Bates, solicitor, Conservative election agent and chief party organiser for Belfast from 1832 until his death in 1855. His conduct of the July 1842 general election was marked by widespread corruption and other irregularities, leading to the unseating of the successful Tory candidates. Town Clerk and Town Solicitor to Belfast Corporation from 1842 until he resigned when a Chancery suit exposed municipal financial irregularities in June 1855 (Budge and O'Leary, *Belfast: Approach to Crisis*, pp. 44–62.)

64 Brother-in-law of Peel and former MP for Derry City. He attracted widespread Orange criticism in August 1828 by a speech temporising on Catholic Emancipation and praising the besiegers of Derry as well as its defenders (R. M. Sibbett, *Orangeism in Ireland and throughout the Empire* 2 vols (London, 1939), II, pp. 3–5.) The *Vindicator* recalled this in mocking him as "George Orange Chameleon Dawson". Describing the meeting in a letter to Peel, Dawson praised Cooke's eloquence and expressed the conviction that he would have beaten O'Connell in debate. (Holmes, *Cooke*, p. 149.)

65 The Grand Orange Lodge of Ireland had dissolved itself in April 1836 after Radical MPs alleged the existence of an Orange and ultra-Tory plot to supplant the future Queen Victoria with her uncle Ernest, Duke of Cumberland and Orange Grand Master. The *Vindicator* accused the whole Conservative Party of participation in the alleged plot, and hailed Victoria's marriage and the birth of Princess Victoria as finally shutting out "the tyrant of Hanover" from the British throne. (*Vindicator*, 25 Nov. 1840).

66 *Hudibras*.

67 The "noblest and bravest" was Frederick, Duke of York, heir to the throne until his death in 1827 and an outspoken opponent of Catholic Emancipation. The denunciation of the Duke of York was delivered by Richard Lalor Sheil, and the scandal caused by the speech appreciably delayed Sheil's evolution from Repealer to Whig officeholder.

68 O'Connell's refusal in later life to accept challenges to duels often produced accusations of cowardice. (MacDonagh, *Emancipist*, pp. 125–6).

69 The Orange Order. The Verner family, small Armagh landlords, had been connected with the Order since its foundation in 1795; Colonel Sir William Verner, MP for Armagh, had been County Grand Master of Armagh and Deputy Grand Master of Ireland. In fact, only the central leadership was dissolved; the Order continued to operate at local level and Verner resumed his County Grand Mastership on its official reconstitution in 1836. Verner was removed from the magistracy in 1837 for toasting the memory of "The Battle of the Diamond", in which he had participated. (Sibbett *Orangeism in Ireland*; Billy Kennedy (ed.), *Steadfast for Faith and Freedom: 200 Years of Orangeism* (Belfast, 1995), pp. 8–9, 17–18. The *Vindicator* cited Verner's speech as proof that the whole assembly was an illegal Orange meeting which ought to be investigated by the authorities.

70 David R. Ross, merchant, Liberal MP for Belfast 1842–7.

71 James Emerson Tennent, Conservative MP for Belfast 1832–45, subsequently Secretary to the governor of Ceylon; merchant and Fermanagh landowner.

72 Alleged to have composed a radical address in the 1790s beginning "We, the people of England".

73 Conservative MP for Belfast 1835–41; first mayor of reformed Belfast Corporation, 1842.

74 Henry Grattan junior (1789–1859), son and biographer of the celebrated Patriot politician of the Irish Parliament. MP for Dublin City 1826–30 (Whig), for Meath 1831–52 (Repealer).

75 Robert Stewart (1783–1852), Cooke's friend, college contemporary, principal ally and party organiser in the Subscription controversy.

76 In the June 1835 Carlow by-election O'Connell recruited Alexander Raphael, London financier and sheriff of Westminster, as a candidate. Raphael paid O'Connell £2,000; after being unseated on petition he accused O'Connell of cheating him and published their correspondence. A parliamentary committee investigated O'Connell for corruption; although he was able to show that the money had gone on Raphael's election expenses, the tone of the correspondence damaged O'Connell's reputation. (MacDonagh, *Emancipist*, pp. 139–42).

77 A Dublin Liberal journalist and politician.

78 The devils' palace in *Paradise Lost*.

79 The issue of 20 January 1841.

80 O'Connell wore a wig in later life, occasionally waving it in public or taking it off to display the formation of his skull.

81 Cooke had long been on bad terms with the Belfast Academical Institution, which he accused of spreading heresy and religious indifferentism.

82 During 11–21 September 1835 O'Connell held a "mission to the people of England and Scotland"; at meetings in Manchester, Newcastle, Edinburgh and Glasgow he called for the House of Lords to be replaced by 150 popularly elected peers. (MacDonagh, *Emancipist*, pp. 133–4).

83 Since 1831 Achill Island—in MacHale's archdiocese—had witnessed stormy attempts at evangelisation and counterevangelisation by the

Protestant missionary Edward Nangle and Catholic preachers. (Mealla Ni Ghiobuin, *Dugort, Achill Island 1831–1861: The Rise and Fall of a Missionary Community* (Dublin, 2001)—especially pp. 17–21).

84 Possibly Fr. James Hughes, parish priest of Claremorris, Co. Mayo (in MacHale's archdiocese); for his activities during the Famine see Donal Kerr, *A Nation of Beggars? Priests, People, and Politicians in Famine Ireland 1846–1852* (Oxford, 1994), pp. 61, 134.

85 Forged sixpences (rap) when detected were nailed to the counter by shopkeepers as a warning to other potential passers-off of forged currency.

86 Liberius (352–66), was pressurised by an Arian Emperor into disowning Athanasius, the defender of Trinitarian orthodoxy (to whom Cooke was often compared by his admirers) —he has often been used as an argument against Papal infallibility; Hildebrand (Gregory VII, 1073–85) was widely condemned for Protestants for his assertion of the Church's independence from lay control, symbolised by his humiliation of Emperor Henry IV at Canossa in 1077; Pope Joan—apocryphal figure, supposedly a learned woman who disguised herself as a priest, secured election as Pope, but was discovered when she gave birth during a solemn procession; Julius II (1503–13) led armies to battle to extend the Papal States, his warlike activities were widely criticised as unbefitting a priest; Sixtus V (1585–90) issued a 1588 Bull deposing Queen Elizabeth I.

87 John Bale (1495–1563), scholar and dramatist of European fame, encountered widespread local hostility (described in his *Vocacyon*) to his attempts to impose Protestant practices during his reign as bishop of Ossory 1552–3. William Bedell (1571–1642, bishop of Kilmore 1629–42) was revered by Cooke and many advocates of the nineteenth-century "Second Reformation" because of his pioneering and frustrated efforts to preach Protestantism to the Gaelic Irish in their own language.

88 Catherine Macaulay (1731–91), radical historian; published *History of England from the Ascension of James I to that of the Brunswick Line* from 1763.

89 John Doyle (HB) (1797–1868) was a celebrated political cartoonist whose lithographs marked the transition between the savagery of Regency visual satire and the restrained Victorian style. Although Doyle was himself a Catholic (his son, the *Punch* cartoonist Richard Doyle, resigned from that journal in protest at its anti-Catholic coverage of the restoration of the English Catholic hierarchy) he held conservative political views and believed O'Connell's attacks on the Established Church violated an implicit understanding on which Emancipation had been granted. His caricatures of O'Connell grew steadily more hostile throughout the 1830s; they were often praised in *Times* editorials and played a significant role in shaping hostile British stereotypes of O'Connell. (James N. McCord, "The image in England: the cartoons of HB" in Maurice R. O'Connell (ed.), *Daniel O'Connell: Political Pioneer* (Dublin, 1991), pp. 56–71, with inset plates.) Doyle's cartoons may have inspired the satirical line-drawings with which McComb decorated *The Repealer Repulsed*. Doyle was the grandfather of Sir Arthur Conan Doyle, creator of Sherlock Holmes.

90 In Laurence Sterne's *Tristram Shandy*.

91 Gregory XVI (1830–46), fiercely supportive of the European alliance between throne and altar. Although O'Connell's support for religious and political freedom extended so far as to join Evangelicals in denouncing the persecution of Jews in the Papal States (William D. and Hilary Rubinstein, *Philosemitism: Admiration and Support in the English-Speaking World for Jews, 1840–1939* (London, 1999), pp. 13–14), Gregory continued to favour him because of his political stature and fidelity to Catholicism. European Catholics who wished to reconcile the Church with political liberalism were not always so fortunate. The *Vindicator* denied that any such encyclical existed, but Cooke is clearly referring to the 1832 encyclical *Mirari vos*, condemning French Liberal Catholicism and arguing that liberty of expression leads not to the triumph of truth but to religious indifferentism.

92 During the 1828 Clare election.

93 *Paradise Lost*

94 David Stow (1793–1864) Scottish Presbyterian philanthropist and educationalist. The "one step higher" presumably involved religious education.

95 Parody of a popular ballad "The Beggar Girl" ("Over the mountain and over the moor") by H. Piercy.

96 Queen Adelaide, widow of William IV, was known to be sympathetic to the Tories, whereas Queen Victoria was at this time strongly attached to the Whigs.

97 The Chartist John Frost (1784–1877), a draper and Justice of the Peace in Newport (Monmouthshire) was transported for life after leading the unsuccessful "Newport Rising" of November 1839, when a crowd of miners attempted to rescue Chartist detainees and were bloodily dispersed by the army.

98 The Whigs offered judicial office to O'Connell in 1830 and 1838. (MacDonagh, *Emancipist*, pp. 42–3, 175.)

99 A Luxembourgeois (d.1819) based in Dublin during his later career, who developed a system of education based on memory training. His name gave birth to the American slang term "finagle" = cheat.

100 Term applied to the half-human Caliban in Shakespeare's *Tempest*.

101 Zetzel = Johan Tetzel, the friar whose sale of indulgences triggered Luther's original protest; Cajetan (1469–1534) the Papal legate to Gemany who tried to persuade Luther to abandon his protest.

102 A history of Ireland by Thomas Moore written in the form of the memoirs of a hereditary Whiteboy chieftain, claiming that all Irish rebellions were caused by British misrule and oppression. Its appearance in 1824 provoked numerous literary imitations and counterblasts (the latter often attributing Rockite and Whiteboy activity to a Catholic conspiracy).

103 Cooke confuses William Parnell with his older brother Sir Henry, a Parliamentary advocate of Catholic Emancipation and Whig Cabinet Minister, ennobled as Lord Congleton in 1841. (This was a frequent mistake: Foster *Parnell*, p.19) William, who died in 1821, could not have been influenced by Taylor's work, which appeared in 1831.

104 A. J. Macrory, a prominent Belfast solicitor, member of Cooke's May Street congregation, and legal adviser to the Presbyterian Church.

105 In December 1830 Montgomery spoke out strongly in favour of parliamentary reform and vote by secret ballot. O'Connell responded by praising him extravagantly and expressing the hope that he would join in advocating Repeal. In January 1831, the day after O'Connell was arrested on the grounds that his pro-repeal declarations violated emergency legislation, Montgomery and other Non-Subscribers presented the Lord Lieutenant with an address declaring their support for the Union. O'Connell (who was rapidly released) denounced Montgomery as a timeserving sycophant motivated by desire for government assistance in obtaining a favourable division of the Presbyterian synod's property after the schism, while the O'Connellite Press attacked the Non-Subscribers as Unitarians and unbelievers. Montgomery retorted with a stinging letter pointing out that his religious beliefs had been the same when he antagonised the Tory government by campaigning for Catholic Emancipation, and claiming that O'Connell's intolerance of criticism showed that Repeal under his auspices would produce a dictatorship. The controversy is described, and the text of Montgomery's letter reproduced, in Crozier *Montgomery*, pp. 417–36, 581–99. Cooke's praise for Montgomery reflects the Conservatives' attempt to persuade the Liberals that their best interests lay in a pan-Protestant front.

106 Alexander Leopold Hohenlohe-Waldenburg-Schillingsfurst (1794–1849) an Austrian priest later Bishop) from an old aristocratic family, allegedly performed many miraculous healings by prayer for the afflicted person. His activities gave rise to widespread controversy in Europe and America, with many Catholics claiming them as divine endorsement of Catholicism, while Protestants and freethinkers attributed them to suggestion or imposture.

107 Bruen took the Carlow seat from the Whigs in a by-election on 5 December 1840.

108 During the general election of December 1832–January 1833 a crowd of Louth peasants encamped on a hill outside Newry for two days, threatening to enter the town and kill every Conservative voter. They were dissuaded by a local priest. (Angus MacIntyre, *The Liberator: Daniel O'Connell and the Irish Party, 1830–47* (London, 1965), p. 118).

109 In the Book of Numbers the prophet Balaam is bribed by the king of Moab to curse the Israelites, after having been forbidden by God to do so. After his donkey is divinely inspired to warn him and the angel of the Lord threatens him with death, Balaam blesses the Israelites instead of cursing them. In Deuteronomy Balaam advises the heathen to attempt to seduce the Israelites into idolatry through intermarriage, and is subsequently killed by the Israelites. Balaam is regrded by Christian and Jewish commentators as the crowning example of the misuse of divinely given abilities; by calling the bribe "the Moabitish rent" Cooke equates it with O'Connell's Catholic Rent.

110 Xenophon's *Anabasis* describes the successful retreat of the "Ten Thousand"—Greek mercenaries brought into Persia by a claimant to the throne and left stranded by the death of their employer.

111 From Walter Scott, *The Lady of the Lake*. The *Vindicator* replied to these taunts by ascribing Catholic quiescence to forbearance, and claiming that on previous occasions the Hercules Street butchers alone had shown themselves capable of dispersing the entire Belfast Orange mob.

112 O'Connell suffered an accident to his carriage at Annan in the Scottish Borders, referred to in Cooke's letter. Cooke belonged to the pre-millennial Recordite section of the Evangelical movement, called after the London paper edited by his friend Alexander Haldane (1800–82), which believed that God frequently intervened directly in human affairs. (McComb's apocalyptic writings show that he was a premillennialist.) This is probably related to his support for Tory paternalism, as distinct from the political and economic liberalism of those postmillennialist Providentialists who believed that God laid down His laws for the world at the beginning but thereafter generally refrained from direct intervention. For the difference between Recordites and postmillennial optimists, see Boyd Hilton, *The Age of Atonement: The Influence of Evangelicalism on Social and Economic Thought, 1785–1865* (Oxford, 1988), especially pp. 211–15. Porter, *Cooke* contains extensive material on Cooke's close relationship with the Haldane family.

113 This resolution reflects the longstanding bitterness between O'Connell and the Chartist leader Feargus O'Connor.

114 The *Vindicator* claimed that Cooke passed through the crowd while it was gathering, was cheered by it, and made no attempt to persuade it to disperse.

115 The testimonial raised £2000 (Holmes, *Cooke*, p. 149).

116 "Lochiel's warning" by Thomas Campbell is cast as a dialogue, shortly before the 1745 rising, between the Jacobite chieftain Cameron of Lochiel and a Highland prophet who foretells his defeat. It became a longstanding favourite of schools and reciters. "Old Ritchie" was Dr. John Ritchie of Edinburgh, who engaged in a marathon debate with Cooke in March 1836 on the issue of Church establishment vs. Volutaryism. The exchange was regarded as one of Cooke's greatest triumphs by his admirers; Ritchie wrote to O'Connell on 23 January 1841 claiming that his Belfast debate had been disrupted by an Orange mob, and suggesting that O'Connell should highlight the fact that Cooke had been unwilling to debate Ritchie on the same subject in Edinburgh. (O'Connell Correspondence vol. VI; Holmes, *Cooke*, pp. 129–32). The "one duel-stain" is O'Connell's killing of John D'Esterre in a duel on 1 February 1815. (James Kelly *That Damn'd thing called Honour: Duelling in Ireland 1570–1860* (Cork, 1995), pp. 243–4. O'Connell made frequent public expressions of remorse for the duel.

117 This is occasionally described as a genuine example of the millenarian O'Connellite ballads composed in the period (e.g in Catherine Hirst *Religion, Politics and Violence in Nineteenth-Century Belfast: The Pound and Sandy Row* (Dublin, 2002), p. 50). In fact, it is clearly a parody of these ballads, combining the mockery of pseudo-erudite hedge schoolmasters and ballad-writers found in its prototype, Richard Milliken's "Groves of

Blarney", with the loyalist tradition of presenting nationalists as ignorant buffoons driven by infantile credulity, violence, and greed.

118 From Richard Brinsley Sheridan's *School for Scandal*.

119 Isaac Van Amburgh was a celebrated animal-tamer (John M. Mackenzie (ed.), *The Victorian Vision* (London, 2001), pp. 280–1, 293.)

120 A parody of Wolfe's "Burial of Sir John Moore".

121 A Protestant working-class area at the top of the Shankill Road.

122 An area in South Belfast inhabited by Protestant unskilled labourers; an Orange stronghold.

123 This parodies one of Macaulay's "Lays of Ancient Rome". William Joseph O'Neill Daunt (1807–94) was a Cork landowner, convert to Catholicism, and leading Repeal activist. Goshen was the region of Egypt where the Israelites lived during their captivity in Egypt; in the Book of Exodus God exempts it from the ten plagues inflicted upon Egypt.

124 A parody of Scott's "Young Lochinvar". Belfast was called "the Northern Athens" by admirers.

125 Urachree—on the site of the Battle of Aughrim.

126 Another travesty of "The young Lochinvar".

127 Sam Slick was created by the Nova Scotian politician and judge Thomas Chandler Haliburton (1796–1865) in *The Clockmaker* (1836) to satirise American manners from a conservative standpoint. The book and its sequels were international bestsellers, widely pirated and imitated. Jonathan Crane's proposal, as well as reflecting the marital metaphor often used for the Union, reflects the contemporary reputation of upstate New York as the site of numerous religious and social experiments (such as Mormonism and the Oneida Community) often involving new forms of marriage. "Loco-focos" were radical Jacksonian Democrats.